Dedication

To Dan, Naledi, Akelo and Manu
To my parents, Emmanuel Omondi Ligaga and Alice Obiero Ligaga
and to Hilda Croxford, with love and appreciation

About the Series

The African Humanities Series is a partnership between the African Humanities Program (AHP) of the American Council of Learned Societies and academic publishers NISC (Pty) Ltd. The Series covers topics in African histories, languages, literatures, philosophies, politics and cultures. Submissions are solicited from Fellows of the AHP, which is administered by the American Council of Learned Societies and financially supported by the Carnegie Corporation of New York.

The purpose of the AHP is to encourage and enable the production of new knowledge by Africans in the five countries designated by the Carnegie Corporation: Ghana, Nigeria, South Africa, Tanzania and Uganda. AHP fellowships support one year's work free from teaching and other responsibilities to allow the Fellow to complete the project proposed. Eligibility for the fellowship in the five countries is by domicile, not nationality.

Book proposals are submitted to the AHP editorial board which manages the peer review process and selects manuscripts for publication by NISC. In some cases, the AHP board will commission a manuscript mentor to undertake substantive editing and to work with the author on refining the final manuscript.

The African Humanities Series aims to publish works of the highest quality that will foreground the best research being done by emerging scholars in the five Carnegie designated countries. The rigorous selection process before the fellowship award, as well as AHP editorial vetting of manuscripts, assures attention to quality. Books in the series are intended to speak to scholars in Africa as well as in other areas of the world.

The AHP is also committed to providing a copy of each publication in the series to university libraries in Africa.

Published in this series

WOMEN, VISIBILITY AND MORALITY IN KENYAN POPULAR MEDIA

DINA LIGAGA

Published in South Africa on behalf of the African Humanities Program
by NISC (Pty) Ltd, PO Box 377, Grahamstown, 6140, South Africa
www.nisc.co.za

First edition, first impression 2020

Publication © African Humanities Program 2020
Text © Dina Ligaga 2020

ISBN: 978-1-920033-63-7 (print)
ISBN: 978-1-920033-64-4 (PDF)
ISBN: 978-1-920033-65-1 (ePub)

Manuscript mentor: Prof. Lynette Steenveld
Project manager: Peter Lague
Indexer: Sanet le Roux
Cover design: Advanced Design Group
Cover photographs: © agsandrew/Shutterstock (front),
                   © Flamingo Images/stock.adobe.com (back)

Printed in South Africa by Digital Action

Contents

CHAPTER 4: Scandal, surveillance and the spectacular 'wicked' woman   82

CHAPTER 5: Consumption, good time girls and violence in public discourse   100

Acknowledgements

The manuscript for this publication was prepared with the support of the African Humanities Fellowship Program established by the American Council of Learned Societies (ACLS) with a generous grant from the Carnegie Corporation of New York. I am also grateful for funding from the National Research Foundation of South Africa which assisted in bringing this project to fruition.

I am indebted to the African Humanities Program (AHP) postdoctoral fellowship for the opportunities it made available to me. In 2014, I participated in the AHP Manuscript Development Workshop (MDW) held in Dar es Salaam. I would like to thank Andrzje Tymowski, International Program Director at ACLS, who has always gone above and beyond to ensure the success of the program, and for the stimulating conversations at the MDW. I would also like to thank Eszter Csicsai who was the program coordinator of the AHP at the time, as well as the AHP advisors — Adigun Agbaje, Innocent Pikirayi and Steven Feireman — for their constructive feedback and insight. To my co-participants, Adebayo Mosobalaje, Harrie Bazunu, Eliah S. Mwaifuge, Ifeyinwa Genevieve Okolo and Abosede Omowumi Babatundi — thank you for your continued support. In 2017 I was African Studies Association (ASA) Presidential Fellow. During this period, I had the opportunity to visit Rutgers University. I would like to thank Stéphane Robolin, Chika Okoye, Thato Magano and Ousseina Alidou for welcoming me. I would also like to thank Mona Mwakalinga and Uni Dyer for companionship, laughter and intellectual exchange. To the AHP book series editors, Fred Hendricks and Adigun Agbaje, thank you for your patience. I am indebted to my manuscript mentor, Lynette Steenveld, who worked tirelessly to help me turn words into a book, always with patience and grace — I felt I had to finish this project as a way of saying thank you. To Barbara van der Merwe who believed in this project way before I knew it was one. I am grateful for your continued support. My thanks also to Peter Lague for your keen eye and engaging feedback during the last leg of editing the book.

My thanks to Grace Musila for friendship and support. Your detailed feedback on my various drafts, attention to detail and brilliant suggestions remain invaluable. I am also grateful for the 'roadside tutorials' you and Flo allowed me. To Carli Coetzee, who read an early version of the book draft, and gave honest yet affirming feedback — thank you for being a constant in my life and for the 'parallel desk'. To my sisters in work and play: Mary Immaculate Odongo, Danai Mupotsa, Pumla

Dineo Gqola, Polo Moji, Sarah Chiumbu, Natasha Himmelman, Flo Sipalla, Grace Musila, Carli Coetzee and Sharlene Khan — thank you.

To all my friends who are probably tired of hearing me go on about my need to find time to write – Fouad Asfour, Dee Marco, Lynda Gichanda Spencer, Tina Steiner, Collins Miruka, Godfrey Chesang, Sean Rogers, Godwin Siundu, Tom Odhiambo, Jacob Akech, Chris Ouma, Khwezi Mkhize, Anthony Ambala, Neo Musangi, Dorcas Wangare, Khwezi Gule, Ghairunisa Galeta and Margaret Atsango — yes, I finished, finally. To my dear friend George Were, I did not get to say goodbye, but I trust you have found rest. To the Karin Barber Lab members, I appreciate your support and collegiality. I would like to thank my colleagues and friends who have heard versions of my project in forums and shared thoughts with me. They include George Ogola, David Kerr, Karin Barber, Stephanie Newell, Liz Gunner and Ranka Primorac.

To my mentors and friends, both at Moi University and Wits University, words cannot begin to describe the appreciation I have for you and the help you extended my way. At Wits, I had the opportunity to work with Isabel Hofmeyr and James Ogude. Both were excellent mentors, and they helped to shape the way I think and write. To Bhekizizwe Peterson, always available for consultations, and to Ruksana Osman for continued support, my grateful thanks. I will always be grateful to Joyce Nyairo for everything and more. To the Moi University community: Tom Michael Mboya, Peter Amuka, Tirop Simatei, Tobias Otieno, Basil Okongo, Solomon Waliaula and Busolo Wegesa — all of you influenced who I have become. Thank you. To my colleagues and friends in the media studies community, Tawana Kupe, Dumisani Moyo, Wendy Willems and Nixon Kariithi — thank you, too.

Thank you to my colleagues in the Media Studies Department at Wits University — Dee Marco, Katlego Disemelo, Ufuoma Akpojivi, Nicky Falkof, Mehita Iqani, Glenda Daniels and Iginio Gagliardone. To Merle Govind, always friendly and helpful. To Valerie Kilian and to Marilyn Jousten — I appreciate all the help you have extended to me over the years. To postgraduate students, past and present, with whom I thought through some ideas: Viraj Suparsad, Prinola Govenden, Eddie Ombagi, Justin Jegels and Vidhya Sana — thank you.

To my family: my father, the late Emmanuel Omondi Ligaga, eternally present. To my mother, Alice Ligaga, and my siblings, Carl, Judy, Margaret, Petty and Olga Ligaga — you all rock. To my South African family: Achieng, Miriam, Zuri and Nina, and to Walter and Rhoda Ojwang and all my clan in Kenya and elsewhere — I appreciate all of you. My appreciation also to Thenjiwe Ntshingila, without whom I would be lost, and to Julia Ntshingila (may she rest). To my children, Naledi Akinyi, Akelo Hawi and Manu Odongo, my babies who teach me so much every day, and to you, Dan Ojwang, my steady companion — you all have my love and appreciation.

Foreword

The birth of this book is a typical tale of the dynamic of women's visibility and invisibility in private and public life. Indeed, the binaries do women's lives an injustice, because our lives demonstrate the accomplishment of a 'both and' approach to life. While writing this book, the author, a Wits University professor, gave birth to twins, and thus began the process of both nurturing her babies and writing the book. As the manuscript mentor, I was in some ways a 21st-century antenatal and postnatal guide and support: we communicated intimately at a distance through email. Our mediated connection and the relationship we developed, speak, in part, to the way in which women negotiate their place in a mass-mediated world that shapes the ways in which we make our lives, become visible or invisible, and how we are seen by others.

This book takes us into that mediated world of the 20th and 21st century media: radio plays, newspapers, television and social media platforms such as Instagram, Twitter, Facebook and YouTube, that all exist simultaneously in our contemporary world. It explores how these media in Kenya have historically both shaped, and been shaped by, Kenyan ideas about the meaning of Kenyan womanhood. The book demonstrates the author of *The Second Sex*, Simone de Beauvoir's, comment that 'One is not born, but rather becomes, a woman'. More specifically, the book engages with the way in which the media shape how Kenyan women's roles are pre-determined. It demonstrates how different media circulate ideas about womanhood, thus showing how they mediate, as Ligaga explains, the 'relationship between the state and other dominant social institutions and the media on the one hand; and popular culture and everyday life in Kenya, on the other.' Institutions like the church, and other traditional forums, provide 'scripts' or culturally normative ways of pronouncing what it means to be a Kenyan woman, which are then reproduced in popular cultural forms like songs, plays and journalism, and circulated by the media.

Despite all manner of social advances, African women are still 'the second sex': not regarded as important in our own right, and always subservient to what 'people' think we should be, and how we should act. Key to 'becoming a woman' are the social understandings of sexuality, for 'becoming a woman' is understood in relation to deeply held ideas about patriarchy, and in this case, Kenya's colonial history which propagated a moral understanding of womanhood. Deeply embedded in Kenyan culture are notions of the asexual 'good woman', often referring to a rural woman who represents the ideal of 'nurturing motherhood', who is contrasted with the 'good-time girl', or urban hussy who leads men astray because she shows that she too has desires of being and becoming, which include sexual desires.

As part of a broader, national, cultural system, the media circulate cautionary tales about what befalls women who try to step outside of culturally prescribed roles. In these tales of sex and retribution, women become objects to be gawked at, shamed, and belittled. One tale is about how couples become 'stuck' during sex — often accomplished with the help of a 'witchdoctor' as a means of punishing one of the participants who is engaging in an 'illicit' activity. Another narrative probes what women do at chama, traditionally rural women's economic self-help groups, which have become increasingly popular in the cities, and are now framed in the media as opportunities for women to escape the sexual bounds of their husbands. More recently, through social media we see the rise of blessers and blessees: the latter, women 'blessed' with the patronage of men (for transactional sex) which enables them to escape economic and other confines. In particular, they celebrate their sexuality as a way of being 'modern', in contrast to the asexual associations of the traditional, good, Kenyan woman. A common social media trope that captures the essence of this 'new femininity' is the university-educated, middle-class young woman who does not have the 'excuse' of needing a 'sugar daddy' for money and other material benefits, but nonetheless enters into compensated relationships. Finally, there are stories of the 'difficult woman': she is simply larger than life, 'hypervisible', and refuses to conform to the 'norms' of good Kenyan womanhood. In short, the book explores women as 'spectacle', through the spectacular tales that are told about them in Kenyan popular culture.

Using Black feminist and other perspectives, Ligaga offers readers a way of seeing these representations of contemporary womanhood as signs of social crisis. Why is there a big media brouhaha about a young, well-dressed woman who doesn't pay her bill at an expensive hotel? Why are married women often the subject of 'sex scandals'? Why is it scandalous for a married woman to have an extramarital affair, but for men it demonstrates their 'manhood'? Why is sexual desire 'normal' for men, but 'immoral' for women? Why are young, university-educated women framed in social media as money-grabbing hussies? What does it mean that women are challenging social norms about their place in society, and how they ought to conduct themselves? What are the social meanings of the media's cautionary tales about the punishment meted out to women they mark as 'wicked', 'loose', 'immoral', 'wild', 'difficult', educated, when they step outside of patriarchal conventions of what it means to be a Kenyan woman?

What if these same stories demonstrate the chutzpah, or daring of these women, so that we read them instead as 'trickster figures' who challenge patriarchal cultural conventions and offer other ways of imagining what it means to be a Kenyan woman? This is the vision that Dina Ligaga offers in her book, showing us new ways of reading Kenyan popular culture. Indeed, in this digital media age, women are no longer confined to former nationalist constructions of womanhood but become 'citizens of the world' and thus able not only to construct themselves imaginatively in boundless ways, but also to circulate these ideas themselves on social media.

The media may indeed be social regulators that attempt to contain femininity by working with stereotypical scripts, but they succeed only to the extent that we, as readers, unquestioningly take up their interpretations of social actions and identities. Ligaga thus invites the reader to see the media as complex social systems that necessarily interact with their context in order to be commercially profitable, but are also vulnerable to the vagaries of social change forged by the very people they create stories about, and their readers' freedom to make their own meanings of the stories told.

Ligaga innovatively shows us how we can read Kenyan women's 'transgressions', not as moral flaws, but rather as demonstrations of how they negotiate the constraints of national cultural conventions and, in so doing, offer new ways of 'becoming' a Kenyan woman.

Lynette Steenveld
Associate Professor of Media Studies
Rhodes University
Grahamstown

Preface

Five years ago, when, as part of the AHP I was presented the opportunity to write a book, I planned to write one about radio drama in Kenya. The book would be based on my PhD thesis, and I would flesh out some of the ideas I had spent three years working on. I was fascinated by the idea of the 'moral narrative' which I had explored in detail in my doctoral dissertation as the mode through which radio drama constructed its publics. I was also intrigued by the centrality of everyday life as an organising principle in thinking through the link between culture and ideology in Africa. In my book, I would therefore problematise the relationship between state ideologies, institutions and everyday life and, following Michel de Certeau (1984), look for possible sites of resistance to problematic ideologies. However, when I began writing, I realised that a different matter bothered me. I could not reconcile the women in radio drama, constructed in the melodramatic fashion of high drama (Brooks 1976) as either 'good' or 'bad', with the women I encountered in tabloids or the entertainment pages of newspapers and magazines or on social media. The women on social media, for example, were daring to exist in public in ways previously unknown. They were 'divas', 'socialites', 'slay queens', '#blessed' and 'sugar babes'. They were talking back and refusing to be shamed into silence. The disjuncture between these various representations struck me as odd, especially in a context in which violence consistently disrupted the lives of women. Media reports of women being stripped naked in public for dressing indecently were on the increase, accounts of female members of parliament being harassed, physically harmed and taunted in public were becoming familiar, and stories of women being murdered for obscure reasons related to money and older men were on the increase.

I realised that the only way I could begin to make sense of what was happening to women in this context of violence in Kenya was to understand how public culture worked. I cannot say that I completely understand it yet, but this book is the beginning of a journey of questioning the familiar, taken for granted assumptions about women in Kenyan public culture. It looks at examples of popular texts — radio plays about everyday life, sensationalist tabloids and spectacular modes of self-representations — examples that may at first seem one-dimensional but are in fact multi-layered with multiple perceptions and realities for intended readers as well as wider publics. They may appear simplistic but are in fact extremely important. As Grace Musila (2015) so eloquently shows us, the terrain of informal networks, rumours, gossip and scandal generate intriguing ideas about power. These are the untapped resources of knowledge, the heart of popular culture.

Against this backdrop, this book seeks to answer two interrelated questions. First, why are particular women's bodies (those interpreted as transgressive or unruly) significant symbolic sites for the generation of knowledge on morality and sexuality? And second, related to this, why is it that for knowledges (of femininity, and how to be a good woman) to circulate effectively, such knowledges must embrace the melodramatic, the spectacular and the scandalous? In attempting to answer these questions, I return to the familiar construct of femininity in this book to assess the ways in which femininity circulates in discourse, both stereotypically and otherwise. I assess the meanings of such discourses and their articulations in various public spaces. I think about pre-convened scripts that contain or condition how women can in fact circulate in public. It is my hope that this book opens up discussions about ideas that circulate in the public domain about women — often taken for granted — that are harmful to their wellbeing in Kenya and elsewhere. In a society where femicide is more common than ever and where domestic violence no longer evokes outrage, there is need to revisit what we know and to question traditions and institutions that enable violence against women.

1

Women and the politics of visibility in Kenya

Introduction

On 18 February 2015, a story broke in Kenyan media revealing that a 27-year-old woman had been arrested for failing to pay a hotel bill. The story spread quickly on various media platforms, including television, radio, newspaper and social media sites. Indeed, in days, she was one of the most talked about people in Kenya. Two leading newspapers, *The Standard* and *The Daily Nation,* reported that Laura Oyier had been arrested and charged with obtaining credit under false pretences.[1] Ordinarily, this would have been just another news story. Because this incident happened to a woman staying at one of Kenya's high-end hotels and had occurred on Valentine's Day, and because the unpaid bill had come to approximately two thousand three hundred American dollars, the story became spectacular. There were multiple speculations about what could have happened prior to the news event. The narratives circulating on social media and online tabloid websites such as *Ghafla!* and *Mpasho*,[2] stated that there was a mysterious man at the centre of the scandal. They suggested that Oyier had been left in the lurch to teach her a 'lesson'. They also suggested that she was a 'socialite', a 'party animal' and a 'good time girl'.[3] Oyier was turned into an example of a 'bad' woman who had defied public expectations of good feminine behaviour. Appearing undaunted by the fuss the media created following her arrest, her loud and opinionated responses helped to fuel this perception. Indeed, Oyier's confidence and refusal to feel shame made her visible, but in an unexpected way. Not long after the media furore surrounding her arrest and eventual release had died down, she was offered a job as a radio disc jockey.[4] In addition, her hotel bill was settled in full by sympathisers, among them well-known media celebrities, and once again she was in the limelight, both as an object of curiosity and of mirth. This time, the public were curious and amused, and endless jokes were shared at her expense about how she looked, her confidence and her refusal to feel shame.

I begin with the example above to signal the preoccupations of this book. It is a book about Kenyan public cultures on sexuality and morality, with a focus on political, cultural and economic influences on constructions of femininity. The book critiques public constructions of femininity in Kenyan mediascapes, in which public scripts act as screens for reading women in public spaces. It dwells on what such public interfaces mean, how they are constructed in Kenyan public imaginations, and eventually how these constructions circulate in discourse. I argue that there is a link between these constructions and the increasing violence against women, particularly as performed in public. The book asks questions about what visibility means for women in such contexts, and engages with various dynamics between institutionalised moralities, and emergent counterpublics. The main questions that I pursue then are: in what ways are women policed in Kenyan public culture, whether in political, cultural or socioeconomic contexts? What are the interfaces between constructions, circulation and counterpublics of femininity in these public cultures? When and how are women visible in these cultures, and with what kinds of repercussions? How are their narratives articulated in popular media forms, whether as pedagogic or advice columns, cautionary tales, 'tragic' news or through other forms of sensationalist reporting? Lastly, what does the ubiquity of public scripts suggest broadly about the theorisation of women, morality and sexuality in Kenya? How does such a theorisation enable a better understanding of the connections between gender, sexuality and violence in Kenya? The public script and how it circulates stereotypical representations of femininity provides an important entry into understanding Kenyan public culture. I use feminist scholarship on women, sexuality and morality to engage gender and sexual politics in Kenya. The idea of a public script regarding gender and sexuality in Kenya defines a publicly endorsed moral narrative that is supported by existing structures of patriarchy and tradition. It suggests that femininity is regulated via popular culture as well as other institutions to ensure control of women's social behaviour in public.

Two significant points emerge for the book: firstly, women's bodies are significant symbolic sites for the generation of discourses on morality and sexuality. Secondly, for such narratives to circulate effectively, they operate through melodramatic, spectacular and scandalous forms. These elements create a pattern for narrating gender and sexuality in the Kenyan public sphere and emphasise the need to discipline the female body in public in order to generate its morality discourse. I borrow the idea of the script from John Gagnon and William Simon (2017) whose labelling theories identify sexual scripts as ideological constructs that 'shape what is seen as sexual or non-sexual, normal or abnormal, pleasurable or painful; and which offer signposts for human interaction' (Weeks 2014, 6). Similarly, public scripts discursively define what is morally acceptable in terms of public behaviour. For Gagnon and Simon, sexual scripts operate at the level of language and symbols, and act as guidelines to sexual conduct (2017). In this way, scripting is not static, but is produced and reproduced 'at personal, interactional and cultural-historical levels' (Plummer in Gagnon and Simon 2017, xiv). Scripting suggests some form of invented structure. In this book, I use scripting to suggest mediation of public sentiment towards women's social behaviour aimed at regulating such behaviour.

I draw on existing scholarship on sexuality in Kenya, acknowledging the various bodies of work that explore varying ideas on sexuality, including the links between, for instance, adolescence and sexuality, sexuality and HIV/AIDs, and sexuality and anthropology, among other themes. Moreover, I am specifically drawn to bodies of work that explore cultural constructions of sexuality in Kenya. In relation to this, I find Rachel Spronk's (2012) work particularly useful. I am drawn to the link she makes between sexuality and anxiety, which troubles easy readings of sexual moralities in Kenya. According to Spronk, sexuality entails the interface between social conventions upheld in public, and sexual pleasure; 'a tension between practices and ideologies, between personal experiences and public opinion' (2012, 13). The tension, as she argues, rightly captures the nuances of sexuality in Kenya. She urges a recognition of the ways in which young Kenyan professionals (a group that she studies in detail) both defy and conform to 'normative discourses of femininity and masculinity, in that they both comply with and challenge common sense' (2012, 15). She adds that 'their narratives are structured by accounts of love and desire, where sex is related to notions of contemporary womanhood and manhood' (2012, 15). A complex reading of sexuality is important if one is to understand the Kenyan public imagination on sexuality. As Spronk argues, there is a tension between sexuality as socially constructed and how it circulates among individuals. While Spronk focuses on ideas of selfhood and personhood in a broader context of cultural production of sexuality, I focus on public productions and circulations of sexuality and morality, and what these public interfaces mean in reading productions of violence against women in Kenyan media. In other words, I focus on the ways in which texts circulate meanings of sexuality in public, and how one can understand that circulation as an interface between public sentiment, disciplinary regimes and subjective positions on sexuality. I argue that the public imagination is shaped by a variety of factors, both institutional and in everyday life.

The book is premised on two related strands of thought. The first has to do with the relationship between the state and other dominant social institutions and the media on the one hand; and popular culture and everyday life in Kenya on the other. I argue that there is need for a closer examination of institutionally endorsed cultural productions in Kenya that generate narratives of gender and sexuality during moments of social crisis or change. The second idea develops from the argument that popular cultures circulate using public scripts to control and manage narratives of gender and sexuality. As Danai Mupotsa (2011) reminds us, discourses of gender and sexuality are embedded in culture, tradition and nationalism, which in turn affect how women and their experiences are interpreted. The state, the media, the church and other similarly dominant institutions contribute to the generation of public scripts for reading gender and sexuality, which are then sustained by circulation. Popular scripts circulate as narratives, songs, utterances and jokes among other modes consumed in everyday life (Barber 2018, Ogola 2017). As demonstrated in the example cited earlier, humour is a form of articulating social anxieties. Laura Oyier's audacity to exist outside a heteronormative expectation of femininity made her an object of ridicule in ways that aimed to discipline her. My engagement with this aspect of the public script is a mode of illuminating patterns of representation in the Kenyan mediascape. My assertion is that by examining how popular narratives circulate as public scripts, I can critically engage the intersections between familiar and well-known stereotypes of femininity; and the disruptions posed by the women represented in such narratives.

In the chapters that follow, I select examples from radio drama, tabloid newspapers and social media. I find that these three media sites map out a general pattern of representation of femininity, while also making apparent temporal and spatial connections between state-endorsed media content and public articulations of the same. While other media forms — such as television — exist, radio drama, tabloid and entertainment newspapers and social media each represent historical standpoints in Kenyan media history that allow for a tracking/tracing of practices in relation to gender and sexuality. I also selected a range of forms — audio, written and visual texts — that help me navigate a variety of narrative terrains and how each engages with central themes of morality, sexuality and gender. The corpus of data that I deal with is based on a set of themes that usefully characterise the public script in relation to normative constructions of romance and intimacy, marriage and (in) fidelity, and other sexual and gendered behaviour in popular culture and media. I also explore the possibilities of counter-readings, and what transgression of norms in heteronormativity looks like. In this case, I use feminist criticism to articulate what happens when women refuse to fit neatly into normalised heterosexual categorisations. I explore scandal, shame and hypervisibility, both as punishment and transgression.

Specifically, radio drama provides a glimpse into state broadcasting, and allows me to engage with the colonial context of its beginnings in Kenya. I use radio to map constructions of modern African identities in a colonial past and a postcolonial present. The radio plays I analyse offer normative fictional narratives of gender and sexuality, presented via a state-endorsed mainstream media channel. These are produced for the Kenyan state broadcaster Kenya Broadcasting Corporation

(KBC), from the 1990s and early 2000s. I have deliberately selected plays from this period because of the political context in which they are steeped. I examine a radio programme called *Radio Theatre*, which was produced for KBC from 1982.[5] The plays were aired weekly, with each radio play based on a theme drawing on everyday life in Kenya. The moral narrative forms the structure on which these plays were based as they pursued seemingly simplistic themes on marriage, love and sex. I consider the metanarrative of the moral narrative present in all the plays and link it to the ideological function of the plays in a heteropatriarchal state. Arguing that this moral narrative presents a form of public script from which audiences are encouraged to read, I critically analyse the ideological assumptions embedded in the plays produced by drawing together what I perceive as 'patterns' in the production of morally acceptable themes. It is interesting to note how much even randomly selected radio plays enact heteronormative discourses. In one play titled *My Aunty Weds* (2002), two women get married in order to honour the lineage of a man who has passed away without leaving behind an heir. There is a clear lack of intimacy between the women, and a general understanding that the younger woman is free to get into relationships with men in order to bear children for the dead man's family. Such an adaptation of a cultural practice that aligns with a national heteronormative framework, demonstrates the dominant patterns of production of sexual narratives in Kenya. I do take note of radio's intimate connection to the everyday lives of listeners that makes it possible to explore such narratives in ways that may deviate from the normative script (see Fardon and Furniss 2000; Gunner, Ligaga and Moyo 2011; Gunner 2019).

In addition to radio, I look at a number of newspaper articles from different sources in the genres of tabloid and entertainment reporting. This is to signal a general mode of representing women as sensational objects — objects of derision as well as of curiosity, as seen in the example at the beginning of this chapter. The examples I use are drawn randomly from the period between 2010 and 2019, to highlight what I argue is a *continuation* of conversations already apparent in the media about women. For instance, in reading media representations of women in public in the 1960s and 1970s, Christine Obbo (1980) signals how punitive the discourses on particular kinds of women were. To exemplify, she explores how single women in Uganda and Kenya were portrayed in binary moralistic terms that aimed to shame and call to order those who were identified as deviant. These trends of representation seem to have persisted, and warrant another look. In the context of contemporary Kenya, similar to what Obbo described in a 1960s East African context, the bulk of newspaper articles circulating show themes that lament the increasing number of single women, who are deemed problematic. Titles such as "Who will marry the increasing number of single mothers in Kenya";[6] "Why most Kenyan women want to have boyfriends but not husbands";[7] and "How young Kenyan women suffer in the hands of a sponsor [sugar daddy]"[8] are not uncommon in most entertainment pages of mainstream newspapers and in tabloid newspapers. Such titles demonstrate a superficial engagement with women's issues, issues which double up as entertainment. These titles are sensationalist, alarmist, didactic or even simplistic. They offer varying accounts of sexual scandal and melodrama, with the ultimate aim of sensationalising the stories and creating spectacle. In many ways, they represent gender and sexuality in ways that are arguably sexist and stereotypical. However, I am aware that tabloid newspapers generally have all too easily been dismissed as trashy due to their dominant style of reporting. As a growing body of scholarship on popular culture in Africa is beginning to show, tabloids, like other forms of popular culture, tap into informal networks of knowledge in order to engage with publics previously excluded from the mainstream public spheres (Barber 1997). Herman Wasserman's work on tabloid journalism in South Africa offers a comprehensive sense of how the tabloid genre can be taken seriously (2010; see also Strelitz and Steenveld 2005; Steenveld and Strelitz 2010). If this is the case, then a deconstruction of the public script in the tabloid genre makes it possible to generate alternative understandings of newspaper reports that I analyse.

Lastly, I choose to read digital platforms as generative of public scripts. An increasing number of young women have become digitally perceptive, and in a context such as Africa, this stands at odds with largely rural, traditionalist cultures, huge class divisions and a normative embrace of gender roles. Even so, more women are taking to online platforms to curate versions of themselves as part of their embrace of global trends, but also as expressions of freedom (Ligaga 2012). While I argue that the digital space remains heterogeneous enough to register varying meanings of femininity, I acknowledge that the public script of morality dictates how the visible bodies of young women that appear online are publicly interpreted. As such, the women who curate themselves online do so with the knowledge that they are going against normative practices of respectability. I use examples of hypervisible women as crucial in engaging a project of voicing and making visible femininity outside of dominant public scripts. I am interested in how these women weave into and out of discourses of acceptable and desired femininities. I choose to work with women in the public eye, such as Vera Sidika, Huddah Monroe and Akothee, who have been publicly dubbed 'divas' or 'socialites'. I engage with the possibilities that digital media have created to allow such voices to emerge, disrupting the normative representations and expectations of desired femininity.

In this chapter, I explore the theoretical frameworks that I use to engage the various questions I pose above. I look at public scripts as derived from public sphere theories, and extend this reading as engendering ideas that control and police discourses of femininity. I argue that the public script exists in a context of controlled sexuality and where respectability defines constructions of morality. Using a cultural studies approach, I then engage with the idea of a disruptive public. This in many ways makes it possible to offer counternarratives to dominant ideology. Using visibility and popular culture as key sites of analysis, I argue that a disruptive public that exists in a violent context provides key clues into understanding questions of agency in Kenya. By reading these using the format of the moral narrative, the chapter then develops ideas of narrative continuity across genres. I explore ideas of transmediation and intertextuality to engage questions of morality as dominant discourses through which sexuality and gender are shaped in Kenya. Finally, the chapter explores the methodological approaches used in the book. These predominantly focus on the text as generative of discourse, and map the symbolic use of language across the various examples used herein.

Public scripts and gender policing

The public script is generated from broader theories of the public sphere. If, as Alan McKee argues, we approach the public sphere as a 'metaphor that we use to think about the way that information and ideas circulate in large societies' (2005, vii), then public scripts can be thought of as consisting of public sentiments about morality, gender and sexuality as normative. I follow McKee's argument that the public sphere can be theorised through a mapping of popular as well as academic conversations on public culture. In my formulation, I argue that although it is important to think of public spheres, it is also important to acknowledge that *a* public sphere can be created from sentiments of morality. I suggest a consideration of a dominant public sphere (where I derive the idea of the public script) in Kenya in which masculinist discourses of gender and sexuality circulate as a norm (Musila 2005). This normalisation has in many ways enabled a dangerous and violent discourse to seep into public discourses of gender and sexuality. Wambui Mwangi (2013), for instance, writing on the idea of public decency, postulates that 'the violent masculinism acting in the name of public "decency"…has launched a pedagogy of violence and terror against Kenyan women using women's bodies as its teaching instrument' (2013, 17). Mwangi adds that 'these "lessons" are administered through public media showing public spectacles enacted in public spaces and fuelled by public commentary' (2013, 17). Mwangi questions the role the media plays in enabling, sustaining and encouraging ways of reading women publicly as sources of 'lessons'. Citing one example, Mwangi shows how in April 2013, a woman in Nyeri town in Central Kenya was attacked, stripped naked and raped for being 'indecently' dressed. Mwangi reproduces the words in the original newspaper article:

> Traders and other passers-by had a free movie to watch as they gathered to
> witness as the drama was unfolding…women and mothers were warned not to

> let their daughters walk out of the house without their approval. What a lesson!
> (Mwangi 2013, 22)

What Mwangi identifies here is unfortunately not an isolated story. In Chapter 5, I explore the connections between discourses of sexuality and violence in Kenya, generated from the belief that women who do not observe the rules of public decency deserve punishment, meted out predominantly by men. The problematic and narrow frames of reference to femininity contribute to the reductive ways in which consequences are articulated in the media. Such kinds of narratives show a predominant sense of policing by the media, which are positioned as sources of moral authority in Kenya. The silence of the ruling elite in cases of violence shows an unspoken endorsement of the media's participation in this policing role. The symbolically entrenched cultures of violence that accompany public representations of ordinary women in the media through discourses of morality and decency form the core of public culture in Kenya. In exploring femininity through the moral narratives that emerge in the media every time women's sexualities are involved, I explore both the participation of the media, as well as the different ways in which specific media genres enable a rupture in this discourse (Gamson 2001a).

What emerges is the role that the media play in setting the agenda or framing issues that circulate in the public sphere. Where agenda-setting refers to the media's ability to focus the public's attention on a few issues, in essence 'priming the public' (McCombs 2002, 12), framing refers to the deliberate gate-keeping role of the media and the deliberate structuring of an issue in a particular way (Scheufele 1999; Fairhurst and Sarr 1996). In thinking through ideas of framing and agenda-setting, I acknowledge the hegemonic discourses on gender and sexuality in the public space, circulated as sources of moral values by the media in Kenya.

Sexuality and respectability

If women's bodies are sites of contested discourses of morality, it is important to engage more closely with the politics of respectability that frames them. Normative approaches to sexuality suggest that the regulation of sexuality takes place in multiple locations, including the family, the school, church and the media. During moments of moral panic, the media, for instance, becomes an important site of social control.

Stan Cohen (1972) has argued that specific conditions or persons can emerge as a threat to societal values and interests, during which time such conditions or persons become pariahs couched in stereotypes by editors and other moral police, sometimes causing change to happen. As Jeffrey Weeks shows, sexuality 'has had a peculiar centrality in such panics, and sexual "deviants" have been omnipresent scapegoats' (1981, 14). The idea of control through sexuality becomes an important way of engaging with how women's representations are regulated.

In Kenya, the politics of respectability are tied to religion as well as to colonial attitudes towards sexuality (Tamale 2011; Nzegwu 2011). Victorian sexuality was idealised as the norm, while African sexuality was read as brutal, primitive and backward, following a deliberate 'stigmatisation of black women inherent in the sexual scheme' (Nzegwu 2011, 253). Nkiru Nzegwu (2011) explores the re-writing of African sexuality through an engagement with the erotic, arguing that a Western-based perception has, over time, influenced how one engages African sexuality, creating a sense of universality. According to Nzegwu, the 'European-derived sexual scheme' presents women as 'objects of pleasure rather than subjects who ought to have pleasure' (2011, 254). Nzegwu points out the disjunctures in sexual genealogies that heighten particular narratives over others, creating a façade of commonsensical knowledge. In fact, interventions by religious institutions, especially Christianity and Islam, meant that Africans had to let go of their 'uncouth ways' and embrace more chaste and 'civilised' approaches to sexuality and social behaviour. This affected other avenues, such as public health research in colonial Africa, which focused, for instance, on 'disease, pregnancy prevention and curbing sexual excesses and perversions' (Tamale 2011, 16). The gendered nature of such interventions affected women in very specific ways. Nzegwu, for example, discusses the historical ways in which religion and the state reinforced an ideology of sex as the purview of men, such that 'the idea of female sexuality and eroticism acquired overtones and attracted moral strictures from the church and state' (2011, 255). The projection of African women's hypersexuality and lasciviousness 'rationalised black women's subjection to rapes and sexual exploitation and the lynching of black males for the imagined ravishing of white women' and what Grace Musila terms 'the shadows of the "black peril"' (Nzegwu 2011, 255; Musila 2015, 64). Imperialist and colonial views of sexuality in Africa led to the view that sex in the context of black bodies was perverse and promiscuous, while white women were presented as 'paragons of purity and beauty and deserving of love and affection' (Nzegwu 2011, 255). It is no wonder that the ideal woman constructed within normative moral narratives pursues this ideal of respectability. Women who 'fall outside' of chastity as a framework automatically symbolise immorality, priming themselves for punishment. This kind of framing embraces the singular history of sexuality that emphasises women's subordination. African scholars have now pushed back on this argument, arguing that the recognition of the matriarchal social ideology in most African societies provides avenues for exploring a different history of sexuality (Diop 1978; Amadiume 1987). In the postcolonial context, the advent of HIV/AIDS brought about a re-theorisation of African sexualities as permissive (much like in the colonial era), in a bid to explain the rampant spread of the disease on the continent (Tamale 2011). Such stereotypical renderings have influenced policy in immense ways. Indeed, as Weeks (1981) has argued elsewhere, a society's identification and classification of deviance reveals hidden attitudes, prejudices and thoughts on what are considered 'good' sexual behaviour.

The need to control sexuality is therefore connected to how it is represented. Stella Nyanzi (2011) outlines different categories through which she reads sexuality in Africa, some of which are sampled below. The first is Foucault's theory of governmentality, which emphasises processes through which governments 'produce governable citizens' to create 'a happy society' on the one hand, and how citizens respond through 'organized practices' such as techniques, mentalities and rationalities, 'to the modes through which their conduct is governed' (Nyanzi 2011, 481). Following Foucault, governmentality takes place in intricate ways, both through coercion and through other modes, such as what Foucault elsewhere has referred to as 'technologies of the self' (Foucault 1982, n.p.). The idea is to engage in what self-governing means outside of centralised power. As Nyanzi argues, Foucault's idea is useful in studying African sexualities precisely because it makes it possible to understand the relationship between broad institutional practices and internalised notions of sexual conduct (Nyanzi 2011). Foucault's ideas help to explain how social behaviour comes to be normalised. A different approach has to do with the idea of surveillance. The surveillance of people's sexual behaviours leads to the formation of general assumptions about those groups of people. A third approach is the charmed circle model developed by Gayle Rubin (1984), which explores hierarchies of sex. Often, what is considered good sex (or good sexual behaviour) is muted in public discourse. Often good sexual behaviour aligns with good moral behaviour. There is no excess. Behaviour that is demonised also often exposes what Rubin identifies as bad sex. In the case of women, this predominantly involves extramarital affairs, same sex relations, sex before marriage in a heterosexual relationship and so on. Sexual stereotypes also provide a way of understanding how regulation works. Stereotypes provide a language or pattern through which general assumptions of people are made. Stereotypes are often reliant on conventional knowledge and leave little room for diversity and difference. The above approaches are useful for thinking about the place of conventional sexuality in the public sphere, and in tracing the patterns of knowledge production about it in the media.

Visibility, popular culture and disruptive publics

The above theoretical outline shapes how we can read the public script as constructed through dominant ideas. Yet, can one speak of a singular public script without acknowledging the numerous ways such a proposition can be contested? I look at the idea of the public as generated by the text to provide a different kind of interest in a heterogeneous interpretation of women, and the possibility of a pushback to problematic discourses. Where a public script suggests a static, monolithic, construct against which all meaning is generated, I acknowledge that media messages are invariably heterogeneous. As such, I interrogate the idea of the 'public' in the public script, to signal what Mikhail Bakhtin (1981) terms heteroglossia, the multiple variations of language. I use Michael Warner's idea of a public not merely as a social totality or a concrete audience, but as that which 'comes into being only in relation to texts and their circulation' (2002, 50). The discursive location of publics allows them to be recognised as existing in multiple planes, sometimes simultaneously, in different texts. A close reading of selected texts maps the kinds of disruptive publics constructed through the discourses of femininity across a number of texts. It is also possible to imagine a counterpublic that reads the dominant codes differently. A counterpublic, according to Warner, exists through discourse as a public that marks itself as against a dominant cultural horizon. Important in Warner's theorisation of publics is a second useful idea, that of agency. Warner argues that publics are self-organised, that is, they exist 'by virtue of being addressed', and this means that no external forces such as the state or the media can organise them outside of themselves (Warner 2002, 50). In other words, the strength of this public lies in its generation through discourse: 'it is self-creating and self-organized, and herein lies its power as well as its elusive strangeness' (Warner 2002, 52). Agency, he argues, is located in discourse, where the possibility of being addressed and the possibility of action are contained in that discourse. This is juxtaposed with 'formally organized mediations…defined by pre-given frameworks, by institutions and law' which, according to Warner, 'is the image of totalitarianism' (2002, 52). Warner's formulation is particularly useful because of the over-arching methodology that I choose to use in this book. I read the public discourse circulating through media forms and articulations of subjectivity as evident in the text. My interpretations of the texts are based on the possibilities of texts generating disruptive publics.

It would be naïve, however, to think about disruptive publics without considering the intersecting experiences of oppression and social inequality that affect women in Kenya. In this case, disruptive publics are read as existing in a context of violence. One method of surfacing these publics is by looking at how women become visible, and to consider what such visibility means, both in terms of disruption and vulnerability. As such, I want to argue that the idea of visibility captures the complexity of publics as generated as text. Increased visibility of women in the media in Kenya in the last two decades or so, can be celebrated as a positive development in on-going feminist conversations about gender, power and society. Visibility, often read alongside notions of voice, suggests an increase in awareness of gender differences, and the need to address intersections of oppression along racial, sexual, gender and class lines. As Sarah Banet-Weiser (2015, 55) describes,

> The politics of visibility usually describes the process of making visible a political category (such as gender or race) that is and has been historically marginalized in the media, law, policy, etc. As a politics of visibility, this process describes what is simultaneously a category and a qualifier that can articulate a political identity. Representation, or visibility, takes on a political valence. Here, the goal is that the coupling of the qualifier and 'politics' can be productive of something else — hopefully, social change. 'Politics,' then, is a descriptor of the practices of visibility, where visibility will hopefully result in political change.

Visibility as a feminist agenda is the desire for women to be seen, recognised, and acknowledged; for their choices to be taken seriously; for their contradictions not to be highlighted for purposes of shaming, but as markers of being human, and doing the work of 'living'. Feminist scholarship has emphasised the need for continuous interrogation of everyday experiences of women and the spaces they occupy in order to better understand the power dynamics generated through problematic normative gender discourses. This kind of interrogation is a process of making visible the experiences and realities of women that are often deliberately invisibilised. Visibility can also be understood as a refusal to conform to norms that restrict one's ability to be properly human. Both visibility and invisibility are important tropes in feminist thinking, because, as explained by Ilya Parkins and Eva Karpinski, they symbolise the 'feminist desire for presence' (2014, 3). Both presence and absence address the questions of women's participation in public spaces, whether through activism or other modes of representation. The politics of visibility are about a project of recuperation and revision that inspire new feminist epistemologies that make clear 'invisible, marginalized knowledges' (Parkins and Karpinski 2014, 3–4). In this configuration, the 'ability to be heard and seen has come to signify as the foundation of empowerment' (Parkins and Karpinski 2014, 4).

Even as one engages with meanings of visibility, a competing strand of thought has been the subjects of invisibility, voicelessness and absence. In looking at black women's bodies, Mowatt, French, and Malebranche (2013) argued that questions of invisibility make reference not just to their exclusion from mainstream discourse, but also to the ways in which these bodies are reduced to stereotypical, sex-objectified forms. This can include the placement of black women on display through a minute focus on specific parts of the body. This book engages with the kinds of scrutiny that black women face in the public space, and the methods of policing that define their femininity. The book, in acknowledging the contextual space in Kenya, draws attention to the punitive measures taken against women who choose to make themselves visible, even when faced with threats of shaming, violence and in some cases, death. In the age of social media and the availability of mobile telephony, young women are becoming more brazen in their engagements with the public.

I use a black feminist approach, as well as a cultural studies engagement with popular culture to examine this complexity with visibility in Kenya. Black feminist theories have long signalled the inadequacy of mainstream scholarship in dealing with black women's subjectivities in different contexts. The body of work in this field engages more broadly with questions of marginality, and calls for a reorientation of theory into reading subaltern subjectivities. This body of work also signals alternative ways of knowing that are not properly elucidated in mainstream scholarship. Scholars such as bell hooks (1997) and Patricia Hill Collins (2000) for instance, have suggested ways of engaging with this gap. As an ode to Audre Lorde (1982), hooks suggests the use of experimental genres such as biomythography as a space in which to 'invent the self' through 'dreams and fantasies' in order to 'challenge notions of absolute truth' (hooks 1997, xix). This approach disintegrates notions of a single truth, and acknowledges other truths that are the collages and pastiches of these women's lives (hooks 1997). To re-narrate one's story in this way is to reclaim one's identity. It is to re-coup the black woman from the margins of knowledge, and re-introduce her into the realm of public knowledge, through lenses that make her visible and legible. In line with such a re-narration is what Stuart Hall (1993, 105) refers to as 'the global postmodern'. According to Hall, the global postmodern registers shifts in dominant culture

> …toward popular practices, toward everyday practices, toward local narratives, toward the decentering of old hierarchies and the grand narratives. This decentering or displacement opens up new spaces of contestation and affects a momentous shift in the high culture of popular culture relations, thus presenting us with a strategic and important opportunity for intervention in the popular cultural field. (1993, 105)

I find Hall's invitation to disrupt normative cultural practices useful as a theoretical and methodological inroad into my work. The popular, as Hall argues, engages with the underside, informal aspects of culture, and is a site of alternative traditions (Hall 1993). The popular also allows a different kind of conversation about culture, different from a dominant national culture. The popular is, however, not linear. It is contradictory because, inasmuch as it captures the potential for rejuvenating narrative, it is also the site of commodification through the recycling of stereotypes and the formulaic (Hall 1993). This contradiction is important in explaining the various ways in which femininity has circulated discursively in Kenya, and how that affects a reading of women.

The emphasis on popular culture is deliberate. As argued by scholars of popular culture globally, and in Africa more specifically, a study of popular culture yields information about culture's muted, nuanced and understated aspects. Popular culture records the particularities of the everyday. Even then, as has been argued by scholars such as Michel de Certeau (1984), it is in understanding the everyday that one can begin to grasp broader connections to the global. A study of the practices of everyday life, as explored in detail in the work of De Certeau and others, begins to engage more deeply with a space that is often ubiquitous, and seemingly random and disconnected. Spencer, Ligaga and Musila (2018, 3) define the popular in Africa as 'the dynamic culture that speaks to ordinary people's concerns'. For them, the popular is a valuable site of meaning making in which everyday aspirations and desires can be mapped. Karin Barber (2018) identifies the popular as the unofficial site of the everyday from which ordinary people can contest, agree with and negotiate life. The popular is a vibrant site of cultural production in Africa. Popular culture establishes a clear understanding of how stereotypes of ordinary women in Kenya circulate in the media. The bulk of these stereotypes centre on questions of morality and sexuality. The popular culture genres that I explore project stereotypes of femininity onto the public sphere, and interrogate the binary mode of representation of the morally good and the morally deficient, and how these are often considered so, based on gendered and sexual behaviour. This dichotomous logic and its possible violent connotations is central to my work.

Intertextuality, transmediation and the moral narrative

So far, I have demonstrated how the 'moral narrative' structures the way narratives of femininity emerge in different popular media platforms. The idea of the moral narrative stems from the broader genre of the morality tale and is a well-established form. I draw ideas both from African oral literature (Okpewho 1992; Finnegan 2012) and from Western morality tales in which function is central to understanding the form. Oral literature, which consists of 'riddles, puns, tongue-twisters, proverbs, recitations, chants, songs and stories' creatively use language to engage lived experiences of members of a community (Okphewo 1992, 4). Oral narratives have didactic functions as well, used demonstratively to shape conduct and offer lessons. Like the Western morality tale, the African oral narrative portrays a struggle between good and evil and offers a lesson in the end. The genre of the moral narrative is often linked to children's narratives of a particular period in European history. Similarly, the bulk of morality narratives in Africa stems from a long tradition of oral storytelling, in which 'virtues and morality are deliberately and systematically inculcated by adults into younger generations' (Insaidoo 2011, xvi). The moral narrative reiterates the rules about virtue and evil, in the hope that social order is maintained. It is not lost to me that the oral narrative or morality tale, with its simplistic format, was addressed to children. Yet what are the modern ways in which it has been recuperated? I consider forms such as the melodrama useful in shaping certain genres, like the soap opera, which draws on the structural uses of virtue and vice, and heightened drama, to articulate the plot of the story. In this way, I consider the moral narrative as taking over the function of the morality tale in the context of contemporary modes of telling, such as edutainment television in several developing countries; and how it can be used across media forms to transmit specific messages (Singhal et al. 2004). In this case, 'narrative' as opposed to 'tale' invokes a looseness of genre that is far more theoretically useful in its application to reading a disparate corpus of texts.

In reading texts across a range of platforms, I therefore aim to engage narrative continuity as a mode of expressing femininity. The moral narrative becomes a form that is referenced across texts, but that also structures the very texts that contain it. It becomes possible to identify the moral narrative through its format (plot, characters, storyline) in radio drama, as well as in tabloid reportage. If we return to the story at the beginning of this chapter, we see a formulation of a moral narrative in which different actors perform different functions. Oyier is a villain who gets punished for being a 'bad' woman, while the man speculated to have abandoned her is a hero for 'teaching her a lesson'. The design to embarrass Oyier in public, as well as her arrest, form part of her punishment. She is rescued from this scandal by sympathisers as part of her rehabilitation. She is offered a job and restored back into society as a 'normal' woman. The possibility of identifying good and bad in such a story forms the core of the moral narrative genre. It cuts across formats, and becomes easily recognisable. I attempt to map this connectivity by engaging with theories of intertextuality and transmediation. I hope to explain how the moral narrative can exist in different media formats as well as function in different technologies.

Specific bodies of scholarship have attempted to theorise the interconnectivity of narratives that share similar storylines and formats, or which demonstrate the ways in which the media and communication worlds are increasingly converging. Conceptually, this connection between texts in which they continually reference each other is called intertextuality (Chandler 2002). Conceptualised by Julia Kristeva (2002), intertextuality is used to identify shared codes between texts through which referential meaning can be gleaned. It points to the instability of the text, a post-structuralist concept that opens up the possibility of reading phenomena across texts. In popular culture, intertextuality has come to play an important role in the creation of frameworks or genres through which to understand the context of textual production.

Another useful concept to explain the phenomenon of connectivity of narratives is transmediation. Jennifer Jones and Brenda Weber (2015, 13) argue that the expansion of the mediascape makes it possible to study phenomena across a range of media platforms through the manner in which they form traceable narratives, what they refer to as 'transmediated continuity'. Transmediated continuity refers to the 'intensification of stories across diverse media platforms, such as the internet, tabloids, and social media' (2015, 13). They here refer to the convergent cultures emerging particularly in the era of digital media. Traditional media converge in unique ways with other media platforms to make any kind of fixed identification of technological sites impossible. As Jones and Weber argue, television, for instance, 'no longer references a square box in a living room but now refers to a host of mediated screens — from phones to tablets to computers to flat screens — and programming is becoming more dispersed across network, cable, and online modes such as Netflix' (2015, 13). Addressing a similar phenomenon, Marsha Kinder (1991, 1) writes on 'transmedia intertextuality' to refer to the 'expanding supersytem of entertainment' forging connections across media. Similarly, Henry Jenkins (2006) speaks of transmedia storytelling 'which has come to indicate the technique of creating a connected narrative experience across multiple platforms and formats in a complex form distinct from traditional sequels or adaptations' (Jones and Weber 2015, 13). While each of these authors addresses slightly different experiences with narrative continuity, what is emerging strongly is the possibility of reading narrative across platforms. Jones and Weber explain this replicability of narrative that 'creates a "now-ness"' in which ideas circulated at one moment continue to have relevance in another, blending with new forms in new times to structure an eternal present. In so doing, transmediated continuity often recrafts a notion of what existed before (Jones and Weber 2015, 14–15).

The moral narrative is a continuous and persistent narrative that remains relevant across platforms and across time and can be identified as fitting in a particular genre, and containing a recognisable structure. At the same time, applying a post-structuralist reading allows one to read beyond these patterns and to explore different interpretations and ways of reading. A moral narrative, according to Mark Tappan and Lyn Brown (1989) is a genre whose main purpose is to procure moral education and moral development. It explores conflict and offers resolutions, inevitably reflecting a society's moral values. Embedded in the moral narrative are three ideas: narrative in relation to the everyday life experiences; narrative in relation to moral conflict and narrative in terms of lessons that can be learned from it. In the genre, conflict and resolution are demonstrated in dramatic and highly visible ways, with the purpose of highlighting the lessons that ought to be learned. The idea of lessons is therefore important, for, as Jeffrey Turner (1991) argues, this is a key element of the moral narrative and is what enables moral self-understanding.

The moral narrative and its connection to moral lessons in everyday life are central to understanding how popular arts in Africa function. Media forms of radio drama, tabloid newspaper articles and online or digital modes of (self) representation as popular art reflect various cultural values belonging to those who produce, circulate and consume them. This is the significance of popular culture in producing a disruptive reading of the public script. It encourages a reading not just of production of dominant ideology, but also of reception. Popular culture in Africa, following Winfried Fluck (1987), Karin Barber (1987) and Johannes Fabian (1978), among others, emphasises the 'active production of meanings, and consequently, an expression of genuine cultural attitudes and values' by 'a large segment of the population' (Fluck 1987, 31, 32). The possibility of a counterpublic expresses ways in which the moral narrative can be engaged beyond its dominant function. It can become, as has been argued, a source of self-reflection and self-engagement, and it can become a source of resistance. Fluck reads the African popular text against another idea of the popular as mass culture. Unlike the suggestion that the popular insinuates active production of culture by 'the people', the popular as mass culture centralises culture industries that impose dominant ideas on seemingly passive recipients.

It is therefore a challenge to explore texts produced by media institutions and read them as popular culture. Radio drama is, for instance, produced mainly for the state or commercial radio stations in Kenya. Similarly, print newspapers and digital platforms are owned by large conglomerates whose main aim is to earn profit. However, popular forms such as radio drama, tabloid newspaper articles and social media cultures fit theoretically in the frame of popular culture as circulating among potentially active recipients precisely because of their engagement with everyday cultures that are familiar and ordinary. George Ogola usefully reads popular fictional media as popular because of its ability to draw on informal and ordinary narratives that comment on the Kenyan polity (2017). My reading of the popular is likewise influenced by scholars of popular literary cultures such as Stephanie Newell (2000) and Joyce Nyairo (2004) who, while reading different modes, namely popular fiction and music respectively, emphasise the need to understand the interaction between producers of popular forms and content and their contexts of production which engage with everyday realities that are familiar to potential readers and audiences. Newell, for instance, argues for a closer look at the Ghanaian context in which local publications circulate, and how these intertwine with the lives of both book sellers (often also the publishers of the books) and readers / buyers of the books. Similarly, in a different context in Kenya, Nyairo demonstrates the importance of popular music texts whose interaction with their context enables an understanding of how these forms mediate everyday realities in Kenya.

The nuanced readings of moral narratives as popular allow for a rich engagement with the contexts of production and reception, given the centrality of mediums such as radio in the lives of ordinary people in the African continent, the popularity of tabloid newspapers, and the possibilities for agency presented through the upsurge of digital cultures. Indeed, Bodil Frederiksen (2000) highlights the importance of popular media in the lives of young men and women in Kenya who appropriate popular cultural modes to engage with everyday life and attain a semblance of equality in a society that is still highly unequal and conservative. In her analysis, Frederiksen discusses how popular narratives offer young people an opportunity to negotiate real life situations in spite of limited economic and social opportunities. The moral narrative can, in the context set out above, be read as a popular genre. It is a ubiquitous form that permeates several African forms of narration, whether popular music, art or performance. It circulates narratives that are familiar and reflective of ordinary life. As art, it circulates modes of entertainment that require an uptake of lessons dramatised in it. Yet, to explore it as a form means to explore its melodramatic nature. Peter Brooks (1976) highlights as its key characteristics: elements of 'excess', 'heightened dramatization', 'extravagance' and 'intensity of the moral claim impinging on their characters' consciousness'. Narratives of everyday life are elevated to 'heightened and hyperbolic drama, making reference to pure and polar concepts of darkness and light, salvation and damnation' (Brooks 1976, ix). In other words, melodrama brings with it exaggeration, sensationalism, and oversimplification through linear plotlines and stereotyping of characters.

Methodological considerations

I use a text-based research and not an ethnographic account by and with the women I refer to. Yet as feminist studies consistently show, experiential research is useful when reading women in order to bridge the gap between the researcher and the researched (Mupotsa 2011). To paraphrase Mupotsa, experiential knowledge also answers ethical questions about studying women and their experiences in situated ways (2011). While I find this kind of research method invaluable, I wanted to explore questions of representation that I consider deliberately harmful to the wellbeing of women. As a feminist researcher and a media scholar, I am particularly alert to the casual circulation of news items that contain taken-for-granted assumptions about women. I explore familiar texts that harm women not just physically, but psychologically. I explore items that affect public sentiment about women, and which, when left unnamed, continue to foster violence against women. This is a project against myths of femininity that do harm. By naming aspects of myths in circulation even today, I map problematic articulations that need to be attended to rather than dismissed. In many ways, my work is influenced by feminist scholarship that is located in women's everyday affective encounters, marked prominently in the work of Sara Ahmed (2017); Pumla Dineo Gqola (2015; 2017); and bell hooks (1997), among other black feminists.

In many ways then, a text-based research remains useful for me for a number of reasons. Speaking specifically about media and communication studies, Sara Mckinnon (2014, 2) states:

> While many qualitative researchers assemble instances of communicative action from people themselves, through methods of data collection such as interviews, focus groups, and observation, other qualitative researchers examine texts as sites of people's use of symbols. A text can be understood as any instance where symbols are being used to convey meaning to an audience. In this vein, texts may be written words in the strict sense of the term — such as books, magazines, manifestos, or pamphlets — but they may also be verbally delivered speeches, music, television sitcoms, photographs, or buildings.

I am interested in the symbolic messages assembled through the media, and the pattern of meanings generated through these texts. Subsequently, I am interested in how these meanings refuse to remain embedded in a typology of morality. These texts are leaky narratives, to use Keguro Macharia's formulation (2015). This 'leakiness' allows me to read the multiple publics that are addressed in the texts, and the various alternative meanings of femininity that are made available (Macharia 2015, 69). The leakiness also enables a critical intervention using feminist theory, in which mapping becomes a form of unsettling (hooks 1996). In her work on black films, bell hooks identifies the significance of interrogatory work done by cultural scholars studying black films / filmmakers. She argues that 'the interrogation of the very sign of blackness by contemporary left cultural workers ruptured the critical complacency surrounding fixed assumptions about the black aesthetic that had for the most part constituted the conceptual framework in which most critical writing by black thinkers about film took place' (1996, 8). My book offers a necessary dismantling of frameworks for reading gender and sexuality as circulated in Kenyan popular media. I am also drawn to textual analysis because I understand texts as part of something larger that are incomplete in themselves. They are what Michael McGee terms 'fragments' of a larger discourse (1990, 279). The context in which the texts are produced therefore remain paramount to my research. This kind of research 'gives the analyst special insight into the symbolic actions, nuances in meaning, and textual forms that are present in the text. Studying theory also provides analysts with ideas about what their own text might say concerning culture, politics, society, or the world around them more generally' (Mckinnon 2014, 3).

Structure of the book

In the remaining chapters, I engage with various debates, histories and textual readings that further elucidate the ways in which popular texts can be located more centrally as cultural clues in Kenyan histories of women and sexuality. In Chapter 2, I consider scholarship on femininity, its construction and theorisation, in order to think about the role that stereotypical views play in the construction of women and sexuality in Kenya. I argue that it is important to map various articulations of femininity, temporally and spatially, in both colonial and postcolonial contexts. In an era of globalisation, new articulations of femininity emerge, and demand new configurations. This is an era of choice and freedom, yet femininity is still located in a neoliberal set-up. What does this mean, when pursuing a theory of disruption and speaking back? What does it do to the theorisation of voice and agency?

Chapter 3 focuses on the institutionalised form of the radio play in Kenya and uses this as a backdrop against which to look at African womanhood and its normative construction during colonialism in Kenya. I use the opportunity here to think about postcolonial modes of gender representations more generally in Kenya. Radio drama is used to index the various ways broadcasting participated in the formation of modern African womanhood. I use radio to engage moments in Kenyan history that were significant enough to influence patriotism and nationalism. I centre conversations about gender in this context. In the same chapter, I perform a close textual reading of selected radio drama plays and their embrace of normative femininities. I am interested in the form of the moral narrative, its structures and functions and the way in which it shapes everyday ideas of womanhood through romance, sex and other themes related to gender. I show how the radio drama programme of choice follows a formulaic structure, which in many ways aligns with a dominant state-endorsed narrative.

Chapter 4 examines the genre of the newspaper tabloid. I focus on stories that often draw attention to themselves as points of learning through unruly femininities. Tabloids signal the use of melodrama, speculation, spectatorship and other forms of excess attached to the narration of women's sexual stories. This is a chapter that dwells on the work of scandal. I attempt to mount an argument for the consideration of a counterpublic that reads against the expected mainstream interpretation.

In Chapter 5, I continue this analysis of the tabloid genre, this time focusing on discussions on love and money relationships in Kenya, and how these have shaped discourses of young women's sexualities. The chapter also draws links with the ongoing violence against women, often engaged with publicly, both with shock and regret. I am drawn to this narrative of shock and regret, and the subsequent circulation of particular narratives as cautionary tales.

Chapter 6 explores the idea of hypervisibility in the age of social media. Looking at a number of figures of women who have risen to public notoriety because of their public displays and articulations of their sexualities, I read them against the backdrop of the arguments of morality as a key disciplining narrative. They epitomise unruly femininities in their transgressive practices of self-presentation. I look at the different ways in which these women 'transgress' the norm and how they create new spaces for themselves in a context where their visibility is frowned upon. By locating these cultures in broader arguments that the internet needs to be read as an emerging site for popular culture productions, I take into consideration both the successes and limitations that make it possible to apply such a reading to this space. Considering examples from social media such as discussion forums, Facebook and Twitter, I look at a number of examples that 'shocked' Kenyans, not only because of the transgressive behaviour displayed in such spaces, but also because of the refusal of those involved to apologise for their transgressions. The ensuing scandals that accompanied the displays of sexuality fade in comparison to the manner in which these women chose to embrace their ideas of personal freedom and choice. I borrow from literature on postfeminism, but push the argument further to find the role of agency in such self-representations.

Notes

1 Several newspaper articles circulated the story of Laura Oyier during this time. She was a minor sensation, appearing on TV shows, radio programmes and social media. See for instance: Faith Karanja. 2015. "Woman charged over failure to settle KSh229,505 [about $2 000] bill at Intercontinental Hotel on Valentine's Day." *Standard Digital*, February 18. Accessed 17 September 2019. https://www.standardmedia.co.ke/article/2000152118/; Richard Munguti. 2015. "Woman charged with failing to pay Sh230K Valentine's bills in Five Star hotel." *Nairobi News*, February 18. Accessed 17 September 2019. https://nairobinews.nation.co.ke/news/woman-charged-for-failing-to-foot-valentines-bills-in-five-star-hotel

2 Tabloid newspapers sustained intrigue around Oyier. See for instance Caren Nyota. 2015. "Where the hell is the serial defaulter Laura Oyier?" *Mpasho*, December 14. Accessed 17 September 2019. https://mpasho.co.ke/hell-serial-bill-defaulter-laura-oyier/; see also Edward Chweya. 2015. "Laura Oyier is a fame seeker, controversial singer roasts the intercontinental hotel woman." *ghafla!*, March 16. Accessed 17 September 2019. http://www.ghafla.com/laura-oyier-is-a-fame-seeker-controversial-singer-roasts-the-intercontinental-hotel-woman/

3 In this book, I use the idea of the good time girl to signal ways in which modernity and gender intertwine with consumerism in the Kenyan public imagination.

4 Henry. 2015. "Laura Oyier and the Intercontinental Hotel Valentine's day drama, was it just a blessing in disguise?" *Crazy World Times*, March 17. https://blogjob.com/crazyworldtimes/2015/03/17/laura-oyier-and-the-intercontinental-hotel-valentines-day-drama-was-it-just-a-blessing-in-disguise/

5 This is the information given by one of its long-term producers, the late Nzau Kalulu. According to him, this was the official date of production. However, *Radio Theatre's* generic title suggests that it could have existed before this in other forms. I discuss this aspect in Chapter 3.

6 In the Standard Media: UReport section, readers can post their stories online. In this one, accessed 13 November 2018, a Nelson Mandela, May 2017, raises alarm about the increasing number of single mothers: https://www.standardmedia.co.ke/ureport/story/2000202158/who-will-marry-the-increasing-number-of-single-mothers-in-kenya

7 Some articles use celebrity women to justify their arguments. In the article by Anne Muiruiri (2017, October 9), for instance, the idea of women exercising choice is intriguing enough to draw attention. "Why most Kenyan women want to have boyfriends but not husbands." *Eve Digital*. Accessed 13 November 2018. https://www.standardmedia.co.ke/evewoman/article/2001256812/why-most-kenyan-women-want-to-have-boyfriends-but-not-husbands

8 In this article, Honesty Oimbo details how young women looking for compensatory relationships suffer. Oimbo argues that it is often the young woman's greed that destroys her, with cases of men poisoning and even nearly killing women. This article was published soon after the gruesome death of Sharon Otieno who was in a relationship with an older married man for money. I explore her story and others like hers in Chapter 5. Accessed 13 November 2018. https://www.standardmedia.co.ke/ureport/story/2001297580/experiences-how-young-kenyan-women-suffer-in-the-hands-of-a-sponsor

2

Femininity, stereotypes and resistance in Kenyan public cultures

Introduction

In her essay, *Silence is a Woman* (2013), Wambui Mwangi critically maps women's entry into public space in Kenya, and the ways in which silence has been used as a weapon to define this entry. Mwangi's argument though, is that women in Kenya have historically used the very sites of silence — their bodies — to protest against ill-treatment and to stage dissent. In an androcentric world, women use their bodies as forms of 'public voice' (2013, 16). In analysing the politics of containment therefore, Mwangi does not dispute that patriarchy functions by creating good and bad women, and by constructing good women as the ones who remain silent. Mwangi rather launches an argument for reading how women exist in these spaces, and how they find voice in such spaces of restriction. She traces a history of women who have dissented against patriarchy before, during and after colonial rule. Wangu wa Makeri, for instance, stands as a powerful icon of female leadership. Wa Makeri was a Gikuyu tribal chief, a position she held from 1902 to 1909. She was said to have been authoritarian in her leadership and was forced to resign from her position after a scandal, in which she apparently danced naked in what was supposed to be an exclusively male warrior dance. Power had 'gone to her head'. Some narratives have it that she was overthrown from her position after all the men under her rule impregnated all the women, overthrowing Wa Makeri once she was too weak to fight back. Mwangi draws attention to this narrative of submission that holds women's participation in politics suspect. She argues that

> This carefully circulated and re-narrated cultural 'knowledge' re-inscribes alleged contradictions about women's bodies, power and political possibility. It reminds

women that all our bodies are always available for physical degradation by men. It threatens while inscribing the illegitimacy of women in political authority. It destroys the public power of women's bodies by destroying women's power to use our bodies in a public way. It inscribes the collective memory of matriarchal rule with the mark of illegitimacy and perversion. (Mwangi 2013, 20)

Mwangi's work engages the Kenyan public space as a site that produces narratives of restrictions for women. How women enter into the public space is controlled carefully using narratives that are repackaged for specific purposes. The very site of women's political voice is also the site that is most publicly attacked and called into doubt. The presence of women in the public space is therefore always pre-determined. Women who have occupied the public space, whether ordinary or extraordinary, have always done so against a specific masculinist frame (Mwangi 2013). This masculinist outlook has been sharpened by colonial contact, with white and black men colluding to ensure functional gender hierarchies that work in favour of African men (Ochwada 2007). Anne McClintock shows how women remain at the boundary of the nation-state, where 'national agency is male' (1995, 353). If women do not get the same access to rights and resources, how does this translate in the popular pages of the media? How can one reflect productively on the manner in which women do in fact enter the public space?

The purpose of this chapter is to engage with public sentiments of womanhood contained within stereotypes of 'proper' and 'deviant' women in a complex history of gender power, patriarchal hegemony and heteronormativity. The chapter interrogates the various ways in which femininity is imagined in Kenyan popular culture against shifting constructions of womanhood in Kenyan media. Acknowledging how colonial and postcolonial moments have shaped representations of women in Africa, I explore what it means to be visible and vocal in an era of media plurality. In the chapter, I approach femininity as a normative construction of colonial imperialism, what has been referred to as the cult of domesticity (Berger 2016; McClintock 1995). I also read femininity as a contested category, looking at variations of theories on women in Africa, and use a feminist approach to engage with practices that destabilise normative readings. I argue that these two approaches have influenced the emergence and circulation of stereotypes about women. I use a postcolonial critique to examine the theoretical meanings of stereotypes. I offer a reflection of stereotypes in African popular culture and how their circulation suggests a complex play of meaning in everyday public cultures. I then examine femininity as an ideological concept based on a European/Victorian ethos and consider what new femininities, which enable conceptual rupture, mean in contexts where feminine ideologies seem so fixed. Within an African context, I examine how global meanings and articulations of femininity have influenced the formation of African feminine subjectivities. I look at how these various permutations affect or shape gender politics in Kenya. The woman politician becomes a recurring object of analysis because of her overt exposure to public criticism in the media.

The work of the stereotype

In reading the stereotypical ways in which women are represented in public cultures, this chapter navigates such representations as products of stereotyping, rather than as fixed entities. I pay particular attention to context, as this offers an opportunity to reflect on that to which the stereotyping is responding. In other words, I pay attention to moments when the stereotype is brought into play. Stereotyping as a form of containment, surveillance and control alludes to the function of the public script. One of the reasons femininity continues to circulate successfully in stereotypical and limiting ways is because it is contained in a moral narrative genre in Kenya. This is scripted in a cautionary tale model, using ubiquitous and recognisable figures of womanhood that occupy a distinct place in popular culture on the African continent, and indeed, globally. Femininity is read as a recurring theme in the moral narrative. In this model, womanhood is presented in the broad categories of the 'proper woman' or the 'deviant woman'. The moral narrative presents a useful methodological tool for identifying such patterns of representations, as it allows one to think about sentiment as contained in a type or genre. This kind of approach allows for a questioning of femininity, not as McClintock puts it, 'an invisible norm', but 'as a problem to be investigated' (1995, 8). If we read femininity as invented, then 'it is the inventedness of [such] historical hierarchies that renders attention to social power and violence' (McClintock 1995, 8). An analysis of these kinds of representations allows for a more critical engagement with the ways in which policing and regulation of sexuality works through avenues such as the media. It opens up texts to more complex analyses of the processes of negotiation, contradiction and resistance, reflecting more complicated ways in which women enter into the public sphere.

Work on stereotypes explores how they function in contexts of power to fix and exclude (Hall 1997). A stereotype, according to Chris Barker (2004, 188) is a 'vivid but simple representation that reduces persons to a set of exaggerated, usually negative character traits and is thus a form of representation which essentializes others through the operation of power.' Both Hall's and Barker's observations provoke critical thinking about the role of regimes of representation, whether in reading sexuality, race, gender, or other articulations of cultural difference. Following Richard Dyer's thinking, Hall points out the difference between typing and stereotyping (Dyer 1979, Hall 1997). While a type helps to make sense of something, i.e. using simple, easily recognisable characteristics, a stereotype uses basic characteristics of a thing and reduces everything about that thing into simple and exaggerated aspects. In other words, stereotypes fix difference. Through stereotypes, it becomes possible to exclude those who do not belong to a group, or what Hall calls the 'splitting' role of stereotypes (1997, 258). Splitting enables the closing of boundaries, excluding everything that does not belong and, in so doing, helps to maintain symbolic order. That which is considered polluted or dangerous is symbolically excluded in order for purity to be restored. Stereotypes function in conditions where there are 'gross inequalities of power' (Hall 1997, 258). This power is usually directed at those considered subordinate or as existing outside of the dominant group. In other words, what is considered normative is often reflective of values held by those in positions of power. Heteropatriarchy, for instance, excludes sexual identities seen as different, while ethnocentrism elevates values of one cultural group over others, and so on. In contexts of gender inequality, it is important to recognise who is labelled an outcast and then evaluate their position vis-à-vis normative discourse. The normalisation of stereotypical discourses ensures that the balance of power is maintained. Meanings of gender and sexuality become refined in such stereotypical containment.

In the chapter, I am interested in problematising the stereotype in order to understand subversive women. I find Homi Bhabha's (1994) identification of the paradox in ideological constructions of difference useful. According to him, fixity in colonial discourse both points to the rigidity of colonial discourse's construction of otherness, while also signalling 'disorder, degeneracy and daemonic repetition' (1994, 94). In engaging the concept of fixity, Bhabha identifies the stereotype as 'a form of knowledge and identification that vacillates between what is always "in place", already known, and something that must be anxiously repeated' (1994, 94–95). The stereotype is ambivalent. Ambivalence, according to Bhabha (1994, 95)

> is the force...that gives the colonial stereotype its currency: ensures its repeatability in changing historical and discursive conjunctures; informs its strategies of individuation and marginalisation; produces that effect of probabilistic truth and predictability which, for the stereotype, must always be in excess of what can be empirically proved or logically construed.

For Bhabha, ambivalence enables a methodological shift from analysing the binary rhetoric of the stereotype, that is, whether something is positively or negatively represented. Ambivalence makes possible a productive engagement with context, or what he terms 'the processes of subjection' (Bhabha 1994, 95). What does a thorough engagement with the stereotype produce? What does such an exercise make possible? For as Bhabha reminds us, in order to understand colonial power, it is necessary to 'construct its regime of truth, not to subject its representations to a normalising judgement' (Bhabha 1994, 95). Otherness is then identifiable as an ambivalence

— an 'object of desire and derision' (Bhabha 1994, 95). Bhabha's challenge is then to recognise the stereotype as a 'complex, ambivalent, contradictory mode of representation, as anxious as it is assertive', and to understand that it 'demands not only that we extend our critical and political objectives but that we change the object of analysis itself' (1994, 100). What would a questioning of our own assumptions mean in how we read/locate the stereotypical object of study? If we begin by looking at the object not as other, but as central to our understanding of difference, we begin to appreciate the stereotype in its complexity, and allow for the entry of contradictory readings that challenge our engagement with normative practice.

Stereotypes in African popular culture

Within African popular culture, stereotypes are functional tools for navigating everyday life (Barber 2018; Newell 2002; Ogola 2017). In this case, to pay attention to the role the stereotype plays opens it up for analysis, a kind of window into everyday life. Stephanie Newell (2002, 5) for instance, states that

> [Those] who are disappointed with typecasting in African popular fiction [do not consider that it] relates to the function of these character types and plots, and the way in which they are designed to inspire particular modes of moral commentary amongst readers. Characters such as the good time girl, the barren woman and the gangster surface recurrently in African popular fiction and comic strips throughout the continent. The characters take the form of 'old' familiars, being ethical figures which readers will recognize and judge using existing repertoires of knowledge.

Stereotypes become a shorthand for reading categories of characters, a form of guide through which readers can access moral narratives. Moral narratives thus depend on stereotypes in order to make sense. Familiar tropes are necessary for readers to understand the function that they ought to play.

A way to engage usefully with stereotypes in the media is to identify their narrativity, which subsequently allows one to engage critically with how they function. This also allows us to consider the role they play in shaping historical moments of change. For instance, immediately after independence, many African countries experienced a surge of women travelling to the cities, previously occupied by African male labourers. Several popular forms that emerged functioned as warnings and advice columns that shaped new urban identities at the time. In the 21st century, stereotypical reasoning still acts as cautionary tales using shorthand messages that readers can identify with. However, the escalated changes in gender and sexual dynamics (young women are more educated, more experienced and have access to multiple media) has also meant an escalation in violence to discipline and control. As women become more vocal, more extreme measures are being used to control them, including shaming, beating, undressing and even murder. The moral narrative aids in unpacking how stereotypical genres work in order to enable a better understanding of how these forms participate in shaping discourses of violence against women.

The stereotype of the 'wicked city woman' is a consistent one in African popular culture that features widely in the popular literature and music of 1960s and 1970s Africa. Nici Nelson (2002, 109) notes that the wicked city woman is the 'most powerful and pervasive stereotype' in many of the novels of that period of African writing, and they are used to represent all sorts of women who are considered moral degenerates and socially dangerous. In fact, all urban women in such contexts were considered moral degenerates, collapsing all categories that distinguished them from one another. Nelson, for instance, observes that 'prostitutes, often referred to as "whores", are not distinguished clearly from "good-time girls", who just love the high life of town and drink and dance in bars' (Nelson 2002, 109). The wicked city women are 'often represented in these novels…manipulating their sexual attractiveness to men to entice, tantalize and entrap male characters…or they are represented as sexual objects with nothing to offer a man but sex' (2002, 109). In African popular cultural productions of this period, the stereotype of the wicked city woman highlighted an undesirable character who had to be avoided if one was to survive in the city. Popular culture, in this case, was reflective of the various ways in which women were made to feel unwelcome in the city space, a point I return to later on in this chapter. The culture of unbelonging is reiterated in public spaces in Kenya in more contemporary times. In his work on matatus (public transport vans in Kenya), Mbugua wa Mungai (2003) looks at how matatu culture conceptualises the city space as masculine. According to him, 'the subculture requires crews to express themselves in ways that maximally display their masculinity, which they understand to hinge primarily on libidinous superiority' (2003, 6). Matatu cultures reflect the general attitude towards women as unbelonging, translating a much broader argument on how urban spaces have contributed to a debate on women, bodies and public spaces. Recurring violence against women in matatu hubs, as mentioned in Wambui Mwangi's work, is one such way in which the woman's place in the city is considered marginal (Mwangi 2013).

Onitsha Market literature pamphlets exemplify the argument about popular culture's role in shaping gender relations in the city space.[1] These pamphlets, produced in the 1960s in Nigeria, and sold in the then thriving market of Onitsha, were produced by local presses, and connected with the real lived experiences and anxieties of audiences (Newell 2000). They mainly consisted of stories, plays, advice pieces and moral narratives. They included book titles such as Nathan Njoku's *Beware of women: why women are not trusted* (n.d.); Marius Nkwoh's *Cocktail Ladies*

(1961); Sunday Olisa's *Life Turns man up and down: money and girls turn man up and down* (1964); and Nathan Njoku's *Why boys don't trust their girlfriends* (n.d.). Most of these pamphlets are designed to give advice to young men who were moving into cities. Young women are marked as dangerous, and they either have to be taught to become good wives and girlfriends, or be treated as pariahs. In most of these booklets these young women are merely 'goodtime girls' in need of money to purchase various consumer items — without really bringing much benefit to the man. Citing the work of popular novels such as John Kiriamiti's *My life in crime* and Charles Mangua's *Son of Woman*, as examples, Jane Bryce explores the different ways in which these figures are constructed as degenerates who occupied the city spaces (1997, 119). According to her, against the macho men depicted in the novels, the women appear as sex symbols for the men. While such stereotypical writings about women have become synonymous with a particular historical period, it is remarkable that they continue to play out in the 21st century, re-emerging in narratives of 'blessers', 'sponsors' and 'slay queens' — modern good time girls.

Alongside the stereotype of the wicked city woman is that of the 'proper woman'. These are often depicted as rural women who are 'represented only as wives and mothers…the polar opposite of the wicked urban woman. She is a bridge to a pure past, a talisman which the beleaguered urban man holds up before him to ward off the temptations and obstacles of town' (Newell 2002, 111). She is, as Florence Stratton observes, the 'Mother Africa trope' (1994, 39). Okot p'Bitek's *Song of Lawino* (1972) best captures the contrast between the two character types. In a chapter titled, "The woman with whom I share my husband", Lawino, the main protagonist, laments:

> Ocol is no longer in love with the old type;
>
> He is in love with a modern girl.
>
> The name of the beautiful one
>
> Is Clementine.
>
> Brother, when you see Clementine!
>
> The beautiful one aspires
>
> To look like a white woman;
>
> Her lips are red-hot
>
> Like glowing charcoal,
>
> She resembles the wild cat
>
> That has dipped its mouth in blood,

> Her mouth is like raw yaws
>
> It looks like an open ulcer,
>
> Like the mouth of a fiend!
>
> Tina dusts powder on her face
>
> And it looks so pale;
>
> She resembles the wizard
>
> Getting ready for the midnight dance. (*SoL* 41–42)

Lawino, 'the old type' is a rural woman whose attachments to culture are celebrated as wholesome and authentic, a common stereotype that runs through a number of African popular texts of the 1960s and 1970s. It is useful to contextualise p'Bitek's "Song of Lawino", which was first published in 1966. The poem was a direct engagement with his anti-colonial sentiments, in which he argued that Western scholars and missionaries were 'harmful and destructive' in their conceptualisations of the Acoli people (Gauvin 2013, 44). He had at the time just completed his B.Litt anthropology thesis titled "Oral Literature and its Social Background among the Acholi and Lango" (p'Bitek 1963 as cited in Gauvin 2013, 37) in which he launched a powerful decolonial argument for the acknowledgement of the indigenous knowledges of his people (Gauvin 2013). According to Lara Gauvin (2013), p'Bitek used oral literature to 'correct' the impressions of Western scholars and missionaries and to document Acoli and Lango 'social philosophy, worldview or religion' (2013, 44). "Song of Lawino" went on to influence much of early East African writing, even leading to the founding of the 'East African song school' (Gauvin 2013). Importantly, p'Bitek's work was in conversation with other cultural nationalists who understood that culture could be manipulated, repressed and reinvented (Atieno-Odhiambo 2000; wa Thiong'o 1986; Cabral 1970). An embrace of oral tradition was therefore an embrace of the powerful role it had for 'social action that accounts for how people act and make meaning in the world' (Gauvin 2013, 36). The idea of a modern versus traditional woman emerges from this conceptualisation, in which it embodied specific symbolisms in that cosmology. Clearly, the modern woman is a negative character type whose pretentious attempts at beauty are laughable, while her obvious consumerist tendencies reflect empty aspirations.

The moral narrative thus performs a crucial role in African popular culture. Proponents of education entertainment support its uses as a source of cultural education. In his analysis of pamphlets produced and sold in Onitsha Market in Nigeria, Emmanuel Obiechina (1972, 13) observes that these pamphlets combined 'entertainment with an improving purpose'. Similarly, Donatus Nwoga (2002, 38) notes that the market pamphlets were 'trying to teach people to live a more moral life'. In the African context, the idea of teaching is prominent, especially in narratives that function as development communication which is geared towards initiating, advancing and/or encouraging change in society (Singhal and Rogers 2003). This kind of communication targets existing problems in society and aims to provide suitable solutions. Popular culture forms that use the entertainment-education model fall in this category of communication strategy developed mainly for third world countries (Singhal and Rogers 2003). In broadcast media, forms of melodrama and soap opera in Africa tend to use development communication to 'teach' their audiences. Though identified as 'over-dramatic, under-rehearsed presentation of trivial dramas blown out of all proportion to their importance' (Geraghty 1991, 1), the melodrama and soap opera forms are popular because of their 'emotional realism' (Ang 1985, 45). In other words, they are celebrated because of their close proximity to reality. In the African context, imported soap operas like the American programme *The Bold and the Beautiful* may be described as unreal because of their failure to align with the existing moral order (Amutabi 2007). But as Lila Abu-Lughod (2002) points out in her analysis of soap operas in Egypt, people find refuge in storylines that underline the dilemmas in their own lives. The soap operas maintain links to local realities using techniques that insert contemporaneous events in soap operas (Andersson 2002). As such, scholars of such forms argue that the emotional realism as well as the escapism draw audiences regardless of their material realities (Ang 1985, Geraghty 1991; Brown 1994). The connection between the moral narrative and everyday life can be used to understand this form more generally. Nonetheless, the manner in which women's images are constructed becomes a key point of concern about what this moral form can do. If one focuses on the construction of sexuality and gender, to what extent is the didactic function superseded by a violent discourse of exclusion or shaming?

Femininity, domesticity and moral purity

Pursuing the argument for a complex reading of femininity begins by exploring the meaning of the word. Femininity refers to the 'traits held to be particular to women' (Farganis 1996, 4). These traits, as Sonia Farganis argues, are not static, but influenced by 'a constellation of cultural roles, attitudes, and abilities related to, but not necessarily growing out of biological traits held to constitute being a woman, those grounded in chromosomes, hormones, and anatomy' (1996, 4). Citing Viola Klein's *The Feminine Character*,[2] Farganis explores the feminine as a product of 'a distorted or skewed view of the world' and is concerned with 'the historical views of femininity as historical archetypes or prototypes…operative models of thought through which the data concerning women are filtered' (1996, 13). Farganis's point is important when we think of femininity as a sieve. Women's behaviours are questioned in public because of how their femininities are constructed through stereotypes.

Several ideologies can be referenced when exploring the meaning of femininity. In her book *Representing women: myths of femininity in the popular culture* (1995), Myra MacDonald views these ideologies as myths that can be explored in four categories: 'femininity as enigmatic and threatening, femininity as nurturing and caring, femininity as sexuality, and femininity as a bodily practice (Van Zoonen 2005, 93). These myths in many ways define the ways in which popular representations of women circulate in the media. The idea of women as nurturing and caring is often captured in domesticity. Emerging mostly in nineteenth century Europe, the cult of domesticity was embedded in domesticity that emphasised the spatial separation of gender, so that women were relegated to the private sphere while men pursued careers outside the home (Rotman 2009). At a time of social changes, such as increased dependence on wage labour and reduced possibilities of inheritance from fathers to son, gender 'became the primary means redefining and re-establishing order' (Rotman 2009, 22). Speaking about the middle-class woman in American society in the nineteenth century, Deborah Rotman identifies elements of 'piety, purity, submissiveness and domesticity' as the cornerstone markers of this era (2009, 23). In England, the Victorian age was associated with laws and policies that controlled sexuality, for instance through discourses of social decorum and respectability (Nead 1988). Michel Foucault (1972) suggests that this was a period when institutions of power actively produced knowledge about sexuality, helping to shape new identities of a rising dominant class. The circulation of ideologies of domesticity with clearly demarcated gender roles featured centrally in the process of new class formations. In other words, respectable women who behaved in ways recognised as 'civilised' also belonged to the middle-class community (Nead 1988). Notably, the gendered definitions of morality influenced how femininity and sexuality were articulated in public discourse. Ideas about sexuality influenced behaviour in public. Nead argues for instance, that

> In the nineteenth century gender was a primary category of regulation of sexuality; the male sexual urge was understood to be active, aggressive and spontaneous whilst the female sexuality was defined in relation to the male and was believed to be weak, passive, and responsive. (1988, 6–7)

Where male sexual behaviour was condoned and celebrated as a sign of masculinity, female sexual activities were pathologised as deviant (Nead 1988). This 'double standard' regulated especially middle-class women by emphasising 'bourgeois ideologies of home and marriage' (Nead 1988, 6). The result of such regulations was the emergence of clear references to female sexuality as either 'respectable' or 'fallen';

or through the virgin/whore dichotomy. Such binary identifiers were produced and reinforced through different public platforms 'to create moral boundaries and prevent any possibilities of confusion' (Nead 1988, 6). New regimes of truth on sexuality and class were forged (Foucault 1980). According to Foucault, regimes of truth are

> ...produced only by virtue of multiple forms of constraint. And it produces regular effects of power. Each society has its own regime of truth, its own 'politics' of truth: that is, the type of discourse it accepts and makes function as true. (1980, 131)

In Foucault's argument above, regimes of truth are generated as discourse either through science, tradition or religion and are reinforced and redefined constantly through institutions such as the media, the family, the judicial system, school and the church. Normative social order is created through the reproduction of regimes of truth until it shapes reality. Self-policing, self-surveillance and co-surveillance are a part of this process of reproduction of knowledge (Vaz and Bruno 2003; Fuchs 2015).

Scholars of femininity, however, argue that it is not altogether useful to read femininity as a fixed identity categorisation that cannot be negotiated or whose meanings cannot be re-organised. Stephanie Genz for instance, states that femininity cannot always be seen as 'haunted by a spectre of cultural misogyny that asserts its devaluing and demeaning aspects' (2009, 6). Indeed, she insists that it is a 'complex, multi-layered puzzle that is dynamic in its capacity to change and absorb cultural messages, without being amnesiac and forgetful about previous versions of femininity' (Genz 2009, 8). Genz is concerned with exploring the possibility of reading femininity in resistance, and not merely in the context of passivity. In light of emerging femininities that refuse to conform to any singular meaning of womanhood, Genz argues that it is possible to reinterpret femininity as masquerade, developed in the fields of European and American psychoanalysis and film in the twentieth century. Citing the work of Joan Riviere and others, Genz looks at how the idea of masquerade was used to explain how ambitious, educated, white middle-class women tried to fit in to a masculinised world of work. The problem with this theory, as Genz shows, is that femininity is reduced to a non-threatening performance that fails to 'illuminate female autonomy and creativity' (Genz 2009, 12). But to think of masquerade is to remain open to the possibility of resistance. Citing Judith Butler's notion of gender performativity, Genz argues that the meaning of femininity is redeployed to highlight the 'stylized reiteration of conventions that eventually become naturalized and consolidated' (2009, 13). If, as Butler (1990) has argued, gender is performative, then femininity 'becomes available for a deconstructive practice that uses simulation in ways that challenge the stable notion of gender as the edifice of sexual difference' (Genz 2009, 14). It is important to highlight that the performance referred to here is not by choice, 'for such a construal of performativity presupposes an intentional subject behind the deed' (Genz 2009, 14). Femininity is here still located in heteronormative conventions that generate its meanings. As such, as Genz firmly concludes, to read femininity is to acknowledge these contradictions in which performativity is read as both 'transgression and normativity, empowerment and limitation' (2009, 15). I find this reading useful in opening up ways of engaging with femininity in Kenyan popular discourse. Such an exercise requires an acknowledgement of the contradictory performances of femininity as captured in popular culture. It is to acknowledge 'both the traditional narratives of feminine passivity and more progressive scripts of feminine agency' (2009, 12). This calls for an analysis of both critical discourse on traditional femininity and contemporary modern femininities.

Sexuality and new femininities

In order to understand the complexity of women's lives in Africa, I turn to scholarship on modern and new femininities, which draw attention to new cultures of femininity that allow for more sustained discussions on sexuality, agency, labour and intimacy (Spronk 2012). For Genz (2009, 8) 'the construction of a new femininity organized around sexual confidence and autonomy' captured the discourse of 'Girl Power' of the 1990s that emphasised 'individualism, liberty, sexual self-expression'. In identifying new femininities, she suggests that these identities embrace both old versions of femininity and new versions that emphasise sexual freedom and individual liberties. Theoretically, she suggests that rather than dwell on a separation from the subjugated femininities that exist under extremely problematic patriarchal hegemonies, critical work needs to focus on a more inclusive understanding of both existing and emerging meanings of femininity to make sense of contemporary womanhood. While Genz's work speaks to a white, heterosexual woman, I want to borrow her idea of femininity as a 'complex multi-layered puzzle' (Genz 2009, 8) to read Kenyan women emerging in a society that is still fraught with violence against women.

In this way, to embrace a new feminine identity is to re-signify the meaning of femininity and to adopt an understanding of it that is diverse and more accommodating of the various identities that choose to adopt it. New femininities become transgressive in this way. As Sara Ahmed argues:

> If authority assumes the right to turn a wish into a command, then willfulness is a diagnosis of the failure to comply with those whose authority is given… willfulness involves persistence in the face of having been brought down, where simply to 'keep going' or to 'keep coming up' is to be stubborn and obstinate. Mere persistence can be an act of disobedience'. (2014, 2)

The transgressive femininities that I read in this book are those that are identified as deviant. I am interested in how they circulate publicly and how they defy the rules of normative gender and sexuality discourse. Sara Ahmed's reference to wilfulness captures the subtle acts of defiance that I hope to bring to the surface, even in the case of the women labelled as overtly deviant. New femininities can be read as deviant because of their refusal to conform. They are contrasted with patriarchal femininities that embrace a more traditional approach to womanhood.

One of the markers of new femininities is sexuality as a clear category for identifying how these identities emerge. The terrain of sexuality opens up the morality discourse to criticism in productive ways. Sexuality studies, as Sylvia Tamale reminds us, increase 'our knowledge about numerous issues including: how human beings relate sexually; what influences people's choices of whom they have sex with, how and when; how sexuality influences relationships, laws and policies; how sexualities are reflected in social norms, identities and attitudes; how intimate relationships are regulated and controlled; what causes sexually-transmitted diseases and so forth' (2011, 13). Studies that dwell on intimacy and affection further push the boundaries of the sex-as-taboo argument (Thomas and Cole 2009). Doing sex, being sexual or making suggestions towards being a sexual being, is a core cause of moral panic, depending on who is engaging in it and how that narrative enters the public space. As Cole and Thomas show, the removal of love from the equation reduces discourses of sexuality to that of stereotypical categories (2009). In critically engaging with the idea of love, the two scholars enable a reading of love as unruly, heterogeneous and untidy. As they show, 'by depicting lust as omnipresent and love as absent in Africa, thereby situating blacks as morally and spiritually inadequate…European perspectives established a set of racialized polemics that would inform subsequent discussions and representations of black intimacy' (2009, 8). In a similar tract, Danai Mupotsa's work on heteronormative practices of marriage and its accompanying rituals points to the 'blindness' with which such hegemonic practices and discourses are approached (2014). Beyond reading marriage as the performance of desires and aspirations of the family and the nation through ritualistic practice, Mupotsa argues that one needs to pay critical attention to 'the enjoyment, pleasure, relations, dispossessions, anxieties, expectations, disappointments and negotiations attached to these modes of performing ourselves and experiencing connection with others' (Mupotsa 2014, 7). Mupotsa's work critiques heteronormative practices that are often approached through essentialist lenses. Further, in her review of Sokari Ekine and Hakima Abbas's *Queer African Reader* (2013), Mupotsa argues that heterosexuality is constantly 're-ordered and consolidated as the only basis for citizenship' (2013, 114). She debunks the language of heteronormativity that orders and makes normative social and sexual lives of others. Other studies of sexuality point out that it opens up space for engaging with social anxieties in the lives of young people. Rachel Spronk's work on middle-class sexualities of young Kenyan professionals explores sexuality as a source of anxiety in the context of HIV/AIDs and cultural practices such as genital excision. Weighing these realities against those of pleasure, she engages with the complex ways in which sexuality becomes classed and gendered (2006).

Another body of work that has been useful in interrogating these emerging femininities is on postfeminism. This scholarship includes those who critically engage with postfeminist cultures such as scholars like Angela McRobbie (2007), Rosalind Gill (2007) and Tasker and Negra (2007). Much of this scholarship points to the ways in which neoliberalism constructs the idea of the modern woman, foregrounding a discourse of freedom of individual choice. In a later chapter I explore this idea further by reading Kenyan women celebrities Vera Sidika and Huddah Monroe, both hypervisible bodies in the digital space. I explore the idea of post-feminism to understand how these young women perform their femininities in contemporary society. Caught in what Angela McRobbie refers to as 'double entanglement' of new female subjectivities, I engage with the meaning of the 'freedoms' that such women display. To cite McRobbie,

> [A] seemingly progressive push-forward factor...has seen gay and lesbian partnerships recognized and legitimated, and girls and young women being provided with new avenues and opportunities for achievement in education and employment and with sexual freedoms in leisure. At the same time, indeed as part of this same package, modes of patriarchal retrenchment have been digging in, as these conditions of freedom are tied to conditions of social conservatism, consumerism and hostility to feminism in any of its old or newer forms. (McRobbie 2011, xi)

McRobbie's critique is echoed through the work of other scholars of the postfeminist culture, and its pointed disavowal of feminism. In their discussion of new femininities, Estella Tincknell et al. (2003) identify the growing moral panic over (especially) teenage sex and its impact on young women's morality. As they argue, '...public accounts of shifts in sexual behaviour and attitudes have frequently combined nostalgia for the "traditional" family with an anxious focus on female adolescent sexuality as the source of national moral degeneration' (2003, 47). Postfeminism seems to have brought with it a different form of disruption that is worth focusing on.

Colonialism and African women

In Africa, the myth of femininity was constructed through specific colonial discourses that emphasised a Victorian moral logic through religion, education, and specific consumption practices (Stoler 1989; McClintock 1995; Burke 1996;

Ochwada 2002; Mutongi 2007; Musila 2015; Berger 2016). In her article "Making empire respectable: the politics of race and sexual morality in 20th-century colonial cultures", Ann Stoler argues that the need to assert 'European dominance in the colonies' required a reinvention of European cultures locally (1989, 634). Colonial settlers 'imagined themselves and constructed communities built on asymmetries of race, class and gender-entities significantly at odds with the European models on which they were drawn' (Stoler 1989, 634). For Stoler, 'gender specific sexual sanctions demarcated positions of power by refashioning middle-class conventions of respectability, which, in turn, prescribed the personal and public boundaries of race' (1989, 635). I find Stoler's ideas pertinent to understanding the formation and context in which African women's subjectivities emerged. The African woman was othered in a context in which the white woman's body was imagined as 'mother-of-the-empire', a pillar of moral purity and standards (Musila 2015, 67). Male colonisers depended on their women to uphold moral standards as a form of nation making, and as such, the women had to practise 'sexual restraint and a dedication to their home and to their men' (Stoler 1989, 649). Colonial constructions of sexual morality were therefore central to the formation of African women's identities.

While early colonial and missionary writing on the African woman focused on her apparent sexual wantonness (Tamale 2011), the woman who emerged at the height of the colonial period in Kenya was much more attuned to the social and moral orders of the time (Kanogo 2005). Religion and education were key tools that shaped new feminine subjectivities. This led to a clear divide between educated and uneducated women. Iris Berger observes that the 'colonially-sponsored cult of domesticity resonated with some African women, gaining them prestige and respect at a time when their families faced the threat of disintegration from both internal and external pressures' (2016, 14). Educated women were often ear-marked to marry men who had gone to urban cities to work as clerks, accountants and teachers. Those who did not go to school had little chance of joining the middle class as they were often retained in a dwindling rural economy. Others preferred to leave home so that they could try to earn a living in the city (Berger 2016; Mutongi 2007).

To make a claim that women were seamlessly 'gentrified' through the colonial system is nearly impossible. A number of social changes were taking place affecting women's positions and ability to survive in the changing world. Tabitha Kanogo identifies a number of such changes including 'land alienation for white settlers, taxation, labour migrancy, urbanization, and missionary activities', all of which 'produced extensive social and economic changes' (2005, 3). These changes, she argues, meant that maintaining social order became increasingly difficult, due to the introduction of new pressures at various levels, including gender (Kanogo 2005). African womanhood emerged from these new discourses as a site of contestation, 'where issues of modernization, tradition, change and personal independence were fought' (Kanogo 2005). Modernity and movement were particularly disruptive of existing gender norms (Kanogo 2005). According to Kanogo, 'more often than not, travel and modernity were deemed responsible for women's unacceptable abandonment of "traditional" obligations, roles, and spaces' (2005, 2). Women's agency was not taken into consideration. As Kanogo explains, women tried to control the new contexts in which they found themselves. They 'adopted negotiated solutions, outrightly violated conventional norms, or adopted novel responses to intractable problems' (2005, 2). Women became a threat to social order, escaping the control of both indigenous societies and colonial agents.

The ideal African woman for both the colonial and the postcolonial states was the one who stayed in rural spaces performing gender-normative roles. The gendering of the social role of women led to myths that emphasised women's roles as mothers and wives. Such myths were reproduced in a paternalistic logic on the role of womanhood (Cutrufelli 1983). In her review of literature on motherhood in African literature and culture, Remi Akujobi (2011) concedes that the 'maternal ideals…entrenched and valorized in all cultures…present a woman's central purpose to be her reproductive function and so motherhood and mothering become intertwined with issues of a woman's identity' (2011, 4), generating the female archetypes of Virgin, Venus and Mother Earth. From such myths, the African woman as mother became appropriated much later in narratives of nationhood, for instance, in which these women were selfless, cradle-rockers, nurturers and goddesses (Akujobi 2011, 3).

I suggest that colonial modernity imposed gendered hierarchies in a context that was already structured by patriarchal power (Ochwada 2007). Such hierarchies played themselves out in public, leading to inventions of feminine subjectivities that aligned with imperialist patriarchal logics. Anne McClintock (1995) has argued that feminine subjectivity in Africa needs to be interrogated as a colonial project in which gender, race and class were part of Western industrial modernity. According to her, hierarchies of gender ensured the social subordination of women who were placed in the same category as children. These hierarchies played themselves out well into the postcolonial context of nationhood, in which women functioned as symbolic bearers of national culture. Indeed, to speak of 'akina mama' (the mothers), a commonly used phrase in Kenyan mediascapes, one articulated the idealisation of motherhood as the epitome of respectable femininity. It also signalled older women as bearers of the knowledge of what it meant to be a proper woman. In such cases, women were read as mothers of the nation, as caregivers and as maintainers of peace (Stratton 1994). This logic was useful for British colonialists in Kenya, who used it, for instance, to trivialise women's involvement with the Mau Mau rebellion in the 1950s. The British targeted women as mothers and introduced programmes that would pacify them;

including health and education facilities, clean water and child-care (Presley 1988). They had identified women as staunch supporters of the Mau Mau and needed to excise them from the movement.

The African woman who travelled to urban spaces and embraced modernity was painted as antithesis to the ideal woman. Christine Obbo (1980) shows how the economically independent young woman who was unmarried but sexually active presented a social threat that needed to be disciplined. The woman in such a case was considered a distraction to men, a threat to the family unit, and generally a disruption to colonial and postcolonial orders (Obbo 1980). Such women quickly entered into circulation in the newspaper press and popular culture as 'good time girls' or 'modern girls' (Barlow et al. 2005; Newell 2002; Obbo 1980). The 'modern girl' was identified by her 'explicit eroticism' and use of specific commodities, 'wearing provocative fashions and pursuing romantic love' (Barlow et al. 2005, 245). It was generally accepted that her independence meant that she was also promiscuous, dressed inappropriately to lure 'unsuspecting' men, and brought unwarranted competition for men at the workplace (Obbo 1980). She was blamed not only for creating 'male confusion and conflict over what the contemporary roles of women should be, but for dilemmas produced by adjusting to rapid social change' (Obbo 1980, 11). She was the bearer of sexual diseases, and the cause of broken marriages. Popular cultural narratives carried warnings of such 'good time girls', whom young men were advised to stay away from (Obiechina 1972). While men were able to access opportunities created in the colonial economy, women were not (Kanogo 2005). In fact, as Kanogo argues, 'being a woman in the highly gendered colonial spaces precipitated a plethora of conflicts, contradictions and negotiations' (2005, 3).

In this respect, the lives of African girls and women became, as Kanogo argues, sources of 'public spectacle' (2005, 3). Calls for laws banning certain kinds of female dress considered 'injurious to public morale' (Obbo 1980, 11) were made constantly. In the media, reports 'condemning the exhibition of the female body, and maintaining that it should be a private thing, especially if a woman was attached to a particular man' were circulated (Obbo 1980, 11). Such reports and public discussions encouraged the violent abuse of women's bodies in public spaces, if the woman was deemed to be dressed indecently. Women became the moral bearers of culture with a concerted effort to 'reverse or hinder possible changes in the power and authority relations between men and women' (Obbo 1980, 15). Tabitha Kanogo has argued that women were subjected to unwarranted public surveillance and sanction, such as the forceful removal of an 'undocumented and unaccompanied rural woman' from a city-bound vehicle; the abduction of girls from school for 'compulsory' clitoridectomy (genital excision); and other forms of public violence. These ensured women remained in the constraints of colonial and African traditional practice (Kanogo 2005, 3). There were 'uneasy alliances' that emerged between 'official and unofficial groups that were determined to shape the lives of African girls and women' (Kanogo 2005, 4). Kenda Mutongi demonstrates one of the processes through which the woman was disciplined in public (2007). Referring to a common practice of repatriation of young unaccompanied women in urban towns, she recounts:

> To organize a repatriation, the parents or parents-in-law would locate their daughter or daughter-in-law and then file a formal request with the chief, asking him to help return the woman. If the chief agreed, he would usually send three of the village elders, accompanied by two or three strong young men, to nearby towns in Kisumu, Kakamega, and Eldoret, where they would sit patiently waiting for the bus from Maragoli. If they spotted a suspicious woman, they would grab her, pull her aside into some out-of-the-way corner or alleyway, and begin to interrogate her about her business in town. Almost always, the intimidated woman would surrender without a struggle; if she resisted, the 'strong young men' would body-punch her until she relented. If she did not give what they felt was a 'satisfactory answer,' or if the men remained suspicious of her motives, they would strip her naked and roughly drape a course burlap bag over her naked body; she would then be dragged by her accusers to the crowded bus and forced to sit silent, sullen, and sore until she was deposited in the village to be paraded around for all the villagers to ogle and insult her. (Mutongi 2007, 142)

The incident above demonstrates how young women were considered public property, and subject to public discipline, whether or not they were known to their attackers. Such arrogant appropriations of women's bodies by men is reflective of the overall patriarchal hegemony that informed, and continues to inform, societal attitudes. Such forms of disciplining through public humiliation showed the desperate need to control women at a time of great social change. Importantly, the construction of the acceptable woman depended on the constant reproduction of deviant femininities as a source of lessons to be learnt and adopted. The public disciplining that occurred in the media as well as other public avenues was a form of reclaiming that last hope of an idealised African womanhood.

Women who 'refused' to fit the script of civilised feminine subjectivities are interesting precisely because they disrupted the linear rendering of the colonial archive on African women. Kenda Mutongi (2007), Tabitha Kanogo (2005), Christine Obbo (1980) and Hannington Ochwada (2002; 2007) demonstrate that the African woman negotiated the spaces and economic situations in which she found herself to create a sense of independence and agency. She was never simply a helpless victim, a corrupt woman or a good woman. As Ochwada (2002) has shown, she was a product of colonial conditioning through the church and education, but in negotiation with her cultural traditional role. These various roles did not always align. In her book on prostitution in colonial Nairobi, Luise White (1990) argues that to look at women who became prostitutes through stereotypical lenses, either as victims of exploitation or of male violence, was to render them invisible and passive. She traces the idea of social control and regulation of prostitution to political agendas and public institutions that sought to pathologise while simultaneously sanitising, the bodies of prostitutes for the service of middle-class men in early 19th-century Europe. These ideas were replicated publicly in colonial economies. White's reading of prostitution suggests a much more expanded reading of prostitution as 'a reliable means of capital accumulation, not as a despicable fate or a temporary strategy', and offers a more nuanced understanding of African women's lives in colonial Nairobi (1990, 2). She re-orients analysis of prostitution away from the narrative of degradation and victimisation, and instead focuses on a different methodology in which the prostitutes' oral accounts and narrations offer a different account of their trade. White urges a re-examination of the institutionalised logic behind why women got into prostitution, where the 'generalization that women became prostitutes when family ties were weakened is frequently reproduced in the contemporary literature' (1990, 8). She stresses the idea of prostitution as a means of earning an income in the wage labour economy. She thus demonstrates how women gained new mobilities by controlling their labour power (1990).

Gender and the Kenyan public sphere

The above theoretical and historical reflections on the meanings of femininity as discourse reveal that it is a complex entity marked by colonial and imperialist modernising agendas in Africa. Femininity is also contained in postcolonial constructions of national subjectivity. In such discourses, women remain at the margins of colonial/national imaginations. Whether in traditional, colonial or postcolonial settings, therefore, the Kenyan woman in the public space occupies particular stereotypical positions of femininity in a preconceived moral framework. Women are either good citizens (mothers of the nation, good daughters) or morally questionable, what Joshua Gamson terms the 'virgin-whore discourse' (2001b, 157). These are positions that were deliberately constructed in colonial culture. Grace Musila's (2015) exploration of the various narratives emanating from the murder of British tourist Julie Ward in Kenya in 1988, for instance, offers a substantive example of how these discourses operate. One speculation about her death was about her sexuality, forged from an existing repertoire of colonial and postcolonial social memory. For Musila, the binary demarcation of Julie Ward's character in the public imaginary as either a victim — a 'defenceless white woman at the mercy of lustful black men'; or a 'woman of loose morals' was not accidental (2015, 82–83).

She traces the historical configurations of these discourses as constructed in colonial and postcolonial social imaginaries. I argue that these categorisations emphasise how the woman occupies space in the public Kenyan imaginary. Women in politics offer a good entry point into exploring this idea further.

In her analysis of the female politician as a public figure, Liesbet van Zoonen (2005) contends that one of the difficulties these women consistently face is the false myth that women and politics do not mix. The reigning assumption is that women are held as 'the traditional symbol of innocence and virtue' and that their roles are to offer 'humanity and morality' in a world of self-centred politics (2005, 87). Acknowledging the marginal participation of women in politics throughout history, Van Zoonen explores ways in which women who have been involved with public office have had to navigate public expectations. She uses the figure of the celebrity as a way of understanding women politicians. For instance, female politicians often feature in celebrity press (gossip/tabloid newspapers) as mothers and wives or through their sexual encounters. The family becomes a source of stability, from which conceptions of good women emerge. The link to family life is a double-edged sword because while it shows a form of stability, it also pigeon-holes politicians into particular roles that keep pulling them back into a private sphere. According to Van Zoonen, the 'female celebrity is primarily articulated with the codes and conventions of media representations of women, of Hollywood conventions initially and an amalgam of television pop music, and advertising images later' (2005, 93). In a context such as Kenya, the codes and conventions of media representations are both local and global. As discussed already, a variety of social-cultural and political issues culminate to create myths of femininity that define the space in which women can function publicly. This is why women who contravene these myths become visible, immediately available to being read as defiant and troublesome.

Political women in Kenya are well researched, and their involvement in public affairs well documented. I find here the work of Maria Nzomo (1997), Marciana Were (2017), Shadrack Nasong'o and Theodora Ayot (2007), Barasa Kassilly and Kennedy Onkware (2010) and Lisa Aubrey (1997) instructive. In the various bodies of work, a few issues come up that enable a form of mapping of what the Kenyan political space means for women. Maria Nzomo (1997) for instance, speaks of the attitudes that mostly male political and social elites have that influence how women politicians are perceived, mainly based on their sexuality. Marciana Were's body of work on Kenyan women politicians similarly draws attention to the marginalisation of women politicians in this space (2017). In such cases, women sometimes have to align their interests with those in power — often male (Mama 1995). In an article in which she follows the life of a seasoned female politician, Julia Auma Ojiambo, Were explores the challenges Ojiambo's faced, and the strategies she had to adopt in order to fit in. Were speaks about the necessity for filial relationships, in which Ojiambo occupied the informal title of 'daughter of the nation'. (2017, 492). For Kassilly and Onkware 'as individuals and as groups or class[es], women do not enjoy equal liberties, parties and opportunities in the public sphere…the democratic ideal of "a good political life" is only nominally obtained by Kenyan women' (2010, 79). These kinds of attitudes have of course had a negative impact on women politicians, who are dubbed aggressive and unwomanly when they refuse to conform.

Kenya is replete with examples of 'stubborn' or 'difficult' women who have refused to take their places of silence, as discussed in Wambui Mwangi's piece cited earlier (Mwangi 2013). Famous examples of such women include historical figures, such as Mekatilili wa Menza and Wangu wa Makeri as well as more contemporary examples such as Wambui Otieno, Wangari Maathai and Chelagat Mutai. Mekatilili was a Kenyan woman leader of the Giriama people, who famously staged a rebellion against British colonial authorities. Like Wa Makeri, whom I discuss earlier, Mekatilili was an anomaly, as positions of leadership were not available to women. These two women stand out in history because instead of serving quietly, they rebelled in spectacular ways, refusing to remain marginal figures of history. In more contemporary contexts, Wambui Otieno and Wangari Maathai are often cited as among the most vocal women in Kenya. Both women were activists who fought for causes in which they believed.

Wambui Waiyaki Otieno is recognised as a Mau Mau veteran and a politician. She was born into a prominent family, being the great-granddaughter of Waiyaki wa Hinga, an important figure in modern Kenyan history. The Waiyakis were 'patrons of Christian progress, sponsors of the Church of Scotland mission, benefactors of "Kenya's Eton", the Alliance High School, and individual leaders in many fields' (Lonsdale 2001, 326). She came from a family of well-educated individuals. Otieno attended the African Girls' School in colonial Kenya, currently known as Alliance Girls' school. With her prestigious education, it is confounding that she joined the Mau Mau, taking oaths to transport guns and kill if necessary. Her memoir, *Mau Mau's Daughter*, provides a scope for imagining her life as a rebel, a jailbird and a rape survivor, a political activist and a widow. She worked with Tom Mboya as a trade unionist; and was arrested in 1961 for her 'notorious activism against the colonial government' (Cloete 2006, 115). Even after independence, Otieno remained a staunch member of opposition parties due to what Elsie Cloete terms her 'dissatisfaction with political splits along ethnic lines, increasing corruption and paucity of attention given to improving the lot of women in Kenya' (2006, 115). Although she came from a family of political and social elites in Kenya, she refused the safe haven that her middle-class standing could have provided her. She had opportunities to be co-opted into mainstream politics. For instance, in 1963 she was head of the Kenya African National Union (KANU) women's wing (Cloete 2006). Despite her activist background, it is the 1987 court case regarding her husband's burial that catapulted her into fame. She came to occupy a central place in Kenyan public imaginary in 1987 when she famously challenged her late husband's traditional clan after they demanded the right to bury him in his ancestral home (Cohen and Odhiambo 1992). Otieno drew a lot of negative attention to herself as a result, with most arguing that her behaviour was modernist, Westernised and disruptive, and that it had no place in an African setting. She even earned the name 'bossy whore' (Cloete 2006, 115). She was the face of what bad women looked like. The case went to court and is one of the most highly publicised cases in Kenyan history. Otieno was adamant that her husband had wanted to be buried near the capital city, Nairobi. While Otieno lost the case, her insistence to fight a highly patriarchal system, in spite of the media glare, is often commended as a watershed moment for gender politics in Kenya (Nzomo 1997).

Wangari Maathai was a woman heralded for her commitment to human rights in Kenya. A Nobel laureate, Maathai suffered multiple moments of discrimination, humiliation and intimidation at the hands of former president Daniel Moi's government (Maathai 2007). Her political career was rife with trouble. While she is celebrated for her persistently disruptive politics, she suffered incarceration, name-calling and public shaming throughout her career. In her analysis of Maathai's media representation, Wanjiru Mbure (2018) refers to the various tactics that former Kenyan president Daniel Moi and other male politicians used to try and contain Maathai's interventions regarding the environment and human rights. In a context in which Maathai was thought of as being 'excessive', Moi often called on 'akina mama' to advise her and set her straight. Politicians also referred to a particular type of 'akina mama' [those feminists] who were disruptive and unable to be controlled (Mbure 2018). One of the most well-known cases of disruptive women (also involving Maathai) is the case of the six women who stripped naked at Uhuru Park on 28 February 1992, to demand the release of their sons who were being held as political prisoners. This protest became highly publicised, and as Alexandra Tibbetts (1994, 27) observes, disrupted the very label of 'mama' that had a sanitised connotation. Indeed, nakedness became a form of protest and a way for women to speak in public (Mwangi 2013).

An equally formidable public figure was Philomena Chelagat Mutai. Born in 1949, Mutai was known as an activist and champion for human rights quite early in her life. She led a protest in her high school that led to her expulsion. She went on to become the editor of the University of Nairobi's newspaper, *The Platform*, where she published controversial pieces (Okemwa 2016). So controversial were some of the pieces — including an exposé on police brutality — that she had to go into exile to escape the wrath of the state. Mutai became the first Nandi and Kalenjin woman

MP at the age of 24, and was known as a troublemaker because she consistently challenged major decisions in parliament (Okemwa 2016). She was arrested in 1975 for charges of inciting violence, and served time in jail for this. She returned to her seat in 1978, and continued to be a nuisance to the Moi presidency. Although she died quietly in 2013, Mutai, like the other women mentioned above, made it possible for women to imagine themselves in public as something other than 'the good woman'.

In more recent years, several other women figures have emerged who are just as controversial and who refuse to remain quiet. In the age of social media, the sharp increase in vocal women cannot be ignored. Personalities such as former Nairobi Women representative Rachel Shebesh and current Member of Parliament for Mbita constituency, Millie Odhiambo, stand out as examples of women who push the boundaries of how to be a woman in a man's world. Rachel Wambui Shebesh, at the time of writing the Chief Administrative Secretary of the Ministry of Public Service, Youth and Gender Affairs in Kenya, is one such controversial woman. She is an activist who fights for the rights of women, a recognised environmentalist and a politician. However, her story is reflective of the hurdles women politicians face. For example, in a widely circulated video in 2013 titled 'Kidero slaps Shebesh', Shebesh can be seen involved in a brief but heated argument with then Nairobi Governor, Evans Kidero (K24 TV 2013). Shortly thereafter, the governor is seen slapping her across the face. This violent display of masculine dominance captured the imagination of Kenyans, in what became known in social media and elsewhere as the 'gubernatorial slap'.[3] The assault demonstrated various layers of power. Earlier on, Shebesh had been involved in a protest march with council workers in Nairobi who had a list of demands, including formal pay. Along with the workers, she had marched to the governor's office demanding an audience. This is when the above incident occurred. I am here interested in the responses to the video posted by K24 to map the two broad categories of responses that the incident received. The one interpretation was that she deserved the assault because she was a loud woman who needed to know her place. One respondent, for instance, says:

> Kidero for PRESIDENT…This stupid bitch talks too much. I hope the slap taught her a lesson. I wish Kidero angem-malizia na HEDDI (I wish Kidero had head-butted her to 'finish' her).[4]

The response above, though an individual response, was part of a larger body of comments that showed support for the governor. According to this camp of responses, a woman should not be as vocal as Shebesh was. The idea of discipline comes into play. The clear lack of empathy here tracks back to a longer history, in which female victims of violence are blamed after an assault. Pumla Gqola (2015, 78) terms this discursive industry 'the female fear factory'. According to her,

> The female fear factory is as theatrical as it is spectacular. By theatrical, I allude to its exaggerated performance in front of an audience in terms that are immediately understood. It is spectacular in its reliance on visible, audible and other recognisable cues to transmit fear and to control. Performed regularly in public spaces and mediated forms, it is both mythologised, sometimes through a language of respectability and at other times through shame.

While Gqola is referring to how the fear factory structures rape discourses, I argue that this concept is applicable to other forms of public violence against women, and that it enables a recirculation of disciplinary media forms for women. In this way, the threat of violence becomes 'an effective way to remind women that they are not safe and that their bodies are not entirely theirs' (Gqola 2015, 79). The violence in the video was circulated and recirculated as a warning on what happens to women who are too loud and too visible. The commentator quoted above even suggests that the governor should have done even more harm to silence Shebesh completely. In other words, the post-commentary that Shebesh offers after the attack was unwelcome. In her work on murdered tourist Julie Ward, Grace Musila (2015) highlights this culture in her analysis of cases of women who have been victims of violence. According to popular moral economies, if the woman is perceived as being aggressive (as was the case in both Wambui Otieno and Wangari Maathai) or promiscuous, then empathy is lost (Musila 2015). In the case of Ward and other murdered women that Musila reviews, these women rendered themselves vulnerable 'to violent murder by contravening their men's/society's rules on sexual etiquette' (2015, 86). This is part of a broader discourse in which victims of violence are blamed for encouraging their abusers. In their analysis, Denise Buiten and Elaine Salo (2007) explain that existing discourse suggests the victims were at fault and 'displays a misogynistic virgin/whore dichotomy that legitimises violence against women who do not conform to strict codes of feminine sexuality' (2007, 119). In this discussion I therefore highlight ways in which women in public — even well-known and well-respected women — are rendered victims through a display of masculine violence.

Barasa Kassilly and Kennedy Onkware (2010), Lisa Aubrey (1997), and Shadrack Nasong'o and Theodora Ayot (2007) have variously observed that women politicians consistently suffer political marginalisation based on the gendered nature of the state. As Nasong'o and Ayot observe, 'State power in Africa remains conspicuously male power, ingrained with predominantly male values, ideology and vision of the world' (2007, 170). As a result, many women tend to shy away from politics, for fear of intimidation (Nasong'o and Ayot 2017). In her analysis of Ugandan women's participation in politics, Sylvia Tamale observes that for many male politicians 'women have no business standing for political office' (1999, 1). Women in most African countries who participate in politics are 'defying custom, culture, discrimination and marginalization' in order to be a part of political change in their countries (1999, 1). The few that embrace politics quickly gain reputations for being 'iron ladies', where their political styles are compared to that of former British Prime Minister Margaret Thatcher's. Thatcher gained the moniker for her uncompromising leadership style. The term 'iron lady' is also often used derogatively to suggest that a woman's political style is grossly masculine as opposed to a more natural maternal style expected of women. The small number of women who have been successful in Kenyan politics has had to embrace this tough exterior, including Charity Ngilu, Martha Karua and Millie Odhiambo.[5] I include Millie Odhiambo in this list because of her vocal engagement with masculinist politics and her refusal to back away even when her reputation is at stake. I also include her because of the scandals that have come to be associated with her in the media. Odhiambo, who was nominated as Member of Parliament by her political party, the Orange Democratic Party (ODM) in 2008, is considered one of the more vocal female politicians in Kenya. Despite the numerous contributions she has made as an activist fighting for a more equal society for women and children in Kenya, she is popularly known for her bold comments about her sexuality in social media. For instance, in a Facebook post that has been recirculated several times in various tabloids in Kenya, Odhiambo firmly declares:

> As a woman, I love sex, I enjoy sex, I have sex. You shall not use it as a tool to demean me or another woman. We don't have sex with spoons, biro pens, cooking sticks, snakes or tables. We have it with men, like you. If I have it with one or many men, I will answer to God, not you. The way you will answer to God for having sex with one woman or more, including your daughter (for the depraved). If you are not ashamed of having sex then stand to be counted, after all, I did not invent sex, neither did you so don't blame me for it, same way I will not blame you. Proudly woman enjoying my sexuality and proud of it.[6]

A surface reading of Odhiambo's comments above suggest, as interpreted by numerous tabloids,[7] that she is sharing personal details of her life with the public in ways that disrupt a public moral order. Odhiambo is, however, quite clear that she is deliberately choosing her sexuality as a way of entering the public space. She argues that often male colleagues use intimidation tactics that target women's sexuality to dissuade female politicians from participating in public affairs. If, for Odhiambo, women embraced their sexuality and spoke about it more publicly, then the attacks on them would be rendered useless. In an interview, she explains:

> We must demystify sex. Let Millie be all about sex and the woman after me be about leadership…Someone has to pay the price. Besides, who do women have this sex with?…You can't define me by my vagina. Let's move on to the real issues like drought or the budget.[8]

Odhiambo is clear that she is doing the work of clearing a path for female leadership. Hers is a counter-tactic that engages femininity differently. If women like Odhiambo and Shebesh are read as unruly, I am interested in how this unruliness disrupts public narratives of hegemonic femininity. Their acts of 'disgrace' become critical in understanding how women circulate in public discourse. As such, it becomes imperative to understand the stereotype of the crazy, loud-mouthed, evil woman that defines them. These women refuse the protection of patriarchal femininity. Patriarchal femininity is a type of femininity that conforms to heteropatriarchy in the hope that it can coexist with it peacefully (Genz 2009). Citing Audre Lorde (1984), Stephanie Genz argues that a peaceful coexistence is a fallacy, a pitfall that ensures patriarchal power remains relatively undisturbed (2009). For women like Shebesh and Odhiambo, 'akina mama' discourse is used to rein them in, and dissuade them from behaving like loud, ill-trained women. This is often also accompanied by public displays of violence. In Shebesh's case, she was slapped by a sitting governor. In Odhiambo's case, she had been physically attacked by three sitting MPs whom she claimed even tried to undress her.[9] In a Facebook post, Odhiambo refused to be seen as a victim in the case. She writes 'But I am not of the "ayayayaya you slapped me" fame'[10] (making reference to Shebesh's response when the governor slapped her, as recounted above). Odhiambo proceeds to note that 'I cannot and will not be intimidated using my sexuality.'[11] It is interesting to read Odhiambo's first response, in which she pointedly shows a lack of empathy for Shebesh. To be clear, Odhiambo demands that readers not see her as a victim, but as a fighter, who expects to be attacked while doing her job. She deliberately sees her body as vulnerable but also as a site of battle. Her public persona is one that is not easily intimidated, shocked or diminished by the usual tactics of shame and violence. It is a persona that Shebesh also embraces to a certain extent. In her public performances, Odhiambo is aware of the curiosity regarding her private life, particularly as this has become common fodder in local tabloids. Van Zoonen comments that for the female politician, family life is often constructed as problematic and a source of speculation (2005). As she explains, 'the picture of sacrificing husbands waiting for their wives to come home after a long day in politics apparently does not accord well with the prevalent gender norms in the celebrity press' (2005, 90–91). She adds that 'invariably, the absence of a "normal" family life is brought up' (2005, 91).

In various tabloid and entertainment news, Millie Odhiambo is referred to as 'outspoken', controversial and notorious, among other names. She is the antithesis of a family woman, especially in the way she uses her husband to provoke public debate. In one article titled 'I'm negotiating with my husband to marry a second, third husband',[12] Odhiambo projects herself as a potentially polyandrous woman capable of marrying more than one man. To contextualise, Odhiambo made this statement in parliament during a heated debate on whether a presidential nominee for ambassador should be allowed to serve while holding dual citizenship. Mwinzi Mwende was nominated by President Uhuru Kenyatta in May 2019 to serve as ambassador to Seoul.[13] However, while the rest of the nominees' appointments sailed through the vetting process without trouble, questions were raised regarding Mwende's dual citizenship, with some worrying that she would not be loyal to the position. Odhiambo was among a group of MPs who were defending Mwende's right to hold dual citizenship. Her argument was that her husband is Zimbabwean and the only reason she does not yet have dual citizenship is because she is still negotiating with him so that she can take a second and third husband, just as men do with wives (*Tuko* 2019).[14] Although there is a tongue-in-cheek quality in her line of argument, it should not be taken lightly. She is clearly using controversy to place an important issue — something more fundamental than dual citizenship and loyalty — under the spotlight: the manner in which women, particularly married woman in this instance, are socially and culturally constructed. Whether or not actual matrimonial issues are available for public discussion is unclear. However, the persona that she has created demands that we read her within the private/public split.

The use of controversy is a tool that clearly enables Odhiambo to navigate the male dominated spaces in which she works. In an article published in the online tabloid newspaper *Ghafla!* a headline boldly declares: 'Na nisiambiwe kitu! [Nobody should tell me anything] Controversial MP Millie Odhiambo wants to give birth at age 53'.[15] Odhiambo made this statement after she pushed forward a bill on *invitro-fertilisation* which was passed in 2014. The issue of Odhiambo's fertility has come up numerous times in the tabloid media, an issue that she has addressed in different ways. In this case, she spoke about her age, and that she did not have children of her own, in order to draw attention to an issue that was affecting many women in Kenya. Childless women are still ostracised in communities that see them as worthless (Ngunjiri 2009). As Faith Ngunjiri has argued, motherhood is one of the ways that women navigate the public spaces of politics, and those who are mothers use the social prestige it gives them to present themselves in public (Ngunjiri 2009). Those who are childless have testified to the disrespect their status earns them, including being called 'barren prostitutes'.[16] Odhiambo said she was so moved by women struggling with fertility issues who reached out to her on social media, that she 'sponsored a bill in Parliament on Assisted Reproduction.' (*Eve digital*, 2019).[17] The point I am making here is that Millie Odhiambo has managed to carve out a space for herself in politics, based on controversy. Through the idea of spectacle and controversy, she is able to better communicate her points, while constantly calling men out on their double standards. I read this as a deliberate strategy through which women can engage in the public space.

Conclusion

This chapter engages with the idea of the public female figure and the restrictive ideas of femininity. The chapter argues for a historical contextualisation of femininity, in which a construction based on a colonial and patriarchal regime has lent particular meanings through which women must enter the public space. Reading through theoretical and definitional understandings of femininity, I deal with both how dominant ideas circulate, and how women revise these ideas through individual tactics. The location of popular culture is crucial, as this also enables a re-reading of information available in the public domain. The chapter begins by navigating the complex idea of the stereotype and how it functions, but also how it can be thought of as a more complex site of engagement, what Bhabha (1994) refers to as ambivalence. In engaging Bhabha, I create space for multiplicity of meaning, as well as ways through which one can read the stereotype from the point of view of those who are othered in discourse. I then discuss the circulation of popular stereotypes of women in African popular culture, arguing that it is useful to consider the roles these stereotypes played in a larger context of meaning. I explore the meanings of femininity in its Western location, before engaging more meaningfully with how it translates in Africa, within a colonial and postcolonial context. Lastly, using the figure of the political woman, I explore a number of examples in which women's entry into the media has been through their sexuality. This is significant because it invites us to read how sexual morality has become the site through which women's participation in the public is metered and controlled. From politicians such as Rachel Shebesh and Millie Odhiambo, to young women appearing in the media through social media, women enter the public in very specific ways. I have chosen to focus on stereotypical logic through which such women are framed, and in such cases, the case studies I refer to are those that highlight the sensational ways in which different types of women are represented. I also argue that by focusing on these frames as falling in a broader moral narrative framework, it becomes possible to engage with forms of resistance and push back demonstrated by women who refuse to conform, or to fall victim to patriarchal tactics of containment. Millie Odhiambo offers a good example of this form of push back, where she embraces her sexuality and refuses to allow her male colleagues to use it as a way of putting her down or dismissing her. Several other such examples abound. The point of this chapter is to emphasise the dynamic ways in which femininity can be expanded and engaged with critically. Using ideas from emerging theories of postfeminism, new femininities and sexualities, I engage with the double entanglements of contemporary femininities that link them to historically located patriarchal reasoning, as well as new logics of resistance and renegotiation.

Notes

1 For access to an extensive archive, see 'Onitsha Market Literature archive'. Accessed 30 January 2019. https://library.brown.edu/collatoz/info.php?id=334. Other archives include the Kansas University archive https://exhibits.lib.ku.edu/exhibits/show/onitsha and the Indiana University archive http://www.indiana.edu/~afrcol/onitsha-market-literature

2 Klein, V. 1971. *The Feminine Character: History of an ideology*. Urbana: University of Illinois Press.

3 The moment when former Governor Kidero slapped former women's representative Rachel Shebesh was captured on video and circulated widely. The video link here was reposted on the television station K24 as news. Accessed 30 October 2019. https://www.youtube.com/watch?v=kGL2rSNgsNQ.

4 K24. 2013. "Kidero slaps Shebesh." Accessed 30 October 2019. https://www.youtube.com/watch?v=kGL2rSNgsNQ.

5 Martha Karua is a Kenyan politician, former minister and a longstanding member of Parliament. She is also an advocate of the Kenya High Court. Charity Ngilu is a Kenyan politician who has served in different capacities and ministries.

6 Zipo writer. 2016. "I love sex: MP Millie Odhiambo confesses." *ZIPO*, November 25. Accessed 29 January 2019. http://zipo.co.ke/13836/i-love-sex-mp-millie-odhiambo-confesses/

7 Kepher Otieno (2017). "What is the Big deal? I love sex." Accessed 29 January 2019. https://www.sde.co.ke/thenairobian/article/2000224682/mp-millie-odhiambo-what-is-the-big-deal-i-love-sex.

8 For the full interview, see Soni Kanake. 2017. "Millie Odhiambo: Yes, I have lost my hair." *eveDIGITAL*, April 8. Accessed 29 January 2019. https://www.standardmedia.co.ke/evewoman/article/2001235515/millie-odhiambo-yes-i-ve-lost-my-hair

9 Standard reporter. 2016. "Mbita MP Millie Odhiambo, accuses three MPs of attempting to undress her in Parliament." Accessed 30 January 2019. https://www.sde.co.ke/article/2000145333/mbita-mp-millie-odhiambo-accuses-three-mps-of-attempting-to-undress-her-in-parliament date

10 Standard reporter, 2016.

11 Standard reporter, 2016.

12 Accessed 15 October 2019. https://hivisasa.com/posts/1123-resubmissionam-negotiating-with-my-husband-to-mary-a-second-third-husband-mp-millie-odhiambo

13 https://www.kbc.co.ke/president-kenyatta-appoints-18-new-ambassadors/

14 https://www.tuko.co.ke/307452-millie-odhiambo-sensationally-claims-s-discussing-husband-marry-man.html

15 http://www.ghafla.com/ke/na-nisiambiwe-kitu-controversial-mp-millie-odhiambo-wants-to-give-birth-at-age-53/

16 https://www.sde.co.ke/thenairobian/article/2000158588/why-kenyan-female-mps-millie-mabona-joyce-lay-want-test-tube-babies

17 https://www.standardmedia.co.ke/evewoman/article/2001273738/outspoken-mp-millie-odhiambo-opens-up-on-not-having-a-child-her-wish-to-have-one-by-55

3

Radio and the construction of African womanhood

Introduction

Existing scholarship on radio signals its power by identifying the link it has to national identity formation. Indeed as Michelle Hilmes and Jason Loviglio have stated, '...from its more marginal perch on the media landscape, radio continues to be an important cultural form, troubling the easy distinction between public and private, raising questions about the relationship between the margins and centre of the national discourse, and continuing to emphasize the primacy of voice as a central and often controversial feature of identity' (2002, xii). They also cite radio as an important 'conduit for the education, enlightenment and education of the people', as well as a space where 'intimate relations with the people' are forged (2002, xi). These two elements — its public role and its private role — easily define the power of radio today. Making reference to what Hilmes and Loviglio refer to as 'radio's invisible voices' (2002, xv), this chapter interrogates the role of radio in shaping national consciousness, while also identifying its potential for transgression. I make use of scholarship on radio, both on Africa and on the global north, to map a context for the formation of African womanhood. The chapter takes a historical tenor, arguing that radio was an important medium for the colonial and postcolonial states that used it to shape various colonial and national identities. The chapter then draws attention to radio drama, which I argue is crucial in understanding this exercise of identity formation. Radio drama is, after all, a powerful site of modernity (Crook 1999; Gunner 2019).

In *Radio Soundings: South Africa and the Black Modern,* Liz Gunner (2019) shows that a study of radio can reveal hidden histories of marginalised identities inasmuch as it can draw attention to dominant nationalist discourses. In her study of radio and radio drama in South Africa, Gunner uses radio to trace a genealogy of black life at specific historical moments. Her analysis of the textures of voice, structures of publics and suturing of communities through sounds provides a solid, growing knowledge of an archive on black history in South Africa (2019). Gunner's important reading shows how language and genre played a role in the creation of alternative radio publics in South Africa, in which radio was able to evade, elude and dance around stringent laws in order to communicate with a broad and receptive black audience. Gunner's work is important in mapping publics created through soundscapes of radio in South Africa, but also in Africa more broadly (Gunner 2019; Gunner et al. 2011). Indeed, Gunner, Ligaga and Moyo (2011) ask this question of radio: how does it as a medium of sound 'provide landscapes that both divide and unite, or simply link publics, cultures and communities?' (2011, 1). This idea of public formation, against a reading of a public script, is the preoccupation of this chapter. I interrogate the role of radio in creating publics that address cultural and social issues. I also see radio, and specifically radio drama, as carrying the potential to create subversive publics in Kenya.

The chapter explores the idea of publics by analysing the radio drama, the moral narrative and the circulation of feminine ideologies in Kenya. I explore the connection between manufactured ideals of femininity used to control African women and their subsequent circulation through texts such as *Radio Theatre*. Historically, radio has played, and continues to play, a pivotal role in disseminating state agenda, both colonial and postcolonial. I contemplate what this role is, as it relates to African womanhood. I look at *Radio Theatre*, one of the longest running radio drama programmes in the English language in Kenya. *Radio Theatre* is a programme produced for the Kenya Broadcasting Corporation (KBC) and features one-act plays that run for about 30 minutes every week.[1] According to its former producer Nzau Kalulu,[2] it was first aired in 1982, although there are indications that it could have aired much earlier. Programme line-ups from as early as 1954, for instance, show the existence of a *Radio Theatre* programme that was aired for a white colonial audience (Heath 1986). A Kiswahili language programme aired for KBC called *Mchezo wa Wiki* (Play of the Week)[3] also aired from the late 1970s to the 1980s and was similar in structure to *Radio Theatre*.[4]

Like other cultural forms, such as music and cinema, radio drama is central to the dissemination of public moral values and views. Indeed, theatre as a genre is credited as being one of the most influential mass media forms 'through which general cultural ideas were focalized and disseminated' (Quayson 2000, 110). As a popular form, *Radio Theatre* actively circulates ideas that support the *status quo*, drawing on religious messages, colonial and postcolonial state policies, and everyday moral economies. It focuses primarily on the themes of sexual morality, and functions informally as a regulator of sexual issues. The topics of the plays aired weekly vary. These include immorality and infidelity, girl-child education, same-sex marriages, good time girls, good wives, and more generally, sexually transmitted diseases such as HIV/AIDS. *Radio Theatre* plays transmit their messages through the adoption of heroines/heroes and villains and plot lines of reward and punishment. The themes are frequently repeated as a way of emphasising the moral message contained therein. For radio producers, the moral logic of the dramas resonated across time, and could be transposed into new, emerging situations and contexts.

For instance, one of the plays, *Immoral Network* (1987; 2003), which deals with HIV/AIDS and its spread through traditional cultural practices, was aired for *Radio Theatre* in 1987 and replayed in 2003. While the play's content remained largely unchanged, the producers relied on the power of the message, and its ability to speak to a new public (Kalulu 2006). The play relied on the consistent themes on HIV/AIDS: the prevention and curbing of the spread of the virus, the impact HIV/AIDS has on individuals and communities, the need for a culture of care, the preservation of dignity by alleviating stigma, and cultural practices and their role in enabling the spread of the disease. Set in 1980s Kenya, the play circulated in a context of denial, secrecy, ignorance and stigma. One of the local dailies, *The Standard* newspaper, on 15 January 1985, had this headline: "Killer sex disease in Kenya" followed by another headline three days later: "Horror sex disease in Kakamega". This was the context in which *Immoral Network* was first aired. The play is about the cultural practice of wife inheritance among the Luo of Western Kenya. In the play, Otieno, a lawyer, decides to 'inherit' his dead brother's wife Akinyi to honour the age-old practice of wife inheritance. He contracts HIV and spreads it to his unsuspecting wife. His first wife, jealous of the new wife, starts a relationship with the family doctor as a way of revenge. The string of lovers continues to grow when Otieno also has sex with his domestic worker. In a cruel twist of fate, the couple's son engages in unprotected sex with the same domestic worker, inevitably contracting HIV as well. The play ends when all those caught in the 'immoral network' realise what has happened. There is a dramatic enactment of remorse and regret at the end. In the 1980s, this play fitted within the context of fear, shame and ignorance that marked that era. Kenya, like many countries at the time, was in denial about the urgent need for a national policy on HIV/AIDS. This meant that, lacking adequate knowledge of how the virus spread, most people were not aware of preventative measures they could take to curb its spread. In fact, the government only launched the first comprehensive policy document in 1994, after multiple interventions by different health and human rights advocates. By the time *Immoral Network* was aired again in 2003, Kenya had undergone several changes, including the ushering in of a new presidency. One of President Mwai Kibaki's agendas was a renewed fight against the spread of HIV. *Radio Theatre* producers were able to reach into the archives and re-air the play, whose themes were still relevant. They also produced more radio plays tackling the theme of HIV/AIDS and other new challenges that were emerging. Other themes such as early/forced marriage, equally pertinent to a national audience, also inspired producers to re-air plays. This accounts for the play *Not Now*, first aired in 1995, being re-aired in 2002 (Ligaga 2005).[5]

The gendered thematic framing of the *Radio Theatre* plays signals the developmental agenda contained in the plays that are informed by Kenyan public morality. The plays function as educational canvasses against which society is encouraged to read itself. In many ways, *Radio Theatre* reflects a broad social and moral order in Kenya that defines acceptable behaviour among its citizenry. Assessing the role of radio drama is thus a significant way of determining how it functioned both in colonial and postcolonial contexts in relation to African womanhood, in order to theorise how popular ideas about what it meant to be a 'civilised' woman circulated.

Radio and colonial encounters

Radio is an important historical avenue for probing the context in which the idea of African femininity was constructed. Initially installed for purposes of broadcasting information to colonialists and settler farmers, radio became an important propaganda and educational tool for colonial administrators. The earliest recorded radio station was known as Kenya Radio and was introduced in 1928. At the time, broadcasting 'was primarily intended to entertain its listeners and to provide a cultural link between widely scattered European homesteads and missions and [with] Britain' (Heath 1986, 51). It was only during World War II that broadcasts in African and Asian languages were introduced 'in response to British demands to rally support for the war effort' (Heath 1986, 87). In 1940, a plan to extend broadcasting services for Africans and Asians was established 'to meet postwar demands for economic growth and development posed by Britain and by the colony itself and to deal with pressures for political power and socioeconomic advancement of African Kenyans' (Heath 1986, 87). In addition, as Leonard Doob (quoted in Heath 1986, 87) argues, the mass media 'was being employed to accelerate the process of acculturation' of Africans. The British government explained its decision to introduce and maintain broadcasting for Africans by arguing that there was a need for development and mass education to help Africans cope with changing social, economic and political circumstances (Heath 1986, 129). Radio, in this way, became an aid to the education department whose purpose of community education remained central.

But although seemingly simple, the plan was far harder to achieve in reality. In relation to colonial policies on African women's education, for instance, Joanna Lewis (2000, 2–3) points out that the 'racial, authoritarian, compartmentalized and gendered nature of colonial rule' caused 'colonial practices in social welfare' to take a negative turn. The colonial government envisioned an educated African man who would be prepared for a white-collar job, and whose educated wife would be trained in domestic issues. The reality was different: poverty, cultural constraints, illness, land woes and so on loomed large for the Africans. Colonial policies ensured division of labour in which men were paid low wages, and women became the unpaid labourers (Barnes 1992). This was also a period pre-dating the Mau Mau rebellion, which brought with it serious resistance from Africans (Presley 1988). Convincing locals to embrace so-called development ideas was not as easy as envisioned earlier. That said, radio was a colonial propaganda tool. In 1939, a report on 'nutrition in the colonial Empire', which was intended to further adult education, used 'radio, cinema and "the magic lantern of the gramophone"' because these were seen as 'valuable in the teaching of domestic science to women' (Lewis 2000, 59). Radio was necessary for community building which was threatened by urbanisation and subsequent rapid social changes.

Yet, for the colonial office, the idea of an educated African woman was central to its developmental agenda of 'civilising' Africa through colonialism. To quote Carol Summers (2002, xviii), 'women and ideas of gender, though technically marginal to colonial concerns, were in reality central to colonial debates and initiatives'. The colonial office envisioned African women as the driving forces for development in a rapidly changing world. As early as 1925, advisory committees were appointed to deal with the question of the African woman's education in the colonies.[6] The African woman was to be moulded through formal education and practical instruction to become both a conserver of tradition and a moderniser in her role as wife (Lewis 2000). This seeming paradox — conserver of tradition and driver of modernity — appealed to colonisers who wanted to ease Africans into a more developed future. The African woman thus needed very specific kinds of training. She was to be trained in 'the virtues of womanhood, sewing, mending, knitting, washing, ironing, simple cookery, hygiene, agriculture and child-care' (Lewis 2000, 353). These virtues would help the African woman retain her traditional role, but also accommodate her in the new and evolving world in which she found herself. Cora Ann Presley (1988) gives an account of the Community Development programmes that were set up to help prepare the African woman for a civilised world. According to Presley, at the height of Mau Mau rebellion, the Community Development department set up programmes to 'counteract Mau Mau by providing a course of "general knowledge"' (1988, 520). The information that was circulated 'stressed the positive benefits of colonialism and the evils of Mau Mau' (Presley 1988, 520). The clubs formed under the Community Development project were then essentially used to 'train Africans to be good citizens according to British standards' (Presley 1988, 521). These clubs are the precursors of Maendeleo ya Wanawake (progress among women) Organisation, the largest formal women's organisation in Kenya. During the Mau Mau years, the clubs grew, as they provided food for starving families, and child-care for a lot of women who needed it.

Scholars including Obbo (1980), White (1990), Kanogo (2005), Mutongi (2007), Thomas (2003), Summers (2002), Barnes (1992) and Presley (1988), using methodologies such as life histories and oral interviews, have now shed light on how colonial policies influenced and interrupted the lives of African women. Cora Ann Presley's account provides a harrowing yet intimate texture of women's lives during the Mau Mau years (1988). The interviews carried out speak about pain and suffering, at the hands of both colonial officers and homeguards, for women who worked with the Mau Mau men. Presley's work also gives a clearer sense of the courage and resilience of these women, who were activists, and who's activist work was not always understood. Rather than consider these women passive bystanders of history, Presley engages with their agentic authority during these years, even as they faced severe punishment via detention, jail, beatings and even death. By showing the interior worlds of these women's lives, scholars provide much needed information that complicates our understanding of their lives in the colonial context. Carol Summers (2002) in her book *Colonial Lessons,* looks at the lives of African men who obtained an education under the segregationist state. According to Summers, there is evidence that 'local Africans could…shape colonial agenda and block or force revisions on specific colonial initiatives' (2002, xvii). Paying close attention to specific conflicts and controversies as well as life histories of elite African men, she argues that 'Africans' agency emerged locally, in small ways, in contexts where officials, missionaries, and sometimes settlers needed support and help from specific Africans' (2002, xvii). While her book focuses on men, what is intriguing is the counter-narrative of the colonial experience for Africans that it offers. She uses this site to imagine what agency looked like for both men and women at the time. Her work is in many ways similar to Kenda Mutongi's work on widows in Kenya. In *Worries of the Heart* (2007), Mutongi gives a lucid account of everyday life of Africans during the colonial period, drawing attention to their struggles, choices and other moments of agentic engagement. From the various accounts, it emerges that the African woman's personhood was a contested terrain, with different interest groups trying to gain control over it. Lynn Thomas (2003), in what she terms 'the politics of the womb', explores a variety of ways in which women's reproductive processes became an avenue for control of indigenous, colonial and missionary agents. Similarly, Tabitha Kanogo (2005, 1) has shown that institutions such as 'clitoridectomy, dowry, marriage, maternity and motherhood, and formal education' became sites through which different interested parties sought to gain control of the African woman. Yet the African woman had to exist in these various conflicting terrains. In fact, amid the massive social change that was taking place, women were negotiating 'individual liberties…agency, along with the reconceptualization of kinship relations and of community' (Kanogo 2005, 1).

One of the ways that several historians of gender have envisioned transformation for the African woman in the colonial period is through movement or mobility (Barnes 1992; Kanogo 2005). According to Teresa Barnes in her reading of African women's lives in colonial Zimbabwe, 'physical mobility was a crucial issue in the relationship between colonial rulers and the ruled in Colonial Zimbabwe' (1992, 586). In fact, she argues that the colonial government was 'obsessed with the mobility of indigenous people', introducing pass laws (in the case of Southern Rhodesia) and Kipande system in Kenya. The African woman's physical mobility caused a lot of stress on existing patriarchal institutions that had much to gain from her stasis. These migrations were not just physical, but were also 'ideological, cultural, moral and legal migrations' (Kanogo 2005, 8). Indeed, as Kanogo emphasises, 'any unsanctioned movement by women threatened the elders' control of social capital' (2005, 9). This related to the control of women's productive and reproductive labour, female sexuality, bride wealth acquisition and distribution, domestic and societal authority structures, gender relations, and social order. Because of such anxieties, the state 'made a clear alliance with African patriarchy to control women's mobility' (Barnes 1992, 588). Barnes addresses what she terms 'restrictions on mobile women', including 'girls who ran away from home to escape arranged marriages, and married women who were defining new lives for themselves in the mines and towns' (1992, 591).

In interrogating stereotypes of the African woman of that period, scholars have therefore unpacked ways in which cultural and political institutions were used to retain control over them. As Kanogo points out,

> …in colonial Kenya, the control of women's normative and geographical mobility fell under [the] broad efforts to create and enforce hierarchy and order. The process involved re-definitions and re-workings of the meaning of individual liberties and of notions of home, community, lineage, marriage, work, authority, and property, among other concerns. (2005, 9)

The woman in this context was understood in stereotypical ways as 'perpetual legal minors, chattels, exploited beasts of burden, not too intelligent, gossiping, giggling, idle, shy, vulnerable and dependent social victims' (Kanogo 2005, 9). Similarly, Barnes argues that, by the turn of the century, white settlers and colonists constructed ideas of African women either as victims in need of rescuing from 'heavy socioeconomic bonds imposed by African men' or as 'naturally immoral' (1992, 589). However, for African women, these movements were opportunities to redefine themselves and their worldviews. Summers contends that 'girls and women who ran away from family-negotiated marriages experimented with new economies of sex, and explored new models of mission-influenced Christianity and domesticity' (2002, xviii).

She adds that they 'challenged African patriarchs' authority, created nuisances for white officials, and made new demands on junior African men' (2002, xviii). It was an opportunity to question the very foundations of their knowledge of themselves. It was a moment of self-discovery, but also a time of social threat because they were exposing themselves to new things, and this was not always easy. For instance, many women who migrated to the towns and other vibrant economic hubs were labelled 'prostitutes', suggesting that they went to the city to trade their bodies for money (Kanogo 2005; Obbo 1980). According to this formulation, the African woman who travelled 'had become defiant and obstinate…had crossed the boundaries of respectable behaviour' and was 'at risk of being labelled "immoral" and diseased — evil vessels of contamination' (Barnes 1992, 589–590). Yet African women had a different sense of their realities. New opportunities existed for them in urban areas (Obbo 1980). Women who moved to urban areas specifically for sex work did so for varying reasons that often had more to do with agentic viewpoints towards labour and housing, rather than mere survival and victimisation (White 1990). For many African women, mobility meant a move towards 'self-reliance and having a few material possessions' (White 1990, 1). This rediscovery of independence and need for self-improvement among African women is what caused much strain and created a need for control by indigenous, colonial and mission agents. The factors discussed provide an ample context for understanding why Kenyan women are framed in the way that they are in the media in contemporary Kenya. The desire to retain control of the woman through the avenues of domesticity, sexuality and family are realised in the manner in which femininity unfolds in the media, particularly in radio drama.

Postcolonial politics of control

The visible absence of the Kenyan woman as a key figure in post-independence politics affected the manner in which broadcasting and its programming unfolded. In 1963 the state was interested in national cohesiveness. But it was also encumbered with the politics of control that affected the kinds of programming content that could be aired. The effect of these two issues was that the construction of a national culture took on a masculinist point of view.[7] It also meant that the choice by *Radio Theatre* to adopt a domestic set-up in the bulk of its plays was not accidental. Nationalism was one of the key agendas for the state when it took over from the colonial government in 1963.[8] Achieng Oneko, who was Kenya's first Minister of Information and Broadcasting, maintained that broadcasting provided the new state with a useful tool for disseminating nationalist pride among Kenyans (Heath 1986). Kenya's first President, Jomo Kenyatta, also stressed this point in one of his initial speeches (Kenyatta 1964, 2).

In the construction of national unity, most African countries presented a recurring narrative of brave young men fighting against colonialists, highlighting the absence of women in the national histories of struggle (Samuelson 2007; Berger 2016; McClintock 1995; Presley 1988). This absence affected how institutions such as broadcasting media circulated ideologies of national cohesion. Women were assigned the maternal task of ensuring national cohesiveness, while their role in agitating for political change was ignored (Berger 2016). Cora Ann Presley's account of nationalist women and their contribution to the struggle for independence lends an important historical angle to this debate (1988). According to Presley, most research into nationalist struggles ignores women's contributions from the 1920s onwards. That the British had to devise policies and programmes to wean women from the Mau Mau in the 1950s demonstrates otherwise. Indeed, records exist that indicate that thousands of women were detained during this period for their participation in the Mau Mau rebellion, and interviews reveal that the women involved saw their participation as contributing to the national struggle. They were not just 'passive wings', as the British referred to them, merely hinting at the role these women played in supplying information, smuggling food, clothes and guns, and providing 'lines of transit for recruits travelling from the urban and rural sectors of the Central Province to join the military forces in the forest' (1988, 504).

In both the colonial and independence contexts however, women nationalists were stereotyped as either victims or prostitutes. Their victimhood was explained as being 'forcibly compelled to take the oath of allegiance to the Mau Mau' (Presley 1988, 505). They were 'prostitutes' because of the tactics they used to trick British soldiers, as well as collaborating with African troops to source intelligence and arms (Presley 1988). At independence, attention was drawn to the development programmes — which many women were coerced to be a part of — and women's participation in the national agenda became a developmental one. Women became paragons of moral centredness, replayed in radio programmes such as *Radio Theatre*, as will be seen later in the chapter.

The postcolonial government maintained a tight control of the state broadcaster, Voice of Kenya (VOK). Under the leadership of Kenya's second president, Daniel Arap Moi, broadcasting programming was generally aligned with the state's agenda for a number of reasons. Moi became the president of Kenya in 1978, sworn in just days after the first president, Kenyatta, died. The initial phase of Moi's leadership was filled with tension as several political interests tried to wrestle power from him. There was the 'Change-the-constitution group' of 1976, for example, 'believed to be detractors of Moi' whose bid was to amend the constitution so that Moi would not succeed Kenyatta upon his death (Karimi and Ochieng 1980, 3). Although the group failed to stop Moi's swearing in as president, tensions between Moi and members allegedly belonging to the group remained high. There was also the attempted coup of 1982 in which a group of soldiers from the Kenya Air Force attempted to overthrow Moi's government. Notably, the state broadcaster was one of the first key institutions to be occupied by the soldiers. They had orchestrated a detailed plan to bomb the state house, and for their leader, Senior Private Hezekiah Ochuka, to take over as president. These factors led to what scholar James Kariuki termed 'paramoia', to emphasise what he argues was Moi's paranoia during the period of his rule. The 1980s and 1990s in Kenya were marked by random arrests without trial, assassinations, and a general distrust of the communication sector. Examples of such tortures and assassinations abound (see Musila 2015, for instance). One such example is explored in Wahome Mutahi's novel *Three Days on the Cross* (1991), an autobiographical account of his experiences as a detainee for allegedly circulating *mwakenyas* (seditious publications). This was a period of intense censorship. Theatre was drastically affected by censorship. Ingrid Bjorkman (1989) gives the example of the censorship of writer Ngũgĩ wa Thiongo's plays, including *Mother Sing for Me*, which was so popular that people travelled from afar to watch rehearsals. Weeks before it was to open officially at the University of Nairobi, 'armed police tore down [the Kamiriithu] cultural centre, and a technical school was built on the site' (Bjorkman 1989, viii).

The state and morality in Kenya

In her lucid discussion of the male-centredness of the Kenyan nation, Grace Musila (2009) makes reference to the phallocracies of power operating on the metaphor of the family. According to her, Kenya's first president Jomo Kenyatta 'inherited a legacy of state power that was predominantly a male affair' (2009, 44). The inner circle of the president, she argues, which was deliberately referred to as the 'Kenyatta family', reproduced 'the metaphor of the family homestead at whose throne sat Kenyatta as the old patriarch at the helm of the national family' (2009, 44). He acquired the title of *Mzee* (elder), and as Musila shows, 'with time, the title *Mzee* became firmly embedded in Kenyan parlance as a signifier of respect popularly reserved for figures of authority, regardless of their age' (2009, 45). *Mzee* Jomo Kenyatta had laid the foundations of a patronage politics and authoritarian culture. Both Kenyatta's and later Daniel Moi's regimes were designed on this metaphor of the nation as family, giving them authority to 'protect' the feminised nation (Musila 2009). Among other things, the protection included banning all opposition parties (seen as a threat to national unity), detention of political opponents, and silencing of differences. Where Kenyatta was *Mzee*, Moi became '*baba wa taifa*' (Father of the nation). Patriotic songs echoed this sentiment, while radio and television productions kept pace with the new references to the new regime leader. I go into this detailed description of the nation as family to signal factors that made it possible for radio drama to embrace themes from the domestic space so easily. In her work on family and nation, Susan Andrade (2011) has argued that female writers use the family space to engage broader national issues. To quote her, 'the domestic, where women historically have set their own novels, offers as sharp an analytic perspective on collectivity and national politics as does the arena of public political action' (2011, 1). If we take Andrade's suggestions, it becomes possible to engage critically the relationship between a private domain, the family, and a public one, the state. These interrelations become crucial interpretative tools in understanding how *Radio Theatre* both existed as a 'neutral' entertainment show and potentially as a site of subversion.

I use the context above to locate *Radio Theatre*, which began airing in 1982. Rather than focus on controversial concerns that reflected the politics of the day, the programme dwelt more on domestic themes. When I asked the then producer Nzau Kalulu (2005) about the decision to stay away from political (and often controversial) topics, he commented, 'nobody ever tells you do not. You just know'. *Radio Theatre*'s routine engagements with everyday experiences make it appear innocuous, ensuring continued support from the government. Yet radio drama is a genre that provides many spaces through which plays can be read in alternative ways. Liz Gunner (2000) and Khaya Gqibitole (2002) demonstrate how Zulu and Xhosa radio dramas in South Africa were able to survive the apartheid regime because they hid in the 'thicket of language', where room for several readings and interpretations of the plays resided. In the case of *Radio Theatre*, there are no 'hidden transcripts' that are politically laden, 'encoding the "real", politically subversive message[s] in an apparently innocent tale' (Scott in Barber 2000, 300). These plays focused on morality, in which 'messages about the government, regime or political party are not uniquely privileged or even especially salient themes' (Barber 2000, 300). In the realm of the moral play, what is of utmost importance is the moral lesson that is learnt at the end of the play. Therefore, inasmuch as *Radio Theatre* operated in stringent VOK/KBC policies in the 1980s and 1990s, and despite that it operated in a genre whose creative potential was under continuous scrutiny from the government, it was able to survive any interference from the State. As a survival strategy, *Radio Theatre*, like several other VOK programmes, affiliated itself with the government in order to 'minimize the element of uncertainty' in which it could operate (Heath 1986, 346).

While the state has clearly had a big influence in shaping conversations about morality in Kenya, the role of religion must also be taken seriously. The centrality of religion, particularly Christianity, in postcolonial Kenyan public life was visible between 1978 and 2002 during the rule of Kenya's second president, Daniel Arap Moi. Moi's public performances of piety, which included regular church attendance on Sundays (captured on national television and reported in the news on radio), as well as his embracing of a *Nyayo*[9] philosophy that preached a rhetoric of love, peace and unity, signalled Christianity's permeation into important facets of Kenyan public life. Akoko Akech's reading of what he terms 'Moi's public persona' reveals that specific 'hegemonic cultural powers could have shaped his worldview or consciousness' (2010, 606). He identifies Moi's conservative 'missionary (Africa Inland Church) Christian culture' as one of the influences (2010, 606). This, combined with his Kalenjin masculinity, allowed him to present himself as 'a benevolent, women and children-loving father who brooked no opposition to his rule over the nation of the patriarchal-family' (2010, 608). But Christianity was strongly linked with colonial and missionary presence in Africa that helped sustain the rhetoric of progress and civilisation. Christianity thus informed what was seen as 'modern womanhood'. To be a modern woman was to be *legible* to the colonial and postcolonial state, in essence, to comply with existing laws that ordered what was expected of *decent* womanhood.

Such is the context of media production of gendered and sexualised texts in Kenya. KBC, a state broadcaster and a classic ideological state apparatus in Althusserian terms, embraced the values of Christian religion and African traditional practices, and attempted to use these to regulate and control moral behaviour.[10] Women and men are read as either good or bad, depending on which teachings and values are contained in a particular programme. This control takes place at a symbolic level. For instance, morality is interpreted as modesty in the articulation of sexual intimacy. This modesty is in line with a Christian (often also Victorian) notion of sexuality as 'hidden', muted, or truncated. A sexual scene in radio drama is at best indicated through the sound of lips smacking to show intimacy and pleasure brought about through two people sharing a kiss; and at worst, the sounds of 'low moaning' and sighing to indicate passionate sex. Interestingly, such sounds easily also come to stand in place of 'good' and 'bad' moral behaviour. In *Radio Theatre*, sounds of passionate sex are almost always associated with 'bad' sex, either indicating wantonness or infidelity.

This kind of symbolic language pervades representations of sexual intimacy across the board in Kenya, and contributes towards the developmental function of most cultural texts. Alexie Tcheuyap (2005) argues that in most African countries the presentation of sexuality is done through ellipsis to avoid direct engagement with actual sexual acts while still commenting on how these acts impact behaviour. In her analysis of a Kenyan film *Dangerous Affair* (2002), Florence Sipalla (2004) explores a sexual scene in which the camera panning across a room shows pieces of clothing strewn on the floor, a condom wrapper, and eventually two people in bed, apparently asleep but quite obviously having had sex. Sipalla argues that this is a typical cinematic convention in Kenya that communicates a collective understanding of intimacy in public (2004).

Even so, I am aware that these are very conservative readings of sexuality, not at all reflective of the full spectrum of information available to audiences in Kenya. The rise of the urban FM radio station in recent years has influenced the possibility of a more unrestrained discussion of sex in public.[11] In addition, foreign programming often demonstrates matters pertaining to sex more openly. Among the many programmes are the soap operas such as *The Bold and the Beautiful,* and a host of Latino telenovellas and soap operas. Rachel Spronk's reading of romance and its representation in Kenyan media shows how information on sexuality appears openly in magazines and newspaper pullouts, radio and television talk shows and television music videos, among other spaces (Spronk 2012). My argument is that in KBC's local productions, especially from the 1980s, 1990s and early 2000s, information about sexuality was still controlled, a conservatism reflected in some of the programming.

Transgressing these unspoken symbolic conventions can have dire consequences. In 1986, a popular show, *Usiniharakishe* (Don't Rush Me) was banned because of a sexual scene. This programme, produced for KBC by Hilary Ng'weno, was aimed at adolescents to stop them from engaging in unprotected sex. In its first episode, the programme featured a rape scene involving two young people, Kombo and Raha. Kombo invites Raha to his house (bedroom) and shortly after, pushes her onto his bed. Raha, shocked, slaps him, just as the scene fades and the programme ends. This scene was momentous, given the swift response it received from politicians and the public alike.[12] Comments that were written to the editor of *Nation* newspapers, included those like '[t]his play has brought shame to the families that have watched it', 'the play has introduced prostitution to our children,' and from one Kenyan member of parliament, the programme had shown 'rape and violence, which is embarrassing to both parents and children, and should not be allowed [to continue airing]. The ministry [of information] should withdraw the programme because it is embarrassing.'[13] The then assistant Minister of Information and Broadcasting, Omar Soba, announced in parliament that the programme was 'disgraceful and was likely to mislead youngsters.' He added that the programme was 'supposed to warn children aged between nine and twenty years on the danger of adolescent sex but, as it is now, it is encouraging them to indulge in sex.' The reaction to the *Usiniharakishe* scene was extremely telling. It demonstrated a refusal to deal with sexuality broadly, and particularly young people's sexuality.

Art and culture seen to contain sexual content has elicited multiple responses in Kenya over the years. On 31 August 2003, for example, the Catholic Church lobbied to have three novels withdrawn from the high school curriculum because it found these texts 'morally objectionable' (NDIMA/IFEX report).[14] According to the Network for the Defence of Independent Media in Africa, these novels — Chinua Achebe's *A Man of the People* (1966), and Mohammed S. Mohammed's *Kiu* [trans.

thirst] (1972) and S. A. Mohammed's *Kitumbua Kimeingia Mchanga* [lit. trans. soil/sand in bread] (2004)[15] were considered 'sexually explicit' and were said to contain 'pornography'.[16] Two of the texts above had been used previously in the Kenyan high school syllabus with no issue. That they would raise questions in 2003 was confounding. More recently, the banning of Wanuri Kahiu's film *Rafiki* (Friend) (2018), due to what the CEO of the Kenya Film Classification Board (KFCB) Ezekiel Mutua argues is the 'clear intent to promote lesbianism in Kenya', is yet another testament to the censorship culture in Kenya.[17]

Constructing 'good' and 'bad' women in radio

In a context of censorship and control such as explained above, the construction of femininity signals the work of disciplinary regimes and institutions. The polarities of the good and bad woman are reflective of 'modern residues' of colonial and imperial influences in the shaping of gender and sexuality in Africa (Nnaemeka 2005). Such residues continue to inform how women are configured in the media and other popular culture platforms in contemporary Kenya. Perhaps another way of conceptualising such residues is through Elizabeth Freeman's idea of chrononormativity to capture the forward movement of time and modernity, the language of progress and development, at the expense of those who fall out of step with such temporal modes (2005). According to Freeman, aberrant figures are 'those forced to wait or startled by violence, whose activities do not show up on official timeline, whose own time lines do not synchronize with it' (2005, 57). Such 'chronopolitics of development' are often 'racialized, gendered and sexualized' (2005, 57). Freeman gives the example of Western modernity, which has 'represented its own forward movement against a slower pre modernity figured as brown-skinned, feminine, and erotically perverse' (2005, 57). Acknowledging the location of the radio drama programme *Radio Theatre* as produced for the state, I analyse a few radio plays that are based on the stereotypes of the 'good' woman and the 'unruly' woman. In doing so, I explore the various myths of womanhood that are inherent in the plays, and problematise these using feminist scholarship on African women that insists on possibilities for reading multiple identities in women's social and political representations, or what Freeman refers to as 'erotohistoriography' (2005, 59). Locating the chapter in the Kenyan context emphasises the continuities between colonial and postcolonial state policies and moral orders that continue to influence how women are read in the public sphere.

In the play *3 Times a Lady* (2002), the protagonist, Tabitha, is praised for her chastity and loyalty to her fiancé, James. Tabitha is held up as an aspirational figure of true womanhood after she 'waits' for her fiancé, who disappears for five years without a trace. The radio play's title suggests a narrative of patience, meekness and chastity on Tabitha's part, marking her out as being 'three times a lady'. A section of a similarly titled song by the American music group The Commodores, in which a woman is praised for being 'three times a lady', can be heard playing in the background as the play opens, reiterating this important theme. However, as the play proceeds, it becomes apparent that Tabitha's patience and chastity are not quite as straightforward as initially purported, and in unpacking the characteristics of perfect femininity that she is supposed to exhibit, contradictions arise. Tabitha, for instance, begins to feel lonely and anxious about her status as James's fiancée. This leads her to form a relationship with someone else, having eventually given up hope waiting for James. Tabitha is exceedingly worried about growing older. Although this kind of anxiety is embedded in a problematic gendered logic that relates a woman's age to her supposed beauty, this moment also demonstrates Tabitha's impatience. In the end, just as she is about to marry her new suitor, James returns with an incredulous story about where he has been. The chronopolitics of the play are apparent in the demand made in the narrative for Tabitha to wait. The politics of waiting, for a woman, clearly follows what Freeman (2005, 60) references as the 'cyclical time of reproduction' (2005, 60) which has the female body as 'mute' and 'labouring' eternally in childbirth (2005, 62). There is indeed a return to social order in the end, as James returns just in the nick of time to rescue Tabitha from the hands of the conniving new suitor. The haunting question he asks her: 'has anyone dug out my treasure' reverberates long after the play has ended, marking the strong desire to return to a specific norm. His treasure — her virginity — is the price she pays in order to be redeemable as a 'good woman'.

This example demonstrates how the colonial discourse of domesticity continues to inform contemporary readings of femininity, a discourse that 'sought to shape "proper women" as the monogamous wives of the "new men" produced in mission schools and colonial workplaces' (Cornwall 2005, 6). Idealised femininity brings together a range of meanings that articulate womanhood in restrictive parameters that fail to appreciate the realities of women's lives. Femininity functions in ideologies of colonial and postcolonial patriarchy which inform the meanings of sexual morality. As Drucilla Cornell cautions, there is a 'theoretical need to understand how the symbolic constructions we know as woman are inseparable from the way in which fantasies of femininity are unconsciously "coloured" and imagined in the constraints of gender hierarchy and the norms of so-called heterosexuality' (1995, 75). Such a hierarchy, as articulated in Gayle Rubin's work, signals the construction of value systems that place heterosexual marital relationships that are predominantly monogamous, reproductive and non-commercial at the apex, and relationships such as homosexuality, extramarital relationships, and promiscuous or commercial sex at the bottom (2007). The existence of slay queens, women that I read in a different chapter, completely disrupts this articulation of normative sexuality, with its celebration of practices such as bride price exchanges and reproduction. In other words, women who are aberrant to this normative understanding of sexuality are punished through violence.

The bulk of literature on gender in Africa challenges the polarities of 'good' and 'bad' women in order to highlight what Andrea Cornwall (2005, 4) terms the 'missing dimensions' inherent in 'conventional analyses of gender and power in Africa'. Cornwall points to a growing body of research that problematises the idea of woman as a unitary construct. According to this scholarship, Western analysts and feminists have imposed ideas of gender onto 'particular kinds of male-female relationships — those modelled on heterosexual partnerships and assumed to be hierarchical and oppositional' (2005, 4). It is important to acknowledge that African women's identities are constantly evolving, and are affected by the relationships they come into contact with (Ogundipe-Leslie 1994). Indeed, as Cornwall further argues, 'focusing on other dimensions of difference and dynamics of oppression undermines both the myth of female solidarity and the presumption of universal male domination' (2005, 4). It is much more useful to explore women's 'multiple social identities and identifications — as mothers, as "husbands", as sisters, as leaders, as producers and as "part and parcel" of apparent male dominance' (2005, 5).

This crucial point is methodologically useful in reading the women of *Radio Theatre*. Most of the female characters are mainly constructed in isolation from other relationships. Tabitha, for instance, is extremely close to James, so much so that none of the members of her own family feature in the radio play. In a different play, *Whatever it Takes* (2004), Joy Mbote has no relationships apart from the one she has with her husband, and with Benson Mutia, the man who tries to seduce her. While these could easily be explained as generic problems in the sense that radio drama has a limited capacity to explore multiple characters, it is equally insightful to note how the narratives of women unfold. In both radio plays, the men have family and friends, while the women are often alone. In cases where the women have relationships outside of those with their partners, it is with a friend who supports them in their relationships with their partners. Even then, it is useful to recognise the relationships that these women have outside of their main relationships, even if these are merely mentioned in dialogue rather than acted out. Women's group associations are as important as relationships between girlfriends and sisters in *Whatever it Takes* (2004). Indeed, as Lynda Gichanda Spencer (2014) has argued, female friendships provide women with 'an emotional alternative to the compromising world of boyfriends and potential husbands. The bonds that they forge, and upon which they rely, provide the women with the support that the endless stream of men cannot give them' (Gerhard, 2005, 44 as cited in Spencer 2014, 92). It is useful to take note then, of any form of female-female relationships offered to listeners in the plays.

Romance, marriage and the longing for happiness

In *3 Times a Lady*, Tabitha's femininity is stereotypically constructed on notions of sexual purity, faithfulness and patience. The idea of purity is a recurring metaphor in the three-part play that marks Tabitha as a 'good' woman. In the opening part of the play, that Tabitha and James have not had a sexual encounter is emphasised through dialogue. After James's return, he asks Tabitha if anyone had 'dug out his treasure', referring to her virginity, and whether someone else had had sex with her. Sex becomes the fantasy and promise that holds their relationship together. The play dwells momentarily on the possibility of interruption in Tabitha's relationship with her other suitor, Mbote. However, this other relationship is not consummated, hence preserving her purity. In the meantime, their intimacy is expressed through playful dialogue and sounds of lips smacking together to indicate kissing. This is the totality of their intimacy as shared with listeners, again creating audible boundaries for where Tabitha's passions and desires can reach. Tabitha's is a manufactured notion of purity equated to a 'gift…that even a Vasco da Gama has not discovered', to cite Tabitha. Such an idea of respectability is discussed at length in Ann Stoler's piece "Making Empire Respectable: The politics of race and sexual morality in 20th century colonial cultures" (1989). Indeed, the very idea of empire was based on the regulation of sexual relations. As Stoler notes, 'who bedded and wedded with whom in the colonies… was never left to chance' (1989, 636–637). For Signe Arnfred, other sexualities either held potential for redemption or were considered depraved (Arnfred 2004). Such depictions 'othered' African sexuality, contrasting it with Western European sexualities, but also co-constructing it as epitomising 'modern, rational and civilized' subjectivities (Arnfred 2004, 7). It is this latter characteristic that best explains the choice to contain Tabitha in a colonial reading in which her sexuality is yet to be discovered. This discourse of purity forms a core part of the macro-politics of morality in Kenya. Kenyan moral economies still operate in stringent categories, although the reality of its sexualities far surpasses the tenets of its public discourse (Spronk 2012). Rachel Spronk has argued, for instance, that sexuality has to be understood as a personal, intersubjective and public issue, and that these parts intertwine to create a far more complex reality. People's public projections and perceptions of sexuality are not always aligned to personal sensibilities. This is an interesting observation about the Kenyan society precisely because Kenyans embrace a very purist approach to sexuality, but are also equally obsessive about sex, sexual scandals and any other conversations about sex. Spronk highlights these contradictions as the means through which sexuality could be understood. Tabitha's virginity then becomes crucial to the movement of the narrative, while at the same time, the silences on what could have been (she could have had sex with Mbolu; James could have forsaken her for almost marrying another man), are muted. The possibilities could in many ways align with Freeman's politics of unpredictability, or what she terms erotohistoriography (2005). She says of it:

> As a mode of reparative criticism, then, erotohistoriography indexes how queer relations complexly exceed the present. It insists that various queer social practices, especially those involving enjoyable bodily sensations, produce form(s) of time consciousness, even historical consciousness, that can intervene upon the material damage done in the name of development. (2005, 59)

Not only does Tabitha entertain the idea of another relationship with a man who is not the love of her life, she is 'intimate' with him (a shared kiss). Though brief, this is a moment of interruption worth dwelling on, as creating a different narrative strand for the listener, and momentarily jarring the movement of the narrative. In other words, while she is waiting for James, she engages in something else, another possibility. This in many ways lends her agency in the narrative, thereby complicating her 'legible' feminine qualities.

One of the themes through which her character develops, for instance, is romance. Romance suggests a particular kind of femininity which is admirable, desirable and even achievable. Tabitha is a woman who hopes for happiness in a heterosexual union of marriage, and the intimacy she shares with James is contained in a chaste romance full of this promise. Indeed, it is this promise that holds Tabitha together in the years following James's disappearance. This promise becomes the centre of Tabitha's femininity, where she continues to mould herself into what she imagines as her only ticket to happiness. She tells James, for instance, that she would 'surely die without him'[18] if he were to leave her or not be in her life. As scholarship on romance has shown, the 'happily ever after' promise of romance operates in chrononormativity that positions the woman in a place of perpetual hopefulness and a desire in which marriage is crafted as the ultimate location of happiness (Langland 2002; Radway 2009): what Sara Ahmed (2010, 14) has termed the 'promise of happiness' and Lauren Berlant discusses as 'cruel optimism' (2011, 1). For Berlant, 'one of optimism's ordinary pleasures is to induce conventionality, that place where appetites find shape in the predictable comforts of the good life genres' (2011, 2). The idea of happiness is always deferred, revealing other aspects of emotional reality that work against it. For instance, vulnerability is exposed and becomes an avenue through which reality can be explored. In this way, romance offers a pragmatic avenue for exploring Tabitha's life and anxieties in ways that locate the didactic function that popular cultural forms play, even as they circulate stereotypical forms and themes (Bryce 1997; Muriungi 2004). This in many ways complicates an easy binary reading of whether she is 'good' or 'wicked'.

One of Tabitha's core anxieties has to do with her body, and how it affects her eligibility for marriage. With James gone, she worries that she will miss an opportunity to marry and have children, obviously two important aspects that define her womanhood, what Freeman calls the 'heterosexually gendered figure for progress...the fecund maternal body that engenders natural history' (2005, 61). Two characters who drive home this anxiety are James's mother and Tabitha's colleague, Mr Mbolu. In a meeting with James's mother, Tabitha is made acutely aware of her body and its links to age and motherhood when she is told: 'If there was a button I could switch off in your body to stop you from growing old believe me I would, because I am sure James's disappearance has nothing to do with you, nothing completely.'[19] This is both an accusation (against her ageing body) and a reassurance (it's not your fault). Similarly, in a different meeting, Mr Mbolu who is also an admirer of hers, tells her:

> Time will never wait for you Tabitha, you hear me? It goes on and on until one day no man will be romantically attracted to you. Even if James would come back today, he would go for somebody younger, not you.[20]

Tabitha's body therefore becomes a canvas for social critique on maternity and ageing. It becomes an avenue for exploring popular thinking about women's 'biological clocks', a dated but still present reference to women's fertility. While more recent work on fertility indicates a changing dynamic to the approach equating women's bodies to ticking clocks (see Gergen 1990; Cook et al., 2012), a standard narrative of women's reproductive labour aligns with a patriarchal moral panic about age and infertility.

Tabitha's anxiety is also linked to her fear of being a single woman. As Christine Obbo (1980) and others have demonstrated at length, singlehood for women is read as an anomaly in public discourse. While a lot of single women in Africa lead successful, independent lives, particular dated insinuations still exist that psychologically, if not physically, attempt to round up these women, in a way reminiscent of colonial systems of controlling women's bodies (White 1991; Kanogo 2005; Mutongi 2007). Indeed, as Sara Maitland (2014) has argued, being single is seen as a pathology in a society that fears solitude. Relationships, preferably heterosexual ones, are better. Tabitha's union with a man who harasses her into accepting his proposal, is worrying in this sense. Mbolu is a villain whose negative intentions are signalled in the high-pitched and nervous tone of his voice and the erratic, fast-paced way in which he speaks. The manner in which he preys on Tabitha's fears is undignified, and he is insensitive when he tells her that James could either be dead or married to somebody else. However, Tabitha, because of her desperation, fails to see this evil side of Mbolu and even he becomes an attractive option. He embodies her fantasy of an ever-after.

This moment of seeming desperation on Tabitha's part introduces the idea of choice, disrupting the theme of patience that is contained in the 'good' woman narrative. Freeman articulates such moments in this way: 'against pain and loss, erotohistoriography posits value of surprise, of pleasurable interruptions and momentary fulfilments from elsewhere, other times' (2005, 59). In spite of her undying love for James, Tabitha chooses to move in another direction, abandoning her plans for a life with James. 'Moving on' entails forging relationships with people other than James. She makes friends with James's mother, with whom she discusses her dilemma over wanting to wait for James but worrying that he might have intentionally left her, and also that she was growing old. James's mother is sympathetic and encourages Tabitha to move on. Similarly, her friend Jane is equally unwilling to see her friend continue to suffer, and advises her to move on. By the time James returns, she has been living with another man (though not consummating the relationship), and has even set a wedding date. Her goal seems more set on getting married, than on James. The narrative of the 'good' woman falls short of its promise in this regard.

In using Elizabeth Freeman's idea of chrononormativity and erotohistoriography, as well as other ideas that best capture the interruptions contained within narrative, I have shown how, in a play that presents itself as 'perfect', one can read against the grain to highlight ways in which womanhood can still exist as complex in narrative. *3 Times a Lady* becomes a narrative of chance, as much as it is based on a predictable storyline. One can, in this way, read the play for its potentialities and possibilities, and its interruptions as moments of agency.

Infidelity and the melodramatic mode

In the complex narrativisation of sexuality, infidelity exists in and between the narratives of *Radio Theatre*. This is certainly the case in the play *Whatever it Takes* (2004) in which the lead character, Joy Mbote, gets into a flirtatious relationship with a rich man, Benson Mutia, despite her being married. Her infidelity is implied throughout, never overtly acted upon. What the listener is privy to, however, are the flirtations (demonstrated in the casual conversations between the two) and that the two of them spend a lot of time together. There is also an exchange of a large sum of money in the form of a donation. Lastly, there is a moment when Benson asks Joy point-blank if she would agree to be in a relationship with him, as indicated in the excerpt below:

> Benson: [laughs] so…I am sure that…eh…you will get me out of this situation.
>
> Joy: Uh? Me? [laughs] and how do I do that?

Benson: By becoming my woman.

Joy: Oh [pause].

Benson: Look, Joy. I really, really wanted to tell you this the first time I saw you.

Joy: Mmm…

Benson: You are so beautiful, in both mind and soul, in everything.

Joy: Uh?

Benson: Joy? I am very, very sure that you are the right one for me. C'mon Joy, you know —

Joy: Ben.

Benson: Uh?

Joy: [Laughs nervously] What you want, I am sorry it cannot happen, it's just too late.

Benson: But why? Why would it be late?

Joy: Uhm…because I am married and I love my husband.

Benson: Oh!

Joy: And above that I am a born-again Christian. I can't do anything that…It goes against my faith or that will break my wedding vows.

Benson: Mmm. Oh so you are married?

Joy: Yes.

Benson: You never told me.

Joy: You never asked. If you don't believe it, just look…just look at this [paper].

The excerpt above is the culmination of 'several' days of being in each other's company, having drinks together and ultimately, Joy ending up at Benson's mansion. In the midst of showing off his home, Benson shares his desire to date Joy. Joy of course turns him down, but it is the hesitancy in her response that draws the most attention. She qualifies her response by first citing love and loyalty to her husband, but also, that she is 'a born again Christian'. This latter aspect is important in so far as it places emphasis on her unavailability. Even then, Benson still asks: 'And you cannot love another?' to which Joy replies 'not when he is still alive no. You know we took our vows together and promised to remain together till death do us part' (*Whatever it Takes*, 2004). The dialogue above reveals a number of things. First, it reveals Joy's availability for a relationship, a fact that she verbally refutes. She makes no attempt to rebuff his attention the first time they meet. For her, that he writes her a cheque of one million Kenyan shillings (about $10 000) on their first meeting, is a kind gesture by a stranger. Subsequently, he invites her to his home, a fact that she once again interprets as Benson being friendly. The message Benson gets from her indulgence of his attention is that she is available to date:

> Benson: Mmm. That is a fast one on me.
>
> Joy: I am sorry.
>
> Benson: Well, uhm…what can I say?
>
> Joy: Just keep looking, just keep looking. There is a Miss right for you out there. Just pray about it and the Lord shall bless you one day, just pray about it.
>
> Benson: I…I will I will.

The second issue revealed in the dialogue is that social conventions stand in the way of Joy experiencing passion and desire. Joy's words: 'it's just too late' reveals the possibility of another option. She quickly follows her words by citing marriage and love, and subsequently her Christian faith. However, her response to the question of whether or not she could be available, shapes the rest of the play: 'not when he is still alive no. You know we took our vows together and promised to remain together till death do us part.' This seems like an open invitation for Benson, who has the means to 'do something' about it. This fact is made even clearer when one considers the original narrative on which the play is based. *Whatever it Takes* is an adaptation of a story by the English writer Frederick Forsyth titled *No Comebacks* (1982). Published in an anthology under the same title, it involves the same storyline as the play. *No Comebacks* is a short story about Mark Sanderson, a rich and successful American businessman who realises that despite his riches, he still has no partner to share it with. During one of the many charity events he attends annually, he meets Angela Summers, and is immediately drawn to her. Angela is married, but 'Sanderson could not have cared less; married women were as easy as any others' (Forsyth 1982, 3). He falls in love with her, and for the rest of the summer, they become intimate and spend a lot of time together. Eventually, she has to go back home to her husband. When Mark suggests that she leaves her husband, she answers, 'Until death do us part'. Mark, obsessed with Angela, weaves a plot in which he hires a top-class hit man to find and kill Angela's husband. At the moment the murder is being committed, however, Angela walks in and the hit man kills her as well. He returns to his boss and explains that he killed Angela as well because his boss had asked that there be 'no comebacks' that would trace the murder back to him. Both Mark in the novel and Benson in the play lose more than they had bargained for.[21]

The point of this play is to render moral lessons surrounding the main anti-hero, Benson Mutia. Benson uses his money to try and seduce Joy, who, like Tabitha, is a schoolteacher. The recurrent roles of these women as schoolteachers and community builders is worth noting, especially in the way that these career options are projected as non-threatening options by the radio plays. Such positions also insinuate an inherent maternal role that lends the women the ability to work with children and to serve their communities. In *Whatever it Takes*, Benson's wealth offers a site through which Joy's femininity plays out. She is introduced to the listener as a soft-spoken, mild-mannered woman who is raising money for a community project back in her village. She is part of a *chama* (an informal investment group) of women that has brought together different women whose aim is to deal with community problems caused by drought in her village. Joy is presented as the innocent victim of Benson's schemes to be in a romantic relationship with her at whatever cost. In a grand gesture, he donates one million Kenyan shillings towards her cause. That she accepts money from a stranger is downplayed and an alternative narrative of her naivety and genuine goodness is emphasised. The listener is also introduced to her relationship with her husband. In one scene, Joy tells her husband about the money that Benson donated to the women's group. Like her, James (the husband) is excited by Benson's kindness to their community. In order for the narrative to work, both James and Joy remain innocent bystanders in an evil game of greed and lust, staged by Benson.

The dichotomy between reward and punishment is emphasised in this play, in which, unlike *3 Times a Lady*, infidelity is punishable (in this case) by death. There are parallels between, for instance, Joy and Eve in the Christian creation story, who tempts her partner Adam to eat fruit from a forbidden tree. In the play, the money Joy accepts becomes the forbidden fruit, inviting trouble and death to an otherwise peaceful relationship. The temptation is in the imagination of the possibility of a relationship outside marriage, one that Joy has to cleanse herself of in the end by citing marriage and her Christian faith as the invisible boundaries she cannot cross. She does though, cross other boundaries, allowing herself to be wooed by a man who is clearly interested in her. I argue that the play is interested in keeping Joy 'pure', a good woman, by allowing her to play out her good-natured character via her association with Benson, to whom she does not reveal her marital status the first time. We see Benson's praise of her later as testament to this goodness: 'you are so beautiful, in both mind and soul, in everything'. The dominant masculinist script of this storyline: it is the projection of a masculinist imagination of what a good woman is while simultaneously imagining the woman as sexually available. Certainly, the female character in Fredrick Forsyth's novel is available for sex, a fact that the morality play intentionally holds back on, restraining itself on the boundaries of what is acceptable for it to drive home its message. Benson then becomes the evil one, whose money taints the lives of two 'pure' people. Marriage becomes the haven from which goodness emanates, while the single bachelor must pray to God to receive the blessing of a 'Miss Right'. The conventionality of the play is overshadowed though by the insinuation of infidelity on Joy's part, which I emphasise as part of an interruption of expected behaviour, much like in my reading of Tabitha in *3 Times a Lady*. These are women who toy with ideas of infidelity or seeking out their passions and desires outside of conventionally accepted forums, but always hold back just in time. The plays also highlight the availability of good women to men who imagine them as suitable. The men who pursue these women are often attracted to their virginity and faithfulness (as is the case of Tabitha), or their kindness, non-aggressive engagement with them, as is the case with Joy. While Joy is killed in the play, listeners are still rewarded with the celebration of the good woman against the rich and selfish man, who loses out in the end because of his refusal to respect the sanctity of marriage.

The fate of the cheating woman plays out differently in *Bottoms Up* (2004), a play about a man who is wrongly diagnosed as being HIV positive. Bosco Maele, a successful young university graduate with a young family, finds out during a routine medical check-up that he is HIV positive. The bulk of the play dwells on the stigma he faces, including job loss at a time when most are still ignorant about the adverse effects of stigmatisation. His wife, Maggie, upon finding out, rejects him and moves out of their home, taking their child with her. The straightforward narrative of betrayal and rejection structures the play in a typical morality-play style. The use of characterisation to draw in listeners effectively invites the listener to identify with Bosco, as he is the one who has just received the bad news. Through his stream of consciousness, we learn that he is in fact a family man who has not been unfaithful to his wife. As such, his HIV status is a mystery to the listener as much as it is a mystery to him. Maggie refuses to be associated with him. The moment she rejects him is dramatised in such a way as to turn her into a villain:

> Maggie: I knew it! I knew it, and now see! I knew you had other women in your life! You have killed me and my child too!
>
> Bosco: What are you talking about?
>
> Wife: You have AIDS, don't you?
>
> Bosco: I am HIV positive.
>
> Wife: What is the difference, Baba John? What is it that you lacked from me, Baba John?
>
> [Crying].
>
> Bosco: Would you please listen to me? I swear, I swear Mama John, I have never slept with any other woman!
>
> Maggie: Ohhh! You cheat!
>
> Bosco: I am not lying! Remember we took a HIV test before we got married?

Maggie: Then where the hell did you get this thing from?

Bosco: I don't know!

Maggie: [Shouting] You got it from the air and the water we drink? Eh? C'mon Maele. It is useless to deny this now. C'mon Maele…this, this…

Bosco: C'mon…would you please listen to me? I was hoping to get answers from you…did you sleep with any other man?

Maggie: Oh please!

Bosco: Did you sleep with any other man for the period that we have been married?

Maggie: Listen Maele, eh? You think that because you have been sleeping with other women I have been sleeping with other men? Eh?

Bosco: Maggie…

Maggie: Is that the reason you are putting me at risk and our son? I can't believe you [crying].

Bosco: Maggie? Please…

Maggie: Don't touch me! [Sound of glass breaking].

Bosco: Please…

Maggie: Do not touch me!

Bosco: So what am I supposed to do then? What do you expect me to do?

In his reading of the melodramatic mode, Peter Brooks (1976, 2) identifies it as being in excess of reality, in which hyperbolic reactions and confrontations or what he terms 'superdrama' excites the banal reality in which narratives are drawn. Indeed, this superdrama is presented in Manichean modes, involving intense binaries

> …where every gesture, however frivolous or insignificant it may seem, is charged with the conflict between light and darkness, salvation and damnation, and where people's destinies and choices of life seem finally to have little to do with the surface realities of a situation, and much more to do with an intense inner drama in which consciousness must purge itself and assume the burden of moral sainthood. (1976, 5)

In *Bottoms Up*, the extremities of good and bad play out through the plot lines and characters, where Maggie immediately presents as the impatient, terrible wife that leaves in the face of trouble. She does not give her husband a chance to engage with the news, she does not offer understanding. The play references a different story in the Kenyan public at the time: that of Jane Ngima, the wife of Joe Muriuki, the first Kenyan to go public about his HIV status. In 1987, Muriuki went public about his

HIV status, a time when stigma was prevalent and people had no understanding of the disease. His wife, whom he met in 1989, decided to stay with him after learning of his status, despite facing humiliation and rejection by both family and the public at large. Their story captured the imagination of Kenyans, especially because Muriuki is still living positively, over 30 years later. In the radio play, however, there is a display of impatience, a melodramatic event in which everything becomes 'excessive' (Brooks 1976, 2). For instance, the wife offers her husband no chance to explain himself. She believes the gossip of a workmate, and immediately packs her bags and leaves after finding out neither she nor their son is HIV positive. This superdrama, the 'intense, excessive representation of life', is one of the modes through which the moral world is structured. As Brooks explains further:

> The desire to express all seems a fundamental characteristic of the melodramatic mode. Nothing is spared and nothing is left unsaid; the characters stand on stage and utter the unspeakable, give voice to their deepest feelings, dramatize through their heightened and polarized words and gestures the whole lesson of their relationship. (1976, 5)

The bad woman is thus presented to the listener: impatient; irrational and judgemental. In the meantime, Kanzi, Bosco's workmate who also has to go through the same health check-up routine as demanded by new workplace policies, finds out he is HIV negative. Kanzi maliciously spreads rumours about Bosco's apparent philandering and eventual HIV status (which he finds out after a shocked Bosco confides in him). Bosco loses a wife and a job as a result. Once again, Kanzi is painted as an excessive character, jumpy, vile and unable to learn life's lessons. He unethically reveals Bosco's HIV status to their company boss, and Bosco is fired. The stigma is overdramatised, as he is not allowed into the premises of his workplace. He is deemed contagious, and is therefore completely shunned. Kanzi also rushes to Bosco's wife and lets her know about her husband. On a second visit, he convinces Maggie to have sex with him (because, in a melodramatic fashion, he is insatiable). He has sex with Maggie with no protection, having just been tested HIV negative. During their sexual encounter, and unbeknownst to them, Bosco is at home, having returned to pick up some clothes (he has at the time moved to his rural home). In this extremely dramatic moment, it is clear that Maggie will be punished for her transgressions and betrayal. The listener is by now aware that something is amiss in Kanzi's behaviour. There is a moment of connection with the listener, what Ien Ang identifies as emotional realism, 'the intimate level of feeling' that is the connection between the audience and the melodrama (2007, 19). In the one month of rejection and soul-searching that Bosco goes through, he discovers his own ignorance about HIV/AIDS. He also discovers the extent of prejudice by people with whom he had previously shared relationships. The connection is made through his interior monologues, to which the listener is privy. At the end of that month, he takes another test as he is convinced he has not deliberately exposed himself to HIV. He learns that the clinic where he had taken the test (and where his friend Kanzi had also been tested) had made a mistake and that he had received Kanzi's results by mistake. The play ends as a warning to men like Kanzi and women like Maggie, who are of course 'punished' when they discover they are HIV positive.

Unlike the case of Tabitha and Joy, who flirt but do not cross the line of conventional expectations, Maggie does, and is punished for her sins. While Tabitha gets her happily ever after ending, and Joy returns to her husband (she dies an honourable death); Maggie has to live out her punishment through the discovery of her hasty choice. She is indeed a bad woman who must be punished.

Conclusion

In this chapter, I have focused on radio and the construction of African womanhood, both historically as well as in contemporary media. I identify the power of radio and its centrality in the lives of Africans, especially in rural areas where resources are scarce. Existing scholarship on radio in Africa, for instance, shows that radio is still viewed as a primary source of information and entertainment in many low-income African households, despite a rise in other forms of media (Fardon and Furniss 2000; Gunner, Ligaga, and Moyo 2011). Radio still plays a vital role in suturing communities together and forging new publics and communities through sound and voice (Gunner 2019). In the chapter, I therefore reflect on radio's power to create consciousness, forge communities and lend itself as a tool to be manipulated by the state. I concentrate on the role radio played during the colonial era in Kenya. I dwell on the deliberate use of radio to educate, civilise and develop African women, whom the colonial government was eager to teach how to be good women. Radio was among the means through which information on domestic science and community development was disseminated. I also briefly explore the role radio played in reigning in errant Mau Mau female supporters in the emergency years.

In the postcolony, I place the politics of nationalism and the deliberate re-writing of nationalist struggles that saw women becoming sidelined and relegated to the margins under the spotlight. Women became paragons of morality and agents of national cohesion. I look at how radio played a role in the reshaping of nationalist conversations on who fought for the nation's freedom, and who deserved to be at the seat of power. Radio became central to defining the new nation. I dwell on the Moi years — 1978–2002 — as the years when the media played a role in sharpening public cultures of an apolitical, familial nation ruled by the 'Father of the nation', and the space that Christian religion had in constructing this space. I argue that the context above contributed to the development of conservative notions of sexuality through which femininity was constructed.

The last section of the chapter considers *Radio Theatre*, a long-standing English language drama programme produced for the state broadcaster, Kenya Broadcasting Corporation (KBC). I read the constructions of the Manichean figures of 'good' and 'bad' women in radio and look at the techniques that three radio plays use to engage these categories. Using ideas such as Elizabeth Freeman's chrononormativity, I engage various configurations of femininity, with an interest in reading transgressions in narratives. Transgressive women, I argue, must be read 'outside' of genre and narrative, in the spaces in between narrative, and in the implied sections of the plays, rather than in the dominant storyline. These possibilities become avenues for reading desire and passion, especially as radio for national audiences tends to be extremely conservative and linear. I also consider melodrama demonstrative of lessons: a clear institutional function performed by the radio plays. I am, moreover, interested in the intimate connections such plays make with listeners through sound.

Notes

1   *Radio Theatre* airs every Sunday at 12:30, with repeats on Thursdays at 10:00, with an average of 50 plays a year, providing a wide spectrum of themes that speak to various aspects of everyday life, including gender and sexuality. (This information is based on the production of the programme until 2006. There have been several changes in KBC since, including a change in producers. For instance, Alex Mbathi replaced the previous producer, the late Nzau Kalulu, who was the producer of the show from 1995 to 2006. All interviews herein were carried out between the author and Mr Kalulu.)

2   Interview with Nzau Kalulu, Nairobi, 19 December 2006.

3   *Mchezo wa wiki* is a generic term that means 'play of the week'.

4   Although there is little evidence to connect these various 'versions', I nonetheless read *Radio Theatre* as an umbrella title for radio drama programmes that dwell on and circulate themes of everyday life.

5   See Ligaga 2005 for a full analysis of this play.

6   In 1923, an Advisory Committee was set up to look into the possibility of education for Native Africans. In 1925, the committee presented a memorandum with recommendations, to the Secretary of State to the Colonies. Dependencies, T. A. 1925. *Education Policy in British Tropical Africa*. London: HMSO, 1400, 2374.

7   It is interesting to note that the first cabinet in Kenya was entirely male. It was made up of the President Jomo Kenyatta and 18 cabinet ministers, all men.

8   Radio drama was used outside of VOK premises by the Ministry of Education in Kenya for educational purposes from 1965, and thus was not being produced by the state broadcaster. However, the Ministry of Education worked in collaboration with

the Ministry of Information, and broadcasting for educational purposes was considered better handled in the education ministry. As such, the Ministry of Education, through the Educational Media Service (EMS) at the Kenya Institute of Education (KIE), produced these programmes (Heath 1986).

9 *Nyayo* is a Kiswahili word for footsteps.

10 Althusser 1977.

11 A number of studies exist that are beginning to look at the relationship between FM radio and television's sexual content and exposure to young people. Ngula, Mberia and Miller (2015) for instance, look at how high school students search for sexual information on radio and television.

12 Joseph Ngujiri. 2005. *Daily Nation*. Accessed 28 October 2019. https://allafrica.com/stories/200511210386.html

13 Ngujiri. 2005.

14 "Catholic Church lobbies to have three novels withdrawn from school curriculum." Accessed 28 October 2019. https://ifex.org/catholic-church-lobbies-to-have-three-novels-withdrawn-from-school-curriculum/

15 *Kitumbua kimeingia mchanga* is a Kiswahili proverb that signals conflict. Its literal meaning is 'bread dipped in soil/sand'. The author S. A. Mohammed uses it in his book bearing the proverb as title, to signal domestic conflict in families; tensions between old and new generations; conflicts in marriage, and so on. An article in *Zanzibar Daima* titled "Vita baina ya ukale na usasa kwenye 'Kitumbua Kimeingia Mchanga'" [Conflict between old and new in *Kitumbua Kimeingia Mchanga*] observes that Mohammed's book is about arranged marriages causing intergenerational conflict. This conflict threatens to break up the family. Accessed 26 October 2019. https://zanzibardaima.net/2016/04/24/vita-baina-ya-ukale-na-usasa-kwenye-kitumbua-kimeingia-mchanga/

16 See "Catholic Church lobbies to have three novels withdrawn from school curriculum." https://ifex.org/catholic-church-lobbies-to-have-three-novels-withdrawn-from-school-curriculum/

17 See the article by Caro Rolando titled "Rafiki: ban lifted on Kenyan film that challenges stereotypes at home and abroad." Accessed 28 October 2019. https://ifex.org/rafiki-ban-lifted-on-kenyan-film-that-challenges-stereotypes-at-home-and-abroad/

18 *3 Times a Lady*, part one, 2004.

19 *3 Times a Lady*, part one, 2004.

20 *3 Times a Lady*, part one, 2004.

21 While the play is more or less based on the popular novel by Forsyth, the producer of the play, Nzau Kalulu (2007), denies that it is an adaptation of Forsyth's story. The adaptation of the short story into a radio play shows how global texts often get integrated into local narratives in popular culture. As Arjun Appadurai (1995), Joyce Nyairo (2004), Stephanie Newell (2000) and others have variously noted, what appears to be mimicry often has complex connections with local cultures. In this case, the purpose of the play was to emphasise a moral narrative, achieved in the end through sounds of Benson crying.

4

Scandal, surveillance and the spectacular 'wicked' woman

Introduction

In an article about gendered surveillance and violence, Jessica Murray (2018) argues that women have become accustomed to being monitored and have adjusted their behaviour accordingly. Though she focuses on a South African context, it is possible to apply her notion of the ubiquity of gendered disciplinary structures to reading examples from other contexts. In this chapter, I look at sexual scandal as a form of surveillance of women in Kenya. The woman whose sexuality is discussed in public is often automatically labelled 'wicked' because her behaviour falls outside that of a 'good' woman. The act of public labelling ensures shame and guilt on the part of the woman, while also circulating as a cautionary tale to be consumed as warnings or lessons. I explore what it means to be 'wicked' in a newspaper industry that works to either marginalise women's lifestyle narratives or contain them in pre-formulated structures. I explore the meanings of monogamy in heterosexual relationships that control narratives of femininity, in a context where monogamous relationships are increasingly being tested. I also engage with meanings of tabloids, rumour and scandal, and the role they play in exploding, rather than containing, narratives of individuality, agency and choice for women.

The Nairobian,[1] a popular Kenyan tabloid, published a story titled "Rich married women renting secret pads to meet young lovers". The report continues:

> …*The Nairobian* has uncovered the shocking revelations of women who are now secretly keeping fully furnished plush apartments for escapades away from public scrutiny. The apartments known as 'Spinster pads' or 'bachelorette pads' are quickly replacing high-end lodgings where the fear of getting caught is high. Such apartments have for years been associated with married men. We can now reveal that scores of wealthy married women in the city have taken 'mpango wa Kando' to a new level. A well-known banker with a multinational seems to have been on a roll with a *clande* [clandestine relationship]. The

married mother of four has apparently rented a plush two-room apartment in Mlolongo to quench her loin thirst. Apparently, her 'Spinster pad' is a stone's throw away from her marital home in Kitengela. A source revealed that the married banker visits the apartment at least once a week with her toy boy. 'She is not the type of woman to be seen booking hotel rooms, so she rented the top floor of these apartments and brings her men here,' said our source.[2]

This excerpt reminds one of the figure of the 'wicked' woman that has been used historically in Africa to label and stigmatise women's behaviour in the public sphere. To think about the woman in the story above is to explore the idea of the 'wicked' woman in Africa as '"vagabond," "prostitute," "wayward," "unruly," "indecent," and "immoral"… terms used to label and stigmatise women whose behaviour in some way threatens other people's expectations of the "way things ought to be"' (Hodgson and McCurdy 2001, 1). Dorothy Hodgson and Sheryl McCurdy argue that the so-called 'wicked' woman needs to be unpacked and complicated 'by analysing the processes through which some of the women become stigmatised as "wicked," the nature of their alleged transgressions, and the effects of their actions…' (2001, 2). In their words, 'wicked' women are 'pivotal to transforming gender relations and other domains of social life' (2001, 1), and that 'whether accused of adultery, abandonment, or insubordination, their lives and actions often reflect and produce contradictions and contestations of power in the intersecting and shifting landscapes of the individual, family, community, nation-state, and the global arena' (2001, 2). Methodologically, they suggest that in order to analyse the trope of the 'wicked' woman, her transgressions and the 'paradoxes' she generates need to be interrogated in order to debate and possibly offer more nuanced understandings of this figure in terms of 'gender relations, social practices, cultural norms, and political-economic institutions' (Hodgson and McCurdy 2001, 2). A feminist approach to tabloids that report on women's personal lives and scandals offers a chance to perform a transgressive reading of the ways in which 'wicked' women can be imagined differently. To do this, I analyse the examples of gender representation in the Kenyan press — including mainstream press and tabloids — in order to explore this 'wickedness' in context. What do such actions of wickedness imply discursively in a Kenyan context, where public conversations about women still remain widely conservative? Engaging with the genre of tabloids enables the re-imagining of gendered subjectivities rendered (in)visible through narrative.

A gendered history of the press in Kenya

Tabloids in Kenya emerge out of a mass media culture that has either ignored women or maintained dominant representations of women in traditional gender normative terms. Citing a number of scholars writing in the 1990s, such as Victoria Goro and

Sophie Muluka-Lutta (1991), Leslie Steeves (1997) argues that they suggest common patterns of representation of women in Kenyan media, pointing out, for instance, how advertising predominantly portrays women in traditional roles of mother and wife, or as sex objects. This is a finding that is reiterated in later bodies of scholarship. Mary Mwangi (1996), for instance, carried out a quantitative content analysis of 105 television commercials and found that while more women than men were portrayed as central characters, they also predominantly promoted household products. Men, on the other hand, appeared in car, alcohol and finance commercials. Mwangi's research in this way showed that men were linked to public roles, whereas women tended to take on submissive or passive roles. Even in cases where women were central characters, the commercial was more likely to have a male voice over. While Mwangi's research offers significant clues into how commercials mirror societal gender roles in Kenya, the difficulty with her research is that it does not provide context and history. Steeves, writing about similar kinds of quantitative research, concludes that there is need for in-depth studies that investigate how the media works in specific contexts, since such analyses can reveal 'a variety of ways in which the text reinforces both indigenous and colonial forms of gender oppression, as well as class divisions between elite and poor women' (1997, 9). This is the approach Steeves (1997) adopts in her book *Gender Violence and the Press: The St. Kizito Story*, where she analyses how the media portrayed a tragic event of gender-based violence that occurred in Kenya in the early 1990s.

On 13 July 1991, a group of boys attacked a girls' dormitory at St Kizito Mixed Secondary School, Meru District, in Kenya. According to a report by Kenya Television Network (KTN) reporter Dennis Onsagrio (2013), 76 girls were raped, while 19 were either suffocated, beaten or raped to death.[3] Leslie Steeves (1997) argues that the press was as complicit as the school authorities in excusing the violence during the tragedy. During the trial of the 39 schoolboys held for rape and murder, the deputy head-teacher of St Kizito is reported as saying: 'the boys never meant any harm against the girls. They just wanted to rape.'[4] Apparently, rape was a common occurrence at the school.[5] Steeves interrogates how colonial and postcolonial patriarchal institutions have given control of information to men while marginalising women's issues. She adds that 'political structures and processes in the state control gender relations' (Steeves 1997, 18). This layered reading of gender violence is useful in mapping how they intertwine with the history of the press in Kenya.

The Kenyan press is predominantly identified through its leading newspapers, the *Daily Nation* and *The Standard*. *The Standard* was first published in 1901, and owned for many years by a UK multinational company, Lonrho (Ugangu 2012). According to Gerard Loughran (2010), it was not until 1960, with the establishment of the *Daily Nation*, that divergent views began circulating in the public sphere through the press. Until then, newspapers were under the tight control of the colonial government, predominantly focusing on issues pertaining to the colonial settler communities and completely ignoring the plight of local Africans. The *Daily Nation*, according to Loughran, was instrumental in ensuring a transition from a colonial to an African focus by encouraging Africans to produce their own news and embrace their own issues. In this way, the *Daily Nation* was viewed as the more radical of the newspapers in Kenya. Other influential newspapers include the *Daily Nation*'s sister newspaper *Sunday Nation*, which enjoys wide circulation, as does *Sunday Standard*. Even though these newspapers have circulated as though independent of state influence, scholars have argued that they are closely monitored and prejudiced in favour of the state (Ugangu 2012). In his account of Kenyan media, Loughran (2012) emphasises the various ways in which Kenyan postcolonial leaders attempted to control the entire media platform. These included the use of force, such as arrests, to silence journalists, and attempts by leaders to buy the silence of media practitioners.

The state control of the press coupled with what Steeves (1997) identifies as the 'patriarchal framing' in journalistic practices, influences whether 'women's stories' are included or excluded. Even in cases where women's stories are reported, she argues that issues such as rape and other forms of violence against women are either skirted or dressed in language such as 'the boys never meant any harm' (1997, 56). Newspaper coverage of harm caused through rape still reports on perpetrators as victims of circumstances. A report in *The Standard* newspaper on 16 August 2019 carried a story titled: "Wasted Lives: 15 years in jail for rapist rugby players."[6] The two men who were found guilty of raping a woman were framed in the story as young men who had misjudged a situation and made poor decisions. Social media response to the court judgement also bemoaned the youth and talent of the men, with some commentators arguing that they had received harsh sentences. This chapter acknowledges the persistence of such trends in reporting harm done to women and looks at tabloids as the hub of such kinds of reports.

Tabloids as locations of transgression

Unlike mainstream media, popular press exhibits less restraint in its reporting, representations and portrayals of culture and politics (Bastian 1993). The process of either upholding or subverting dominant ideology is more pronounced in the popular text. It is in this space that critical interrogation can take place. Historically, according to George Ogola (2017), the popular press arose hand in hand with popular fiction, with writers using newspapers to explore, experiment with, and air their views on social-cultural issues. Usually located in the sphere of entertainment, the popular press includes a variety of elements including popular fiction columns (Ogola 2017), tabloids (Wasserman 2010), 'newspapers and magazines that target the widest audience literate in English' (Bastian 1993, 131). Bastian's definition of the popular press covers a broad enough spectrum of the collection of writing that qualifies as popular press in Africa. She writes:

> Within the popular press there are weekly and monthly magazines like *Prime People* which self-consciously attempt to emulate the lifestyle columns of the West, emphasizing human interest stories, photography, health, fashion, society news and advice column features. There are also daily newspapers, both local and national, that divide their column space between 'hard' news and the same type of features found in *Prime People*. (1993, 131)

Like Wasserman, Bastian identifies tabloids as key in the definition of the popular press. In the scandalous stories of tabloid publications, the supernatural and soft-core pornography merge together (Bastian 1993). In Kenya, the popular press carries scandals, gossip, jokes and lifestyle columns containing advice on fashion, health, society news and related issues. These kinds of stories appear in tabloids like *The Nairobian*, *The Star* and *The Weekly Citizen* as well as in several online tabloid newspapers such as *Ghafla!* and *Nairobi Exposed*.[7] Some of these tabloids are owned by mainstream media groups such as the Standard Media Group that publishes *The Standard* and *Sunday Standard*. The Standard Group launched an entertainment website, Standard Digital Entertainment (SDE) in 2013, which carries several digitised versions of its tabloids including *The Nairobian* and *Pulse*. SDE also hosts digital tabloids such as *Crazy Mondays* whose stories have titles such as: "Agony as wife and mpango wa kando (lover) denounce a cheating man", "Mistresses placed as bets to settle debts", "Woman smashes husband's new car, blaming it for his infidelity" and so on.[8] Such stories are presented as spectacle, but also as cautionary tales against particular kinds of behaviour.

Tabloids are spaces for experimentation in their recounting of mundane narratives. The aspects of 'sensationalism, personalization, and the focus on private concerns' that characterise them, make it possible for them to imagine a world that transgresses normative expectations (Strelitz and Steenveld 2005, 267). The very idea of 'excess' that captures their generic structure is possibly also the location where the re-imagination of an alternative world can occur. In her theorisation of popular culture in Africa, Karin Barber (1987), reminds us that what is categorised as popular has the power to speak in a language that is in tune with the everyday realities of those who consume them. These popular artefacts are 'social facts', capturing the nuances of life that defy conventions and structures. They operate in excess, always allowing meaning to spill over and be interpreted in a variety of ways. This theorisation of the popular is useful in reading feminine 'wickedness' in the public sphere.

Tabloids have often been dismissed as tasteless, sensationalist forms that do not circulate any useful or serious information (Franklin 1997). But tabloids, like many forms of popular culture, should be taken seriously in order for researchers to understand the contexts in which they circulate (Strelitz and Steenveld 2005; Wasserman 2010; Bingham and Conboy 2015). Tabloids circulate as 'soft news', capturing celebrity gossip and dramatic human-interest stories, in direct opposition to 'hard news' journalism (Baum 2002). While they are often seen as trivial, studies continue to show ways in which they serve a majority of people for a number of reasons (Baum 2002; Wasserman 2010). In their book *Tabloid Century*, Adrian Bingham and Martin Conboy (2015) show how tabloids in 20th century Britain played a crucial role in shaping politics, society and culture.

In the African context, a number of scholars have called for an examination of tabloids as public cultural forms that go beyond entertainment to engage in issues of social and political significance for those who read them (Strelitz and Steenveld 2005; Wasserman 2010). Indeed, Herman Wasserman points out that by taking tabloids seriously, one 'invests popular culture with legitimacy' (2010, xii). From this perspective, I see their significance in making visible particular cultures of sexuality that are otherwise marginalised. Yet as Wasserman reminds us, tabloids are not merely 'journalistic products to be measured against a scale of good to bad performance' (2010, xii). They are 'social phenomena that tell us something about the society in which they exist and the role of the media in that society' (Wasserman 2010, xii). Wasserman points to the multiple ways in which tabloids remain significant, especially during moments of political and social transition. Reading the South African context, he argues that tabloids 'offer a picture of how popular culture, mediated politics, and discourses of citizenship can converge in a young democracy; and they illustrate how local and global cultural forces interact in shaping media formats and content' (Wasserman 2010, 2). Tabloids in Kenya have not received much scholarly attention. Where they are mentioned, they appear as marginalised forms that did not occupy a visible place on the news-stands until the mid-2000s. Known as the 'gutter press', they were difficult to find, particularly, as Levi Obonyo (n.d.) points out, since they appeared to have no known ownership, and sometimes only appeared to report on one scandal before disappearing from the stands. Referring to them as the 'now-you-see-them, now-you-don't' press, Obonyo describes the tabloid phenomenon thus:

> The sheets are sold on news-stands and often on street corners for less than half the price of the daily newspapers. They are poorly written, poorly edited, poorly laid out, poorly printed, and contain poor pictures. Generally they have no fixed address, no known publisher, and tend to focus on rumour, sometimes making very spectacular claims. They have no clear frequency, will appear out of the blue, make some spectacular claim that regards either sexual or corruption scandal involving a prominent personality, then disappear. They may only occasionally write on current affairs. These are likely to be found in most major towns and in mainly the major languages besides English and Kiswahili. It is said that

sometimes they are sponsored by politicians who use them to launch a smear campaign against their opponents. But there is no way of proving this. These papers have drawn the anger of the Kenyan government in no small way. As a consequence the government is moving to pass a Statute Law (Miscellaneous Amendments) Bill 2001.[9]

Tabloids, as Obonyo points out, are fluid press genres that navigate multiple spheres in search of an entertaining story. In this way, they can be edgy, interesting and worthy of sustained critical attention. With the rise of digital media, they have come to occupy an increasingly prominent place in the Kenyan public sphere. They cater to a 'digital generation' that 'likes to hear that a socialite posted nudes on Instagram, there was a cat fight between this and that on twitter, where the party is at and such' (Gikuru 2014).[10] Samuel Gikuru is of course speaking about digital cultures in Kenya that have created an even bigger public for tabloids, covering issues such as political and celebrity scandals as well as stories of ordinary men and women. To think about tabloid newspapers, then, is to embrace the myriad ways in which they can re-imagine reality, push boundaries and explode understandings of everyday life.

Scandal, rumour and gossip

A key way in which they do this is through scandal, rumour and gossip. In a lecture delivered at the University of the Witwatersrand in South Africa, Keguro Macharia suggests a reading of scandal, rumour and gossip as popular archives of the everyday and stresses the importance of interrogating the language and historicity of these archives in order to make political and cultural claims (Macharia 2017).[11] Referring mainly to the work of Grace Musila (2015) and Luise White (2008), he argues that scandal, rumour and gossip work to reformulate reality and to push forward ways of seeing the world that are located in particular contexts. Musila's work, for instance, investigates the death of a British tourist, Julie Ward, in Kenya in 1988, in which rumour and gossip provide glimpses of 'truth' into her gruesome murder, which remains unsolved to date. Musila argues that the overlapping 'truths' read against official claims by both the Kenyan state and the British government, provide a broader narrative for understanding the Kenyan political scene. In this reading, Macharia lingers on the idea of credibility, and how this helps to highlight why different actors make particular choices in telling the 'truth' through rumour and gossip. One needs to take cognisance of how gossip works through the creation of 'ties of intimacy between those gossiping' (White 2008, 76). The believability of the gossip largely depends on an ability to summarise public opinion (White 2008). So, for instance, White argues that gossip socialises, as 'the very act of talking about others — or oneself — disciplines; the very practices of sorting out the epistemologies that shock and scandalise creates and catalogues ideas about deviance and virtue which are enforced with each telling' (2008, 77). This is a key function of tabloids. Indeed, White's idea demonstrates the ability of tabloids to catalogue ideas, structure ideas and re-circulate and reinforce them through repetition. The tabloid readership is forged through these elements.

While Musila and White refer to individuals as carriers of rumour and gossip, I draw on their ideas to read tabloids as deliberately personifying stories in order to gain an 'insight into the local contemporary context from which they emerged' (White 2008, 82). If one considers the story of rich married women having affairs that opens this chapter, the way in which tabloids function as gossip/surveillance tools becomes apparent. The article offers gossip about a woman who is both a mother and a wife but is having an affair with a younger man, in a flat bought exclusively for that purpose. In exploring the role of gossip, White emphasises the role that it plays in social conventions and behavioural control. For it to function, there must be common understanding of social rules and values. The reliability of gossip is on whether what is said circulates among people who understand what the gossip is about. Indeed, as White claims, 'gossip is a technique for summarizing public opinion' (2008, 76). I take White's ideas as a way into reading the functions of the tabloid genre. Tabloids rely on information already in existence and explode this to create drama and excess in narrative. In this case, the story of the rich women is also a story about their insatiable sexual appetites, their betrayal of their roles as mothers and wives, their secrecy and hypocrisy, and their choices to be in relationships with younger men. The scandal created via the gossip is functional. It shames their behaviour with the hope of bringing them to order. It exposes an event that is getting out of control. The beginning of the story captures an aspect of how tabloids function:

> The saying that 'what a man can do, a woman can do better' seems to be getting a new meaning as some of the city's rich married women are renting love dens to meet their Romeos.[12]

There is the promise of something new and exciting in this piece of gossip, a way to pull readers in. The opening draws together shock, wonder and conflict in the same space, creating what Peter Brooks would phrase as 'the pressure on surface meaning' (1976, 2). The opening is about 'superdrama', an 'intense, excessive representation of life' (Brooks 1976, 3). The melodramatic element of the tabloid genre also relies on intertextuality by referencing a well-known European character, Romeo.[13] This refers to the young men mentioned in the title of the piece. The opening statement has created intrigue, with the promise of much more. The piece continues:

> We can now reveal that scores of wealthy married women in the city have taken 'mpango wa Kando' to a new level.[14]

The article demands that it be regarded as a credible source. White says of credibility and gossip/scandal, 'not everyone hears or appreciates or understands gossip the same way — some gossip and some rumour may be unreliable to some people while sounding perfectly reasonable to others' (White 2008, 75). There must be a connection with the readership. In this case, credibility is in the phrase 'we can now reveal', which promises to link the story to something else that the readership may be intrigued about. The tabloid genre distinguishes itself from other forms of news articles through register and format. It offers surveillance, which adds to the dramatic aspects of the story, ensuring a sustained interest in the affairs of women who are also strangers. The tabloid story is interested in reporting the event of shame and scandal, rather than dwelling on the validity of its claims.

Re-reading 'mononormativity'

A more sustained interrogation of the story above reveals that what is under question is the woman's morality. She disrupts notions of how married women with children should behave. Married women who stray from their marriages are a dominant feature of the tabloid newspaper genre. They are secretive, scandalous, indifferent and disruptive to the domestic ideal and fantasy of the happily ever after fairy tale romance (Finlay and Clarke 2003). Represented through moral narratives with cautionary messages, these women's behaviours are exposed in the most dramatic manner in order to present them as scandalous. It is, nevertheless, possible to offer a counter-reading of these stories by focusing attention on the behaviours of the cheating woman as transgressive. Following the argument presented by Hodgson and McCurdy (2001), such women are disruptive of gender norms, making it possible to review normative practices like marriage. The centrality of monogamy as a practice is increasingly being questioned, as studies draw attention to the structures that naturalise it, such as the Church and the State (Finlay and Clarke 2003). Termed 'mononormativity', monogamist practice refers to 'the complex sociohistoric arrangement and authorisation of particular patterns of relationships over others' (Finn 2012, 124). This privileging of some relationships has repercussions for public discourse, as those who do not fit in automatically become 'risky' and undesirable (Cooper 2002; Farvid and Braun 2013). It stresses the 'monogamous dyad' as 'natural, morally correct and essential' (Finn 2012, 124). Marriage becomes the ultimate site of this kind of union, promoted by the Church and the State through the institution of heterosexuality (Finlay and Clarke 2003; Jackson and Scott 2004). Feminists have long analysed the institution of marriage by drawing attention to the unequal power relations maintained in it (Rich 1980; Jackson and Scott 2004). Earlier critiques focused on the privileges that men have in such arrangements, calling for more sexual freedom and autonomy through practices of non-monogamy (Jackson and Scott 2004). The debate that feminists have had over marriage and monogamy has included the lop-sidedness of such practices, where the marriage contract has been more binding on women than on men (Jackson and Scott 2004). They further argue that marriage is founded on a 'hypocritical morality' of a bourgeois institution that grants men the services of women, whether sexual, reproductive or domestic, and protects the property of ruling-class men as well as their inheritance rights (Jackson and Scott 2004, 152).

The debates on non-monogamy in heterosexual relationships are diverse. Writing on polyamory, Ani Ritchie and Meg Barker, for instance argue that it is emerging as a discourse that can trouble the dominant discourse of monogamy as reproduced in mainstream media (2006). In the face of the dominant discourse of mononormativity regarding partnerships, infidelities and jealousy, they see a possibility of an alternative discourse shaped by the development of 'polyamorous identities, relationships and emotions' (2006, 1). Similarly, in their exploration of casual sex, Pantea Farvid and Virginia Braun (2013) posit that casual sex could offer an alternative to mononormativity. However, even though non-monogamy is celebrated, it is still a negotiated practice rather than a clear-cut, radical alternative to monogamy (Jamieson 2004). Lynn Jamieson, for instance, argues that even non-monogamous couples still insist on identifying as a couple in an ideal domestic space (2004). If, she argues, coupledom is the cherished ideal, then non-monogamy has to be a negotiated act. Any relationship that remains undeclared, such as secret affairs, breaches the trust between two people.

Making women's sexualities visible

The idea of women who have multiple partners and relationships is therefore one that is not impossible to imagine. However, as happens in many African cultures, such liberal approaches to sexuality have to be negotiated differently. Sylvia Tamale (2011) urges us to ask questions about African sexualities, particularly in the way they have been silenced under guises of taboo and other inhibitions. Tamale suggests an unlearning and relearning exercise in order to fully grasp the extent of African sexualities, 'including desires, practices, presentations, fantasies, identities, taboos, abuses, violations, stigmas, transgressions and sanctions' (2011, 5). The process of unmapping and remapping begins with an interrogation of sex scandals in tabloids.

Sex scandals offer glimpses into the sexual lives of women in Kenya. According to Cohen, 'the scandal story, which publicly broadcasts information ordinarily kept secret, supplies a rich vein of cultural material through which to investigate language about sexuality' (1996, 2). This occurs because sexual transgressions, as William

Cohen explains, are still able to 'provoke the most sensational media spectacles' (1996, 2). Indeed, while useful in inculcating 'an understanding of normative behaviour in its audiences, scandal also offers an opportunity to formulate questions, discuss previously unimagined possibilities, and forge new alliances' (Cohen 1996, 4–5). Another way of looking at sex scandals is to see them as institutional morality tales rather than narratives of individual transgression (Gamson 2001b). This distinction is important because the work of the sex scandal then becomes more than just reminding an individual of proper sexual behaviour in public, but an indication of 'institutional pathologies and institutional decay' (Gamson 2001b, 185). To examine sex scandals as part of journalistic practice and institutional ideology is to begin to tackle the strategies that such scandals use to narrate stories (Gamson 2001a; 2001b). Gamson argues that these scandals can be read as genres with specific characteristics: 'a revelation, broadcast, denial and/or confession — and frequently a comeback or an attempted comeback' (2001b, 186). Reading beyond their roles as sexual morality barometers, sexual scandals can be 'generally speaking, carriers of social attitudes about sexual morality' and can reveal and keep hidden various related issues (2001b, 186). As part of heteronormative culture, scandal publicly disciplines through moral discourse (Deem 1999). Importantly, sex scandals are gendered in particular ways, as they are often about sexualising women, rather than men. They have become almost interchangeable with women's public lives (Gamson 2001a).

I consider these various ideas in the reading of the married woman in the context of sexual scandal. In the newspaper articles I analyse, it is clear that the married woman is a source of great moral anxiety in Kenya. Every so often a story appears in the popular sections of newspapers about married women and what they 'get up to' when they take time off from their family obligations. This curiosity often comes in the form of a feature report, as part of an investigative journalistic piece. As I show, such reports on the lives of these women are often triggered by high-profile scandals and high-profile events, or in some cases, following a death. In 2013, the wife of a well-known Kenyan former member of parliament was apparently 'busted' having sex with another man. Shortly after the scandal broke, the wife's lover was found dead in the MP's house.[15]

The scandal surrounding the former MP and his wife led to the sprouting of all sorts of cautionary narratives about married women who kept lovers. *The Nairobian* ran the "Rich married women renting secret pads to meet young lovers" (Odongo 2013) story that opens this chapter. In the story, the phenomenon of the 'Mpango wa kando' or 'side dish' — which refers to women or men who have 'illicit' sex with people who are either married or in long-term relationships — is central. Popular knowledge often alludes to women being the obvious *mpango wa kandos* because of the common belief that men are the ones who cheat on their spouses or partners.

In the case of the story above, it is clear that this pattern has been disrupted by the bold behaviour of women who keep lovers even though they are married. The women described in the article have disposable incomes and vibrant sex lives, both of which subvert traditional gender roles. This disruption of roles is what draws attention to the event. It is scandalous, but also generates social anxiety. The article activates a masculine public that gazes into the lives of these women. The hypothetical scenario created in the article is backed by 'evidence' in the form of 'first person accounts' and 'unnamed sources'. In the story, an unidentified man tells of his encounters with one such 'rich' woman, 'revealing' a 'steamy' affair that ended on the woman's terms. The article also provides evidence of the general location of the 'secret' apartment, details of tactics the woman uses to hide affairs and a statement from the security guard at the apartment.

While this tabloid story works as a source of entertainment through scandalous revelations, it also speaks to Kenyan women's sexualities and pleasures. In a conservative society such as Kenya, sexuality is rarely spoken about publicly. As Rachel Spronk argues, in Kenya 'sexual pleasure often seems in conflict with social conventions' (2012, 13). The tabloid stories introduce the sexual pleasure of women, however marginally, into public view. They make it possible to see women as sexual beings who enjoy sex and want to be sexually satisfied (Spronk 2012). The women in the text are 'wicked' because they defy the stereotype that sexual desire is masculine (McFadden 2003). Sexuality is closely linked to power, according to Patricia McFadden (2003), and as such has led to many women remaining trapped in what she calls 'a hetero-normative cultural and social matrix' (n.p.). She argues that knowledge of sexual pleasure enables a better sense of self, which in turn puts women in better positions to negotiate sexual relationships, especially in the age of HIV/AIDS (2003). The tabloid stories also raise the issue of gender equality and freedom of choice, as the women in the stories navigate terrains of sexuality that open up because they have economic means. This aligns with contemporary feminist arguments that the ability to make choices about one's sexual, economic, cultural and social conditions is an empowering one, 'an opportunity to self-determine' (Snyder-Hall 2010, 205). The tabloid article is therefore more than just a cautionary tale: it is also a glimpse into a different sexual world in which women cross boundaries and thwart social norms.

While the issue of economic success is seen as a contributing factor to the scandalous behaviour displayed by women in the article mentioned above, even women in lower-income groups can pursue sexual pleasure. A story that appears in *The Standard's* online platform, SDE, reports through its column "Crazy World" on a woman who was caught cheating after having tricked her husband by cooking him his favourite meal. The article, "Married woman strays for tilapia"[16] goes on to describe how the husband eventually caught on to the wife's trick:

A fisherman was forced to flee in his birthday suit in broad daylight for dear life after he was caught pants down with somebody's wife. The incident, which occurred at Doho Beach along Lake Victoria at Kanam B Location, Rachuonyo North District, left residents in shock. The man in his 20s and a relatively older woman were spotted sprinting away nude after their midday romp ended unceremoniously. The man had to run out of his own bedroom when the husband to his illicit lover ambushed them following a tip off by a good neighbour. The woman is said to have excused herself out on pretext that she was going to '*we arie tienda matin jokama*' (let me stretch my legs a bit) and left her husband enjoying Tilapia and ugali. The said meal, according to her husband, always satisfied all his culinary imaginations. Other than being his favourite meal, it was one of the best meals — one that gets his taste bud on fire — she had prepared for him this year, her husband later confessed.

This story is a variation of the previous story about women who rent out rooms in secret for their lovers, except in this case the woman in question is in a lower income category. It proposes a moral tale in which women who stray are cautioned that there is always a 'good' neighbour watching who can draw attention to such illicit affairs. The story raises not only the scandal of the woman being 'caught in the act', but also significantly, sexual desire outside of marriage. In the story, the woman in question is deceptive. She performs her wifely duties by cooking for her husband and making sure that he is distracted. She then lies to him to obtain 'permission' to leave the home to meet her lover. She is the tabloid genre's 'wicked' figure who is loathed and punished. The punishment includes the humiliation of being caught and having to run away naked while a crowd watches. It is also contained in the article itself as readers are invited to join in the condemning laughter. The husband is the innocent bystander who is the injured party, and the reader is invited to take his side. This intentional structuring of the tabloid story shows ways in which such narratives mete out punishment via narrative. If one then is to read agency in this, it is to recognise how the wife exists as a trickster figure, defying boundaries of surveillance to have sex outside of marriage. There is a lack of privacy as neighbours are able to track her movements. Her husband is also in close vicinity when she engages in her affair. Bei Cai identifies trickster figures as 'change agents whose status as social outsiders and as cultural critics bestows them not only with the power to defy oppressive social norms but also the creative power to reimagine new concepts of selfhood, gender and race relationships, and community' (2008, 276).

In a context such as the one in the story, the woman-as-trickster reading may seem like an over-investment in a scenario that is simply about deception and illicit affairs. But, to read it as such is to give it new meaning and the possibility for re-interpretation. For Cai (2008), social change can be arrived at if one applies new readings to situations that seem commonplace and familiar. In this way, the article potentially re-imagines a cultural situation in which the woman defies conformity and transgresses social norms. Her marriage has failed to provide her with the sexual satisfaction she needs, and she strays to get it despite difficult circumstances.

Other articles that have appeared in "Crazy World" that dwell on variations of infidelity as a public morality issue include those with titles such as "Narok Lovers Suffer 'Long Glue Stick' Night".[17] In the article, a man 'traps' his wife through witchcraft during sexual intercourse, leading to a painful and shameful attempt by the lovers to separate themselves. An onlooker comments:

> *Huyu jamaa ametupea suluhisho kwa tatizo ambalo limekuwa likitutatiza. Wanawake wajipange sasa* (The man behind this [husband] has given us a solution to a problem that has been tasking our minds for long. Woe unto women who like cheating).[18]

The phenomenon of lovers who get 'stuck' is a recurrent one that has long since been a source of fascination. In a BBC report, William Kremer (2014)[19] asks the question 'can couples really get stuck together during sex?' The article details the condition called 'penis captivus' in which the woman's vagina contracts while the penis is engorged during sexual intercourse. According to the report, while there is a scientific explanation to the condition, the idea of two people getting stuck is fascinating and has been linked to illicit sex. Kremer details how various myths have been created across time around this phenomenon as a form of punishment for 'illicit' sex. In Kenya, news articles about 'stuck' couples frequently come up. It is commonly thought that when this happens, it is often the spouse of one of the couples, usually the husband, who 'ties' the couple with the help of a witchdoctor. The couple then faces public humiliation until the husband 'unties' them. The fact that this narrative travels and is repeated in the media is fascinating because it shows how re-circulation of these stories works to contain behaviour that disrupts normative expectations of sexual behaviour among married couples.

That women are constantly under scrutiny is a key issue in many of the tabloid articles on infidelity. Men remain marginal in these scandal narratives unless they are celebrities. This presentation of behaviour is different from the constructed narratives of *Radio Theatre* as analysed in the previous chapter. In this chapter, the clear dichotomies of good and bad women become blurred as narratives of infidelity become more complex, reflecting the desire by married people to find sexual fulfilment elsewhere. Many of these tabloid stories dwell on the intricacies of women's lives outside marriage. In the stories about getting stuck, however, what is punished is infidelity in the heterosexual relationship. In such a case, even cheating men get shamed. For instance, in 2018, a man and a woman had to be taken to hospital after they were unable to separate from each other after sex.[20] According to the tabloid story, the man was cheating on his wife, and as 'revenge', the wife engaged the services of a witchdoctor. Stories like these about cheating husbands and wives being punished in such public ways draw endless fascination, evidenced by the ways they circulate. Another story that occasionally appears in the tabloid press is about women's group meetings, otherwise known as *chama* in Kenya. This refers to groups of women who come together for a common interest, usually an economic one. However, in the Kenyan popular imaginary, *chama* meetings are also seen as opportunities for women to cheat on their husbands, as one article titled "How women milk *chamas* for illicit love" (Keya, 2013), shows. The article opens with the following lines:

> When your wife comes home late in the night happy, relaxed and tipsy from a *chama* (women's investment club) meeting, she just might have spent a few blissful hours in another man's arms.[21]

This excerpt frames the idea behind the article that follows. The article introduces suspicion about women in general who are involved in such meetings. By claiming that 'she just might' have been with someone else outside of the marriage space, the article acts as a cautionary tale drawing the attention of the 'unsuspecting husband' referenced through the phrase 'your wife'. The disruptive woman who leaves the home in order to seek happiness elsewhere, becomes a threat to social order. Beverly Skeggs argues that 'the loud, white, excessive, drunk, fat, vulgar, disgusting, hen-partying woman who exists to embody all moral obsessions historically associated with the working class', has come to replace the 'single mother as the source of all national evil' (2005, 965). Skeggs is referring to the rise of hen parties, which, like chamas, are made up of mostly heterosexual women. She argues that the threat they pose is not so much one of violence, but one of 'proximity in the space, disrupting safety, comfort and home' (2005, 966). This is the kind of threat that the journalist Linda Keya is concerned about:

> Initially, *chamas* [women's groups for economic development] were the preserve of rural women who gathered in each other's houses once a month to socialize over tea and snacks and buy spoons, cups and pans for each other. With time, however, the meetings — which were frowned upon by husbands who reluctantly funded them — rose in stature. Women began buying livestock, building water tanks, buying pieces of land, paying school fees, investing shares on the stock market and even building houses, courtesy of the merry go rounds.[22]

The implication is that chama meetings originally had a different purpose that grew into something economically more lucrative. It also constructs chama spaces as potentially transformative spaces, especially because women choose them even though their husbands frown on them. However, the reporter is quick to point out that the husband is not accidentally centralised in the chama narrative. He is an important, if non-participatory, benefactor. The *chama* group's success is attributed to his contributions, both economically and socially. Hence the idea of using chama to engage in illicit affairs is painted as a double betrayal:

> But in towns, it has become routine that after a *chama* meeting, the women have one for the road, dance and have a blast. Those in the know say *chama* members, especially the younger ones, discuss anything, including their sex lives in a language as X-rated as what men use in pubs. Their husbands meanwhile love it because they use their wives' absence to paint the town red. As a rule, wives in Nairobi rarely come home before 9pm — all giggly and happy — from *chama* meetings. Virtuous but it now appears some women have turned the once respectable *chama* into an avenue for illicit affairs. Increasingly, the investment clubs are becoming a front and an opportunity for secret love, for the romance some women lack in marriage.[23]

The article shows how women become 'immoral' and 'repellent', momentarily suspending their roles as wives and mothers (Skeggs 2005, 966). Husbands are not spared in this raging moral review. They like it when their partners are unruly because this also means freedom for them. While the 'wicked' women do not stray completely beyond the heterosexual norm, they find moments of freedom outside of the home. These women combine their everyday realities with the spectacular moments of stolen love, sex and romance. Tabloids air these stories as ways of showing up these women, but they also offer opportunity for commentary.

Conclusion

The idea of the scandal as a form of surveillance lends an interesting aspect to the way that newspapers, particularly tabloids, function. Using White's ideas about gossip and scandal as forms of social control and convention (2008), I look at how tabloids participate in the culture of surveillance by engaging in gossip and scandal as sources of news. In a country like Kenya, sexual scandals emerge frequently, provoking public debate and the reiteration of cautionary tales. The one form of scandal that I do not dwell on in the chapter, but which offers constant fascination, is the celebrity scandal involving illicit affairs. Kenya has had its share of celebrity scandals, involving sitting presidents, members of parliament and other kinds of celebrities. While I value these kinds of stories as sites for generating public opinion, I have instead chosen to focus on the non-celebrity scandal and how, in reading this, I can engage more directly with how tabloids perform the role of policing. I do however mention a high-profile scandal involving a member of parliament. The scandal was long and drawn-out in the media, ending with the death of the wife's lover in suspicious circumstances. I choose not to dwell on the details of the scandal since what I am interested in is the kind of narrative an event such as this one generates. My argument in the chapter — and in the book more generally — is that popular culture is productive of discourses that shape moral behaviour. One incident can provoke debate, but what is more interesting is how the discourse is produced and reproduced, circulating as a tale that in turn can generate violence. In the chapter, I analyse an androcentric press media that does not always sympathise with female victims of violence. Instead, these victims are crucified both by the media and societies of which they are part. The St Kizito story shocked many precisely because it revealed underlying assumptions about women's bodies and availability for rape (Gqola 2015). The story of rape and other kinds of sexual violence recur in the media as familiar tropes that highlight the woman as a victim or whore.

In the chapter, I look at tabloids and scandal as avenues for alternative readings of sexuality. Arguing that the tabloid can be analysed as a transgressive site of popular culture, women in sexual scandals can be read as signifying defiance. I consider these women as troubling normative understandings of marriage and mononormative practices. I look at how women who engage in non-normative sex become subjects of gossip, surveillance and punishment. Tabloids, I argue, allow for a crossing of boundaries and engagement with excess. I consider what kinds of excessive meanings tabloids can generate that can allow for alternative readings.

Notes

1   Odongo, David. 2013. "Rich married women renting secret pads to meet young lovers." *Standard Digital*, July 5. Accessed 8 September 2018. https://www.standardmedia.co.ke/article/2000087512/n-a

2   Odongo, David. 2013.

3   KTN News Kenya. 2013, May 11. "Case Files: Black Sunday." Accessed 20 October 2019. https://www.youtube.com/watch?v=1YMr75331Sc. During the Case Files interview, three of the survivors said they were stigmatised after the ordeal and were unable to succeed at school. Some of the men who were accused of violence were interviewed. They maintained their innocence. Most of them served light sentences and have since moved on with their lives.

4   Perlez, Jane. 1991. *New York Times*, July 29. "Kenyans do some soul-searching after the rape of 71 schoolgirls." https://www.nytimes.com/1991/07/29/world/kenyans-do-some-soul-searching-after-the-rape-of-71-schoolgirls.html

5   Perlez, Jane. 1991. Perez writes: 'The principal, James Laiboni, told the reporter for *The Kenya Times*, 'In the past, the boys would scare the girls out of their dormitories and in the process they would get hold of them and drag them to the bush where they would "do their thing" and the matter would end there, with the students going back to their respective dormitories.'

6   Orinde, Hilary. 2019. *Standard Digital*, August 16. "Wasted lives: 15 years in jail for rapist

rugby players." https://www.standardmedia.co.ke/article/2001338404/15-years-in-jail-for-rapist-rugby-players

7   *The Nairobian* is owned by the Standard Group, which runs the more 'serious' newspaper, *The Standard*.

8   "Crazy Mondays", *The Standard* newspaper.

9   Obonyo, Levi. "Press reference: Kenya." Accessed 20 October 2016. http://www.pressreference.com/Gu-Ku/Kenya.html#Comments_66

10 Samwagik. Blog entry. "The battle of the tabloids." Accessed 28 October 2019. https://samwagik.wordpress.com/2014/07/09/battle-of-the-tabloids/

11 Keguro Macharia gave a lecture to the University of the Witwatersrand Media and Gender Media Studies Honours class on 21 September 2017 on the topic: 'Social media, rumour and truth'.

12 Odongo, David. 2013.

13 From English playwright William Shakespeare's play *Romeo and Juliet*. Here, Romeo is used as shorthand for the young male lovers.

14 Odongo, David. 2013.

15 Ombati, Curus. 2013. "Tony Ogunda's wife questioned by police." *Standard Digital*, July 9. Accessed 28 October 2019. http://www.standardmedia.co.ke/article/2000087950/tony-ogunda-s-wife-questioned-by-police

16 Omoro, James. 2013. "Married woman strays for tilapia." *Standard Digital*, August 12. Accessed 28 October 2019. http://www.standardmedia.co.ke/lifestyle/article/2000090730/married-woman-strays-for-tilapia.

17 The story of the Narok lovers in "Crazy World" has since been removed from the website. However, the story was captured elsewhere. See IGIHE. 2013. "Kenyan couple stuck together in sex." *IGIHE*, May 31. https://en.igihe.com/people/kenyan-couple-stuck-together-in-sex.html

18 The article first appeared in "Crazy World" in 2014, but has since been taken off the site.

19 Kremer, William. 2014. "Can couples really get stuck together during sex?" BBC World Service, February 2. Accessed 20 October 2019. https://www.bbc.com/news/magazine-25827175

20 This story circulated in several tabloids around the world. See for instance, "Cheating Husband 'Is Caught' Having An Affair With housemaid after getting STUCK inside her while having sex – VIDEO." Accessed 20 October 2019. http://www.peacefmonline.com/pages/local/social/201806/354637.php?storyid=100&

21 Keya, Linda. 2013. "How women milk *chama* for illicit love." *Standard Digital*, May 20. Accessed 12 December 2015. http://www.standardmedia.co.ke/lifestyle/article/2000084013/how-women-milk-chamas-for-illicit-love

22 Keya, Linda. 2013.

23 Keya, Linda. 2013.

5

Consumption, good time girls and violence in public discourse

Introduction

The recent rise of the phenomena of the 'blesser' and 'sponsor'[1] has drawn attention to social media practices of what Lebohang Masango terms 'compensated relationships' (2019, 7) and Madipoane Masenya terms 'cross-generational partnerships' (2017, 120). These are relationships that combine intimacy, money and gifts, usually between young women and older rich men. I find Masenya's (2017) definition of 'blessers' and 'sponsors' (the Kenyan version of 'blessers') extremely useful in summarising the meaning/s of this term. According to her, 'blesser', the more recent (social media) version of the phenomenon of the 'sugar daddy' (or 'sugar mummy') refers:

> [to] an older man (respectively older woman) who has sexual relationships with young girls (respectively young boys) in exchange for money and/or material goods. The latter may include drinks, gifts, clothes and favourable treatment. The preceding treatment may include various favours such as education, employment, tuition fees payment, financial support for subsistence costs and other kinds of support. The less powerful member of the relationship (cf. especially age and economic disparities) avails her/his body for sex in exchange for gifts. (2017, 120)

Masenya's article sheds light on the phenomenon of female 'blessers', reading this in light of the biblical 'Woman Stranger' in Proverbs 7, against whom young men are warned. In Proverbs 7, the woman (a sugar mummy) lures unsuspecting young men to their death with her sexual wantonness. Masenya compares this woman (Woman Stranger) to sugar mummies in contemporary South Africa and the 'Ben 10' phenomenon.[2]

The idea of the 'blesser' is associated with social media practices in which young women post pictures of themselves showcasing what appear to be ostentatious lifestyles, with the claim that they have been 'blessed' (Makholwa 2017). In her book, *The Blessed Girl* (2017) Angela Makholwa expands on her definition. She writes on the origin of the word 'blesser' as a 'social media phenomenon in which young beautiful ladies posted pictures showing off opulent lifestyles and proclaimed themselves to be 'blessed'" (2017, n.p.). She adds that 'the source of these blessings was soon discovered to be wealthy married men, hence the term "blesser" was coined' (2017, n.p.). Popularly identified through the hashtag movement in social media, that is, #blesser, this phenomenon captured the imagination of many because of its strong visual attachments to material culture. Often contrasted with sex work, cross-generational partnerships or compensated relationships are also about intangible attachments, such as love, romance and loyalty. These relationships are contradictory in nature, and often women identified as 'blessees' (those who receive gifts and intangible rewards from 'blessers') are dismissed as leeches, gold-diggers and sluts, among other derogatory references. Yet young women who refer to themselves as 'blessed' counter societal expectations and moral codes. Sometimes also colloquially referred to as 'slay queens', these women *insist* on being visible amid public calls for them to conform to gender expectations. The link to social media is therefore important in making an argument for the increased visibility of this type of woman who unapologetically flaunts her body while simultaneously claiming that she is using her beauty to acquire expensive goods from her admirers.

This chapter explores media representations of romantic relationships in the context of consumption. It draws on existing scholarship on 'transactional relationships' that have often placed emphasis on the exchange of sex for money. However, more recent studies show that those who become involved in such relationships do so for a variety of reasons, including companionship and consumption. As Leclerc-Madlala (2003) points out, these relationships are formed 'in pursuit of modernity'. Similarly, Cole (2010) and Mojola (2014) urge for an approach to 'transactional relationships' in relation to young women and their relationship to consumerist goods in the context of romantic relationships. According to Cole's investigation of the lives of young women's transition into adulthood in Madagascar, to make moralistic judgement about this process is to ignore a variety of influences both past and present on the lives of these young women. Cole stresses that these young women make particular choices as they navigate life. Mojola, whose research takes place in Kisumu, Kenya, also argues that women in most cases make informed choices regarding romantic relationships and the acquisition of material benefits. One interesting finding, for instance, is that, against the commonly held notion that young women get into compensatory relationships because of poverty and desperation, it is rather those women with the highest chances of negotiating their positions in sexual relationships (for instance, women who have a steady income) who are the most likely to get into relationships for material benefit. Some scholars suggest that this is in a bid to maintain their lifestyles, and to live their lives outside of notions of struggle (Masvawure 2010). In this chapter, I examine the media constructions of young women in such relationships. I argue that such women challenge stereotypes of greed and victimhood. I examine themes of choice and freedom and explore possibilities of reading them outside of stereotypes. In a context such as Kenya, how might such freedoms be interpreted through gendered discourses of violence, punishment and public shaming?

The good time girl

The figure of the good time girl in Kenyan popular culture occupies seemingly contradictory positions. She is young, educated, beautiful, fun-loving, wild, likes to 'party', is 'up for anything' and is willing to trade her body for a luxurious lifestyle. A distinctive aspect of the good time girl is her relationship to modernity, quite like what Barlow et al. describe as the modern girl who circulated globally in the first half of the twentieth century (2005). According to the research relating the good time girl to modernity, what most marked her identity was her 'use of specific commodities' and her embrace of 'explicit eroticism' (2005, 245). The modern girl in this context 'appeared to disregard the roles of dutiful daughter, wife and mother' and instead pursued 'provocative fashions and...romantic love' (Barlow et al. 2005, 245). The modern girl is therefore a transgressive figure.

Similarly, the transgressive character of the good time girl has long defined how she has been constructed in African popular literature and culture. Narratives of the good time girl appear in cautionary tales of popular culture. These are structured narratives with moral teachings designed mostly for children. Yet, this structured format is used pervasively in popular culture in Africa to render moral lessons, both publicly and privately. Indeed, the very idea of African popular culture is linked to the idea of the lesson by example (Barber 1997). In discourses of African popular culture, the good time girl is then, as described by Stephanie Newell (2002, 6), 'a hoarder and private accumulator par excellence...an explanatory figure' used to explore 'the story of a beautiful young woman's misuse of her sexuality' in exchange for material wealth. Newell adds that popular writers 'return repeatedly to the character of the sexually self-determining woman who moves freely around the city, and [that] writers rehearse similar ideological scripts in which materialistic good time girls grab men's money before being punished' (2002, 6). These figures are therefore used not merely to reflect the symptomatic conditions of the time (economic crises, anxiety about sexual morality), but also to 'teach interpretative strategies to readers, ways of reading bodily signals emitted by others' (2002, 6). Newell's arguments suggest a reference point for reading women, where they acquire fixed associations with urbanity, materialism and punishment. These stereotypical underpinnings are further reflected in Onookome Okome's (2012, 167) argument that the persistent recurrence of the image of the good time girl in contemporary African popular forms such as Nollywood films indicates a 'narrative marginality to which women are consigned in the urban African popular imagination'. Okome, like Newell, identifies the stereotypical patterns that make it impossible to imagine the good time girl outside the space of the city, where social change is rapid, and where the links with colonial modernity are clear. As Okome further explains:

> [t]he map of urban relationships is a contrast to that which exists in rural Africa because the city is defined by new sets of social and cultural values. Its discursive template is reflective of colonial modernity, which is defined by access to Western education and religion as well as popular culture, which has been brought to Africa through movies, magazines, television shows, and much more. (2012, 168)

Okome goes on to show how Nollywood films, in the articulation of the city's unpredictability, act as a moral compass where good always triumphs over evil (2012). Okome points to the limiting ways in which the good time girl has been interpreted, but also signals potential ways in which the figure can be read differently. Like Newell, there is an attachment to reading this figure as a source of lessons by which to navigate life.

If indeed narratives of the good time girl emphasise a particular kind of cautionary tale in which good triumphs over evil, as Okoome points out above, then this figure is useful in accessing the various kinds of anxieties that accompany stories about her in newspapers, whether of public shaming or other forms of violence. In contemporary newspaper and other public accounts, such narratives appear in particular modes that report on real life accounts of how young women who desire commodity goods make particular choices, accounts of misfortunes that befall such women, and microscopic accounts of young women's sexual behaviour in public. These categories, though broad, are useful in helping to unpack ways in which particular forms of representations become normalised in the Kenyan public imagination.

Slut shaming and the sugar daddy phenomenon

Lauren Berlant, in *Cruel Optimism* (2011) cites shame as that which one is meant to feel if one steps out of an existing moral frame (2011). Public shame is then a reminder that one has in fact stepped out. The seeming inability to feel shame is a refusal to participate in the illusion of the good wife / the good woman. Public shaming is the punishment. Recent scholarship on slut shaming and social media draw direct relations between a person's reputation and sexual deviancy (Tanenbaum 2015; Ringrose and Renold 2012). Activists have pointed to the violent encounters of young women who are slut shamed, and have related this to negative perceptions of especially girls and young women's sexuality around particular confined meanings. Slut shaming is indeed part of the practice of public shaming. Yet young women demonstrate their desire for consumerist lifestyles by presenting their bodies in hypervisible ways in public. They demonstrate their desire for the fantasy of the good life. In thinking through subjectivity and agency, this chapter reads desire as a demonstration of assertiveness and belonging, where young women create possibilities for accessing material goods. This is an ethic of choice.

A body of scholarship on the 'good time girl', the 'modern girl' or other versions of this figure have linked young women to relationships with older men. Research often stresses the unevenness of these relationships, particularly because of the potentially risky positions that young women find themselves in and the power dynamics inherent in such relationships. In such contexts, young girls are understood as passive, vulnerable participants in relationships involving their own bodies in the age of HIV/AIDS, as well as other risks. In cases where these young women make choices to solicit money, they are often demonised as parasitic, even when these parasitic behaviours are based on the politics of need. A different scholarship has turned attention to thinking of these young women in an economy of desire and want (LeClerc-Madlala 2003; Mojola 2014). Reading young women as consuming subjects, such studies endeavour to locate 'sugar daddy' relationships as a means of navigating an increasingly commodified and globalised reality. I explore narratives of romance and consumption as recounted in popular newspaper columns. Rather than focus solely on the overtly moralising narratives of caution and punishment, I pay attention to female subjectivities and their formulation as 'good time girls' in the narratives. I explore such figures in the complex dynamic between stereotypical representations and questions of agentic practice. In my reading, I am cautious not to romanticise these young women's bodies as sites of political emancipation. I am aware that even as the women navigate their own spaces of freedom, they are vulnerable to various forms of violence that often remain untold for a variety of reasons.

Newspaper articles about 'sugar daddy relationships' offer explanatory narratives of what has been termed the 'sugar daddy phenomenon'. In such articles, the need to offer examples of situations that explore in detail intricacies of such relationships is clear. This kind of microscopic exploration is functional. These articles thrive on providing details of the lives of young women in such relationships. The articles name the usual benefits of being in such relationships, including expensive clothes, cars, homes and jewellery. They also explore the downside of such relationships: that often older men have multiple relationships as they are generally already married, the element of sexually transmitted diseases, violence and other negative outcomes. Using examples of people involved in such relationships, the articles claim to offer a 'balanced' view, before rounding off with advice from a therapist. Indeed, the choice to include information from an expert indicates the pathologisation of such relationships, which are clearly read as anomalies. The experts often dwell on providing reasons why young women indulge in such behaviour, frequently linking the behaviour to self-esteem issues. These women are seen to require emotional affirmation from older men, possibly because they have complex relationships with their fathers, and so on. Such scientific explanations are part of how these modes of narration work in circulating such stories as cautionary tales.

Public shaming plays a role in such articles. Such an article lends itself to being read as a form of spectacle, wonder and, in essence, a site for public shaming. Scholarship on slut shaming suggests the paradoxical positions in which young women find themselves in the era of social media. On the one hand, narratives of empowerment abound, encouraging an embrace of sexual and political freedom. On the other, such narratives send a message, identifying these women as 'sluts' (Tanenbaum 2015; Ringrose and Renold 2012). These contradictions play themselves out in reports that engage with young women who are supposedly in romantic relationships with older, wealthy men for the purpose of empowering themselves financially.

This is the case with the article that appeared in Kenya's *Standard Digital's* "Crazy World" lifestyle section, which carried the following headline: "Meet female medical student whose 11 sugar daddies are company CEOs."[3] The piece immediately promises a 'tell-all' account, and in the context in which the narrative of the good time girl is deemed 'dangerous', a story such as this is of much interest to a majority of popular newspaper readers, especially because it is told from the point of view of an 'insider'. Also immediately interesting is the signalling of her status as a medical student, suggesting intelligence and high achievement on the part of the young woman. In the article, the young woman gives a version of her encounters, and reasons why she prefers to be in 'transactional sex relationships'. She confesses to loving expensive consumer goods, but also points out that she was emotionally unsatisfied with younger men of her age, finding them emotionally immature. The article ends with her saying that she has the full support of her parents.

At first glance, the article sits uneasily in a Kenyan context, precisely because the Kenyan mainstream media is invested in producing a different kind of story, the cautionary tale. This story is one of empowerment and freedom, in many ways capturing what Rosalind Gill (2007) and others have termed postfeminist tendencies. The idea of individual freedom, body policing and donning of consumer goods is a typical marker of a postfeminist body in a neoliberal reality. An online search reveals that the newspaper article was lifted from a UK-based newspaper, and reproduced for the online Kenyan newspaper, *Standard Digital*, in December 2015, a month after the original story was released. The article first appeared in a British-based tabloid newspaper, *Daily Mirror*,[4] where the life of the then 19-year-old medical student, Clover Pittilla, was laid bare for the reader to marvel at. In the article, lifestyle writer Shelley Marsden interviews Pittilla to establish why the young woman has made the choices she has regarding dating older men with money. Pittilla, who refers to herself as a 'sugar baby' in the article, argues that older men pay attention to her, and they offer her a chance at a mature relationship which is something that men her age cannot offer. She also prefers older men to younger ones because they shower her with gifts and give her the opportunity to live a luxurious lifestyle.

The Kenyan reproduction of this story edits out the source of the story, only indicating 'London' as the by-line. It also edits out Pittila's photo (in the original article, a photo is included of Pittila lying on her stomach with head and torso raised, dressed in a bikini and smiling directly at the camera). In place of the original photo is one of a young black woman. It is a photo of her torso with the rest of her body cut off. She is dressed in a black, sleeveless shirt, and is lying down on her back, with her torso facing the camera. The replacement photo constitutes a different public, one that is purportedly black and Kenyan. While the original story seems to give Pittilla agency in telling her own story, the Kenyan reproduction invites the reader to see the story as an object of spectacle. In his book on the phenomenon of media spectacle, Douglas Kellner (2003) argues that media culture has intensified its role of placing fantasies, nightmares, dreams and values on display. By displaying Pittilla's life choices, the article questions her choices, inviting readers to participate in reading it as an element of shock.

The repurposing of the article for *Standard Digital* newspaper, "Crazy World"[5] demonstrates the transmediation process that makes intertextuality possible. It also points to the transnational qualities of the cautionary tale, whose elements can be repurposed for a different context. In many ways, the article suggests how cautionary tales travel, and how femininities that cannot be contained within heteronormative spaces are demonised. The article also makes possible a consideration of how these figures can be read as transgressive. The article, for instance, links to a narrative that was in circulation at the time about the rise of the 'slay queen'. The idea of 'slaying' as popularised in American artist Beyoncé's song 'Formation' references disruption and queering of narrative. It is, as articulated by Marquis Bey 'a modality of troubling the narrative' (2017, 176). According to Bey,

> ...[t]o slay, especially for Queen Bey, is to incite an insurgency from...whatever confines one finds oneself, to shatter the neat lines of boundaried normality, to

queer. Her slay-tastic insurgency is the deathblow to the fire-breathing dragon of the violence of the normal and normative, which manifests in far too often fatal forms of white and male supremacy. (2017, 176)

Beyoncé's music is, of course, suggesting ways in which slaying has become a site of transgression and a mode of survival in heteronormative cultures. Indeed, Lauron Kehrer (2019) traces this phenomenon to queer ballroom cultures in African-American spaces. Slaying also suggests an element of competitiveness among marginalised communities. In reference to popular renditions of slaying, 'slay queens' embrace the boldness and opportunism signalled in popular culture, and refuse to withdraw from a critical public glare. In the Kenyan context, however, the term 'slay queen' signals something less empowering. Nduku Muema (2018), for instance, states that 'a slay queen is a woman who wants to choke everyone else with how beautiful they feel they are and how they do their "cool stuff"' (n.p.). Muema, like several public commentators, seems to suggest that women who identify as slay queens do not have much to contribute to society besides their ability to choreograph how they look online. 'Slay queens' are, as a result, the subject of many jokes in the Kenyan socio-space.[6] Such a reading, I suggest, links to the view of the 'slay queen' as a threat to social order and explains the upsurge of violence meted against her. I contextualise this dislike with a review of the figure of the wilful, educated, university woman in Kenyan public culture.

The fear of the educated woman

The wilful modern girl and/or the good time girl is at the centre of most cautionary tales about cross-generational relationships. As such, she is an important barometer for reading various moral anxieties that accompany understandings of young women's sexualities in Kenya. These are women who privilege material relationships (Hunter 2002; Leclerc-Madlala 2003; Masvawure 2010) and who must face subsequent and inevitable consequences of their choices. Indeed, Tsitsi Masvawure (2010) reminds us that such women who enter into relationships with material benefits do so not always because of poverty but to 'attain an otherwise elusive modern lifestyle, while those from upper middle-class backgrounds used it to maintain an already privileged class position' (2010, 858). It is also possible to read these choices as forms of rebellion against the idea of a good, middle-class girl.

One dominant figure of the good time girl in Kenyan public discourse is the unruly, educated, university woman whose sexual exploits attract derision, condemnation and fascination. This woman is a source of great moral anxiety because of her apparent freedom, living as she does away from the normalising structures of family, church and school. The university is seen as a space where discipline is temporarily suspended as young people become adults, and so also poses a threat to social order. For a young and naive woman, the appeal of freedom and independence is often only limited by her access to money which is still controlled either by parents or through formal national scholarships and bursaries. Sourcing this money through other channels becomes an increasingly attractive option, resulting in a network of 'transactional' relationships. The university woman is seen both as potentially vulnerable to sexual predators and extremely 'mobile' because of her independence. This aspect of university life in Kenya is best captured in popular fictional narratives, such as Wambui Githiora's *Wanjira* (2007). Set in mid-1970s Kenya, the novel is a coming-of-age story of a young woman, Wanjira, who while discovering herself at university, finds out the extent to which young women frequently engage in relationships for material benefit. One such woman, Wangu, sees herself as a good time girl, interested only in the good things in life. The story explores life at the University of Nairobi's female hostels, famously named 'box' and 'suitcase', because of the frequency with which female students are 'picked up' in shiny cars by well-dressed men. It also links, in interesting ways, to stories that continue to shape public narratives of young women's sexuality in the university setting.

While a lot of stories of what these 'types' of university women get up to have circulated in the form of gossip, rumours and anecdotes, the internet has made such stories more visible and easier to track. In the last two decades, stories have circulated via email, discussion forums, chat rooms, blogs and, more recently, on social media platforms such as Facebook and Twitter. One such example is the recycled story of a university woman who confesses to having intentionally 'infected' a large number of men with HIV. This story erupts every two or three years, and each time the woman is from a different university in the country. In one account, a female student from a local Kenyan university is said to have deliberately 'infected' 124 men in 2001 as a way of getting her revenge after an older man lied to her and infected her with the HIV virus. She sets about 'infecting' as many men as she can and then places a list of names of those she has had sex with on a public university noticeboard. This is a familiar story. In 2012, a woman from another Kenyan university apparently circulated the message below on social media:

> I am a student and I am HIV-positive. I swore I would spread the thing because I got infected during my first experience. I have slept with 322 guys in my campus and two outside. I wanted to infect 2 500 people but the guilt is now killing me.[7]

A comment by the male blog owner who re-posted[8] this exposé captures a sentiment shared by most of those who have commented on this story. According to him, this letter shows how academic excellence has now become compromised in the pursuit of sexual immorality, substance abuse and criminal acts. Another similar story broke in 2014, in which a female student from yet another local university confessed to having 'infected' 324 men with plans to infect another 2 000.[9]

Through this recycled story the Kenyan public is taught how to fear the educated university woman whose sexual exploits are depicted as laden with revenge and disease and, in some cases, the threat of death.[10] In turn, this generates a concurrent discourse among the public of the dangers of university life for the young woman, and the hazards of the freedom such a space accords her. In this manufactured media landscape, the university woman becomes a symbolic figure, not only wanton and dangerous, but also gaining power and mobility because of her education. Like the modern woman in the colonial era who travelled alone to the city (Obbo, 1980), this university woman demonstrates independence and an ability to make choices for herself. She thus becomes perceived as a threat to societal order, as she symbolically embodies a disruption of the social expectation of her integration into normative society through marriage and other traditional rituals.

In 2012, the long-held suspicion that the educated university woman was morally corrupt was realised when a Facebook page called "Campus Divas for rich men" was set up, brazenly advertising itself as a 'hook-up' spot for 'campus girls' who wanted to be paired up with rich men. This page accumulated 30 000 followers in the first week or so of being set up. It became so popular that mainstream media picked up on it. Caroline Mutoko, a popular FM radio presenter, issued a warning to listeners, claiming the Facebook administrators were using random pictures of women to advertise on the site, and that young women needed to make sure their photos were not illegally placed on the site. Mutoko who is an advocate of women's empowerment, was concerned about possible predatory behaviour that could affect unsuspecting women. Mutoko's comment read in context, implied that the women the site was promoting were portraying themselves as 'bad' women because of the bold promotion of their bodies for sale to men with money. She doubted that these women would be bold enough as to post their real pictures online, hence the warning.

So popular was the website that the television channel Kenya Television Network aired a documentary: "Facebook: a prostitution ring?"[11] in which they interviewed a series of university men (and a woman) to ascertain whether this group was real or if it was just an advertising ploy for prostitutes. Parallel groups challenging the 'Campus Diva' Facebook page were set up. The logic here was to draw attention to what was being read as morally wrong but also as having potential to influence 'good' girls. A group calling itself "Anti-Campus divas for rich men", for instance, acquired 17 000 likes. The idea was to demonstrate that while some women preferred to identify as women who entered into relationships for purposes of money, there were many more women who were good women, and who did not want to be associated with a corrupt image. Another group, calling itself "Campus Divas for Christ", was set up to signal the immorality of the "Campus Divas for rich men" group. This particular group centred their identity on the Christian religion, purposefully suggesting that not all women were on campus to serve rich men. Other offshoots of 'Campus Divas' included "Campus Divas for rich men — reloaded" (in an effort to reclaim the following that the original group had garnered) and "Campus Divas for every *chokoraa* [street kid]", (a witty parody of the initial group, suggesting that some women were willing to go out with men who did not have money). A similar logic was used to establish the group "Campus divas for *masafaras* [broke men]". While the original group centred on women, other groups were formed to indicate the availability of young men who were willing to get into relationships with rich women, such as the "Campus Hunks for Rich Women", "Campus Divas and Hunks for Rich and Serious Men and Women" and several other off-shoots. 'Campus Divas' became a brand through which various publics could be constituted. It is clear that the internet has facilitated the increased circulation of the image of the good time girl in Kenya. With a high internet access rate, reportedly the third highest in sub-Saharan Africa after Nigeria and South Africa, many Kenyans now have access to the internet.

Regarding the popularity of the 'Campus Diva' website, the reaction of the public was reflective of a general attitude in the public sphere towards women and sexuality. The women were consistently referred to as prostitutes with no moral boundaries whose work was to destroy the national moral fibre. When a short feature titled "Campus Diva — Confessions of a University student" was aired on the television station *Nation TV*, showing a young woman confessing to being obsessed with older men in order to maintain her expensive lifestyle, there was mass outrage.[12] It later turned out that the video was staged and the young woman was actually a medical student struggling economically and had been tricked into accepting a small amount of money to participate in the video. She had also been promised that it would never be made public.[13] The incident with the young woman reveals how spectacle and scandal work hand in hand with young women's sexualities. In an era of fake news, misinformation and disinformation,[14] the desire to publicly shame a woman for her choices is pronounced. While this young woman claimed she was tricked into accepting the role of 'campus diva' by a cunning journalist, her reputation was ruined.

Violence and death

The figure of the 'unruly' university woman, then, is one that has attracted a violent response from various publics in Kenya. In the age of digital media, the violence takes the form of the physical and the discursive. The young university woman becomes a threat because of the power and autonomy she holds through her education. The very thing that empowers her also makes her a target of hate crime. In this section, I look at three cases of women who were murdered and who also happened to be university students. Each case drew the attention of the broader Kenyan public precisely because they were murders, although I am primarily interested in how they played out in the media. What I am interested in is the 'excesses' that spilt into popular media from the original news stories. By 'excesses', I mean those aspects of the original news stories that were exaggerated or highlighted to make the events spectacular or turn the murdered women into objects of derision, or to create shock and stimulate gossip-driven or morbid curiosity. I am also interested in the kinds of cautionary tales that emerged and were circulated as 'lessons' to be learned by observing 'situations' that young women may find themselves in. Such cautionary stories circulated after these women had died.

The medical student who was hacked to death

When news broke in Kenya about the death, on the morning of 9 April 2019, of 26-year-old Ivy Wangeci, what shocked many Kenyans was the violent way that she died.[15] The man who killed her had apparently travelled about 320 kilometres from Nairobi to Eldoret town with an axe, a knife and a clear motive to kill Wangeci. A medical student, Wangeci had just finished her morning ward rounds and was headed to the student hostels when her murderer confronted her. From witness accounts, it seems as though she did not get a chance to react before he attacked her, first swinging an axe at her head, then stabbing her in the neck with a knife. After the attack, the man threatened a stunned and horrified crowd of onlookers, daring anyone to stop him from escaping. The crowd, however, overpowered him as he tried to escape and beat him up, with the intention of killing him.[16] In fact, had the police not appeared on the scene, he would probably have died. Photos of the man bleeding profusely from the side of his head filled social media not long afterwards. It was later reported that Naftali Kinuthia, Wangeci's killer, is a 'quiet man who neither smokes nor drinks alcohol and always goes home straight after work' (Wambui and Achuka 2019).[17] Neighbours and friends told the press that they did not believe he could commit such a heinous crime. Others swore that he was a good man, and wondered if perhaps he had been bewitched, because what had happened was 'not normal' (Wambui and Achuka 2019).

Social media response to the murder was instant. There was the expression of shock at the gruesome murder. Wangeci had died a day before her birthday. Rumours started circulating on social media that she had taken the man's money then turned off her phone when he tried to reach her. Another rumour had it that she had infected the man with HIV/AIDS and that was why he had turned violent. Social media was divided on the issue. Wangeci's classmates came out in numbers to show their support. They swore that she had been a good girl with a good reputation. Newspaper articles carried stories with accounts from her family and friends who swore she had not been in a relationship with Kinuthia. Soon, photos from her social media page were being used to suggest that, in fact, she had deserved to die because she had been a 'slay queen'. Those who suggested she had 'done something' to deserve her death wondered why any sane man would travel from so far just to kill a woman he liked. There was both empathy and contempt, from different camps. The contempt that some people held for Wangeci was captured in a song, released a few days later, by a group called Sheddy Empire, titled "Pigwa shoka". This is a Swahili phrase that means 'hack with an axe'. The men who released the video did so as a joke, capitalising on the moment, while the news about Wangeci's death was still fresh. The video enjoyed a few hours of popularity, and was swiftly shared on social media, including Twitter, Facebook and WhatsApp. It was banned a few days later, after several concerned Kenyans demanded that the government intervene. Despite being banned, the video is still available on Youtube to whoever is interested in finding it.[18]

The lyrics to the song demonstrate how a violent event of gender-based violence was turned into a mockery:

> Slay queen eh pigwa shoka
>
> Leta nyeff nyeff, pigwa shoka
>
> We ni playa, pigwa shoka
>
> Ahhh pigwa shoka
>
> (Slay queen, eh, hack with an axe
>
> Bring issues/nonsense, get hacked with an axe
>
> You are a playa, hack with an axe
>
> Ahh hack with an axe)

The video features a number of young people, male and female, dancing to the song. Scenes include the men wearing torn, blood-stained t-shirts while holding either machetes (pangas) or axes. The young women in the video are seen twerking (dancing in an extremely sexually provocative manner that involves thrusting hip movements) to rap lyrics which include references to Vera Sidika's bottom.[19] The video is a happy video. After Kenyans had demanded that the video was in poor taste and needed to be banned, the male performers were interviewed and they indicated that they had wanted to do something fun and light following the horrifying event of Ivy Wangeci's death. They refused to acknowledge the violence contained in the video.[20]

In many ways, their response to violence against women is not isolated, but is part of a contemptuous culture against women. Their response, in fact, was quite similar to the response the deputy head teacher at St Kizito school[21] gave in defence of the boys who raped and murdered female students: they meant no harm; they just wanted to rape.

Ivy Wangeci's case underscores the primary thematic issues of this book. I am fascinated, for instance, in the way Wangeci's photos and stories about her were circulated post-death when her social media pages were shared. In her pictures, she looks extremely well-groomed and well-dressed. One tabloid newspaper, *Mpasho*, carried a story titled "Photos of Ivy Wangeci, the sexy Moi University student who was hacked to death."[22] In the article, the reader is invited to gaze lasciviously at Wangeci's poses. In the photos, Wangeci is brought back to life as a 'slay queen', as some of the comments on social media indicate. Thus, the public reading of Wangeci as a 'slay queen' is not conjured up out of thin air; it is an image deliberately manufactured by the tabloid, framing her as a 'stock character' in an ongoing catalogue of women who identify or can be visually identified as 'slay queens'.

The pregnant student who was stabbed multiple times

Wangeci's murder followed hot on the heels of another equally public murder of a university student, Sharon Beryl Otieno. On 4 September 2018, Otieno's body was found with multiple stab wounds near a forest. She was 26 years old and seven months pregnant at the time. She had been in a romantic relationship with the governor of Migori County, Okoth Obado. Journalist Oyunga Pala[23] (2018) in his piece "Slay Queens, socialites and sponsors" provided a compelling case for linking the violent murders of young women in Kenya to 'transactional sex'. Sharon Otieno's death was sensationalised and circulated as spectacle. As Pala maintains:

> Both the Sharon Otieno and the Monica Kimani murders become sensational media stories and trending topics on social media. They become compelling spectacles, with their toxic mix of sex, scandal, fame, power and crime. The stories were teased out and milked for their shock value. The public gobbled up the minute details of the developing story that moved into court dramas.[24]

Otieno's story left many enraged, while raising questions about 'sugar daddy' relationships in Kenya.[25] Incidentally, six days prior to Otieno's gruesome death, journalist and film-maker Nyasha Kadandara published an article for the British broadcaster BBC titled "Sex and the Sugar Daddy"[26] in which she highlighted the pervasive 'sugar' culture in universities as well as other city spaces. One interviewee is quoted as saying, 'on a Friday night just go sit outside Box House [student hostel] and see what kind of cars drive by — drivers of ministers, and politicians sent to pick up young girls' (Kadandara 2018). Both Kadandara and Pala link 'blesser' cultures to aspiration and scarcity politics. Pala, for instance, notes:

> Public commentary on Sharon and Monica's deaths began to highlight what is viewed as a social problem. Both young women, who hailed from humble backgrounds, were framed as overnight successes enjoying opulent lifestyles through unclear circumstances. Moral lessons drawn from the incidents leaned towards a refrain to young girls…Avoid dirty old men…young girls, please forget easy money and be safe. Stay away from sponsors.[27]

Otieno's death was circulated both for its shock value and for the lesson it offered. The predominant interpretation in the media was that she was a cautionary tale, a demonstration that the pursuit of money led to violence and death. It also demonstrated the uneven power relations that defined compensatory relationships. Clearly, the 'sugar' culture, while offering women freedom to choose the kind of lifestyles they aspire towards, has also created possibilities for violence.

Graduate student's body found on busy highway

On 18 June 2011, the mutilated body of 25-year-old graduate student, Mercy Chepkosgei Keino,[28] was found on Nairobi's busy Waiyaki highway, having been run over multiple times by several motorists. Mercy had attended a party with her cousin the night before, which had been held at the Wasini luxury apartments in the Westlands area in Nairobi. According to newspaper reports, Mercy had been invited by a distant cousin to a private party that was also attended by a prominent Kenyan member of parliament. The stories emerging after her untimely death were varied, but with consistent strands. She was a university student, she had attended an exclusive party and there had been older, rich men in attendance. While the ensuing criminal investigations surrounding her death are important, I am interested rather in exploring the narratives that were generated about Keino's death, narratives that I argue were distinctively framed as cautionary tales.

Immediately after the first report of how Mercy Keino met her death, her story was framed in a familiar template. This template generated several newspaper reports that linked Mercy's story to other cautionary tales about university women and 'sugar' relationships in Kenya. The narratives that emerged were framed largely around public morality, with various angles being presented to explain why Mercy Keino found herself in certain circumstances hours before her death. Some versions of her narrative show a condemnation of her actions, dismissing her as a good time girl who deserved to die, while other versions sought to find justice, after it was revealed that she may have been murdered. The stories emphasised the risks involved for young women in circumstances such as these. In trying to understand how the story of

Mercy Keino circulated, Keguro Macharia (2011) notes:

> As Mercy's story has unfolded, she has become subject to multiple conflicting narratives and competing attachments. She was, in some stories, a good Christian girl who did not drink or party. Simultaneously, she was a wild party animal, a 'type' of campus girl. She was engaged to be married. And she had 'been seen' with 'certain kinds of men.'…Mercy has also been claimed by the male leaders in the university, as one of 'their' women.

I want to suggest that Mercy's death was used by the media as an opportunity to address a growing social problem, namely the visibility of the wayward female university student. One such account appeared in *The Nation* on 3 July 2011, a few weeks following Mercy's death, titled "The double lives of university students". This article was written by two male journalists, Daniel Wesangula and Nyambega Gisesa, both of whom have worked as feature writers for two of Kenya's leading newspapers, *The Nation* and *The Standard*. The article reconstructs the typical life of a good time girl at university by offering what it imagines to be a typical sex party:

> It was a few minutes to 8 p.m. when Beth's cell phone alerted her to a text message. 'Come with eight girls. Mix them in different styles. Take a cab and let's meet in South B,' it read. Beth, who had been waiting with her friends for the message, was excited. They had to dress scantily, she told the young women who would soon make a short journey to the underworld where illicit sex, alcohol and rich men mix in one of Nairobi's latest fads. The house in South B was tastefully furnished, and the girls, undressed to their lingerie, lay in wait on a couch. The rich men would soon be coming to sample the young women on display and take their pick. Moments later, nine well-dressed men in various stages of inebriation sauntered in, one by one. They ordered their favourite drinks from the well-stocked in-house bar. (Wesangula and Gisesa, 2011)

The obvious male gaze of the story is not lost on the reader because of the way that the young women's objectified bodies are described. The two journalists project a common trend of reporting women in Kenya, and in Africa generally. As Christine Obbo has observed, 'since in Africa there is little investigative reporting on political matters which does not simply reproduce the official line, articles on social issues tend to be what journalists know will reflect the prejudices and beliefs of the (male) people' (1980, 6). A recent newspaper article by one of the journalists, Daniel Wesangula (2013), titled "Beware: another man in your wife's life" is representative of this kind of reporting. It is interested in raising suspicion about what women do with their spare time. Such kinds of stories are sadly part of the normative ways of reporting women in Kenya. It is therefore not surprising that the article on university women cited above emphasises the allure of money, alcohol and wild (fun) sex that awaits the young women involved. There is little attempt in the article to chastise the men who come into the room to 'sample' the girls; instead, it falls squarely on the girls whose 'morals and decency are thrown out the window in exchange for wads of cash that affords them flashy, high-priced clothes, laptops for their course work, high-end electronics for their rooms and money for eating out in restaurants and fast food establishments' (Wesangula and Gisesa 2011). Problematically, the authors do not attempt to engage with the men who make such parties possible or suggest a way of dealing with these men. Instead, as they continue to recount in their articles following the death of Mercy Keino, their investigations led them to a series of 'similar' parties located all over Nairobi:

> In the week-long series interviews with female students, we were directed to houses and apartments in South B, Lang'ata, Westlands, Parklands, Riverside, Lavington, Kileleshwa as well as hotels in various parts of Nairobi and Mombasa that serve as the bases for the parties. Yet others advertise their services — known as escort services — on the Internet. (Wesangula and Gisesa 2011)

The position taken in the article above reflects a desire to offer a clear profile of the good time girl so that those reading the article know how to assess these women. Importantly, the women are painted as ordinary, but as the article ambiguously warns, 'nearly all these students live double lives; their parents, guardians, priests, sheikhs and relatives have not the faintest idea about their underworld activities' (Wesangula and Gisesa 2011).

The article goes on:

> Take the case of Imelda. When you meet her, everything about her seems basic and normal. Her English is neither fancy nor accented. No misplaced words. Her sentences are terse and well-constructed. In a couple of years she would make a great lawyer, but at the moment, Imelda has other priorities; she is driven by an insatiable thirst for money, sex and drugs — the fringe benefits to living life in the fast lane.

Imelda becomes an important aspect of the story, a good time girl who is as calculating as she is charming. She is not poor. According to the report, she is merely charting a course for the life she wants after college. She is extremely aware of the meaning of the double life that she is leading:

> I have two sets of friends. Some know me as the responsible first-born child of a respectable, well-off family. The other set knows me as a high-end, unattached, very expensive escort... (Wesangula and Gisesa, 2011)

The article goes into great detail about how much money she earns and what she does with this money and how she is using it to chart a future for herself. The article then speaks about another student, Lillian:

But Lilian, a student at a private university on Thika Road, says poverty has driven her to do what she does. She said she was so poor she could not afford cocaine. It wasn't a great tragedy, though, because she could still smoke her friends' bhang and get drunk on a 'mzinga' — a 500ml bottle of an alcoholic spirit. For a whole semester she wore someone else's clothes so as to look nice and, on a couple of not-to-be-forgotten occasions, their bras and panties. When a chance to attend a big shot's party in a house in Nairobi's Riverside Drive came up, Lilian could not let it pass. Today she is a regular at the place where she strip-dances and offers massage and sex. 'In an ideal world, I wouldn't be doing this. But it makes me pay my bills and live a good life,' Lilian told the *Sunday Nation*. 'Once I asked for supper and breakfast as payment. The man bought me chips and chicken. My friends keep on telling me that it's a choice. What they don't understand is that this is an obligation.' (Wesangula and Gisesa 2011)

The kind of picture painted in this story encapsulates a series of stereotypes of the good time girl. The details of the story are pegged on money, and why these women engage in compensatory relationships. For the newspapers, there is need to provide varying stories to make them more 'real', a necessary element if they are to be taken seriously. To further emphasise the extent of this 'problem', Wesangula and Gisesa's article shows how even young girls of 15 participate in transactional sex. At the end of the article, the comments offered by the Dean of Students at the University of Nairobi, Dominic Wamugunda, highlight compensatory relationships as problems exacerbated by social media use. According to the Dean, students who choose such relationships are not doing so because of poverty but because they are being influenced by what they see on social media. He suggests that these students bend to external pressures, when they still have the choice to live 'moral lives' and be successful. Articles on university students, though seemingly unrelated, sprouted in the wake of Mercy Keino's death as though to 'explain' what could have led the student to her death. For instance, the article cited below creates a fictional character, Mary, who is a first-time attendee of a 'sex party' involving older, rich men and young girls:

It was in this carefully arranged rendez-vous that Mary found herself with a politician, a man she had only seen on TV debating in Parliament. A first-timer in the business, Mary was embarrassed. But with Sh25,000 in her bag, she forced a smile and vowed never to speak about it. (Wesangula and Gisesa 2011)

In an article appearing in the same issue of *The Nation*, titled "Take measures to protect university women from exploitation and violence", Sylvia Kangara, a university professor, is critical of the lack of responsibility taken by institutions of higher learning to protect young women who could find themselves in risky situations. According to her, the university ought to be a space that allows these young women to grow intellectually and emotionally. The appearance of these two articles shortly after the death of a university student are not random. They both signal a rising issue among young students.

The predominant response that followed Mercy Keino's death betrayed a hegemonic, masculine discourse that was reflective of the presumed negative effect of higher-learning institutions on young women who were seen to be 'too naive'; and too exposed in a space that was away from the protective eyes of family and kinship. The response was based on existing assumptions of the university woman as a good time girl whose goal was to get material possessions from rich, older men. Stephanie Newell, in her reading of the good time girl, argues that the 'negative public feeling about young women's sexuality led to the production of the image of the sugar daddy with his young, educated girlfriend…wielded in the media to criticize unmarried women's apparent greed for material rewards, from workplace managers to corrupt officials' (Newell 2002, 6). Keino's death, while receiving some sympathetic responses, also attracted commentary that suggested that her death was a form of punishment for the alleged lifestyle choice of a good time girl. This is emphasised through a number of responses to her death. In a Facebook post titled 'Keino's fiancé tells of last call to him' (*Daily Nation*, 2012), comments oscillate between those that sympathise and those that suggest she deserved the tragic end to her life. Those that sustain an argument for punishment, justify these arguments by drawing on existing patriarchal logics. They suggest that young women who violate patriarchal norms by displaying 'immoral' behaviour deserved punishment. For instance, one commentator, a senior accountant at a Kenyan government office, posted:

> [Fiancé], u must b a fool of all the kalenjin men me inclusive ur the only stupid man, how cn u let ur woman 2b in bar while ur a sleep? Kumbuf mara ishirini [idiot, twenty times] nkt! (*Daily Nation*, 2012)

The comment above advocates a level of control in order to discipline a woman to whom one is engaged to be married. The commentator references his cultural ethnic location and, at the same time, emphasises the threat to masculinity brought about by Keino's actions. Significantly, the commentator refuses to acknowledge the violence and loss of life here, but is more concerned with offering suggestions about how her fiancé should have disciplined her. Another male commentator said:

> Did the media at sm point say 'escort girls'? Pole sana [So sorry Fiancé]. Next time u want a wife, go to the village, or head to Koinange[29] straight so u knw what u are up against.

The above comment is, once again, an articulation of patriarchal norm. In most renditions of the good time girl in African popular culture, the idea of a return to the rural as a form of idealised space where social order can be restored is presented as a solution. Nici Nelson's (2002) analysis of Kenyan popular novels shows how male authors often sent their city women to the village for rehabilitation. According to the commentator above, the idea of going back to the village to find a wife who has not yet been 'made impure' by urban space is the best course of action for a man trying to find a wife as any other kind of woman can be likened to a prostitute.

Among the comments that associated Mercy with the 'Campus divas', there was the assumption that this was now a familiar shorthand for understanding particular types of university women. One commentator, a female reader who identifies herself as an intellectual, says of Mercy: 'Plain Simple: Dead Divas Tell No Tales!' Another commentator, a Kenyan male in the Diaspora, says: 'She was 4 rich men be grateful GOD SAVED yu from HER everything happens 4 a reason.' This high degree of intertextual fluency illustrates a certain level of interpretative competence of the commentators who are aware of other forums in which a 'type' of university woman has been discussed. That Mercy was educated seems to generate a problem. One man who works in a restaurant said, 'Masomo mingi haifai .tamaa mingi' [too much education is not good. Leads to greed]; while another male commentator said, 'our ladies, learn frm this, u'l always b women. fyt 4 equality bt remember, u r stil WOMEN.' These two last comments view education as the root cause of women's transgressive behaviour since educated women, in their view, forget their place in society. The comment, 'you are still women' demonstrates with finality the way in which even some educated men view educated women. Keguro Macharia (2013), lamenting the lack of critical engagement that Mercy's death occasioned, notes:

> After her death, the mainstream press ran stories about wild campus girls, young women who are little more than avaricious prostitutes — nothing I saw bothered to trace the economic conditions of campus students, especially dwindling state support for higher education over the past 20 years or so that has made campus increasingly difficult, even as Nairobi and other campus locations have become increasingly expensive. Instead, there seemed to be a concerted effort to undermine women's education as a project of nation building.[30]

Macharia's comment addresses the manner in which gender and education are spoken about publicly in Kenya. He argues that, on the one hand, the media and other public platforms are used to informing Kenyans about the need to educate the girl child. But on the other hand, the appearance of reports such as the ones on university women's wayward behaviours invite scrutiny of the extent to which resources are allocated by the state towards ensuring that women obtain an education. Macharia's observations show that there has been little effort to investigate why university women may choose to engage in 'transactional relationships'. Stereotypes are used to categorise, judge and contain them with no interest in finding out how to address what is being signalled as a major problem.

Transgression

In order to read representations of good time girls as transgressive, one needs to keep an eye out for counter-narratives, most of which appear online. Press reports are often limited, and the only way to locate agency is by painstakingly and consciously following comments made by young women who attempt to explain why they choose the lifestyles that they do. While it was nearly impossible to find such kinds of radical voices in newspaper accounts, there were plenty of oppositional voices in online platforms that challenge expectations of what they are supposed to be in public.

The Facebook page, "Campus divas for rich men", offers an important starting point for this discussion. One of the reasons the page was so controversial was that it dared to 'transgress' boundaries of representation. It was one thing to talk about young women's misuse of their sexualities, and quite another to be confronted with visual images of these young women's bodies, with claims that they were actually university educated women. While it is outside the scope of this chapter to ascertain whether or not the 'Campus divas' are actual university students, what interested me in this example was how the Facebook page became visible precisely because of its association with the university as an institution. In many ways, it confirmed the stereotype of the materialistic yet immoral university woman, as shown below:

> Esther is a graduate though tarmacking [looking for employment]. She needs a man who has a business empire, someone who drives either a BMWX6 or Range rover. She believes her looks qualifies her to get whoever she wants. One should be ready to spend but get quality sex. If you believe you have the qualities, present yourself. Jokers and below average will not be entertained. (Campus divas 2014)[31]
>
> …
>
> Chebet…From Egerton University. Hi admin pls connect me to a loaded [a man with money] man in Nakuru to take me out tonight. He will get my goods in exchange. (Campus divas 2014)

Several posts closely resemble the ones above, with requests, seemingly from young women, about how to access men with money. Often a request is accompanied by a picture of the 'diva' and the administrator's phone number.

A close reading of the 'campus divas' page reveals two things. First, Kenyans were publicly confronted with young women's sexualities. Regardless of the moral standpoint from which these women were read and, in most cases, condemned, their voices could be heard in the public domain. Rachel Spronk (2012) has argued that there is discordance between how sexuality in Kenya is spoken about publicly and practised privately in Kenya. Her study reveals the complex and often ambiguous ways in which sexuality is experienced and interpreted at a personal level among young Kenyan professionals. Her study also, importantly, shows how young men and women in Kenya negotiate their sexualities in broader cultural contexts. The kind of agency demonstrated by young Kenyans in Spronk's work is hardly visible in public articulations. The 'Campus Divas', in many ways, has forced a conversation on young women's sexuality. Furthermore, it has created a space for dialogue. If, as indicated through the various commentaries, young women are immoral and in need of salvation, what other conversations can be generated beyond the reductive stereotypical frameworks in which they are read? In a piece titled "An Open Letter to Kenyan Men: Feminism Is Good For You", blogger Makena Onjerika (2014), sarcastically notes:

> It's true and you've been right all along. We, as in women, chicks, chick-ds, dames, ladies, mamas, bitches (and the various other terms you give us, ranging from sweet to derogatory), we are after your money. Why lie? It's just the money plus two or three other things like sex or cuddling or babies, but mainly it's the money...Because let's be serious fellas, you are God's gift to us, but when we really sit back and analyze you (yes, we do have brains and protons knocking about in them), we really can't see the gift part...We've just learnt a few things about perseverance, about giving up our dreams for your dreams, about ambition and why we should have a lot of it in this ridiculous country, about what we need and why the mediocre, sexist Kenyan male isn't it.[32]

Onjerika, the 2018 Caine Prize winner, published regularly for a blog called "WhatifKenya", in order to push for social change. She laments the increase in the number of men who rely more and more on what their patriarchal privileges enable, while claiming to be unable to understand the kinds of choices that some women make. Onjerika's is not a lone voice online. The internet has made it possible to find young university women's accounts of their experiences at university, often contrasting the stereotypes in which they are cast. One such blog, "Diary of a Kenyan campus girl" is fascinating in its detailed reports of daily experiences. In a blog post titled "Remember the time I had a weird Monday", the blogger writes about being sexually harassed by an older man, with details of how she handled the situation. Her account, though humorously told, reflects a common occurrence in many Kenyan universities.[33] Importantly, the blogger's ability to speak about her experiences provides an alternative way of thinking about the university girl. As revealed through a series of blog posts, the blogger enjoys drinking alcohol, dancing, making friends and going to parties, but is acutely aware of who she is and what she wants. She can and does make choices. Similarly, the young women who publish their profiles on Facebook are defying societal norms and expectations. They are willing to state what they want and why they want it.

Conclusion

In this chapter, I consider the phenomenon of 'the good time girl' and consumerism as spaces of transgressive behaviour among young women in Kenya. I read the ways in which this figure appears in public, considering the various meanings of such a visibility. The good time girl provokes curiosity and violence, both aspects of a heteropatriarchal logic to femininity. This is a transgressive femininity, which must be contained in cautionary tales. The phenomenon of the good time girl has a long history. In a consumerist society, it has captured the imagination of the public in what is often referred to as 'the sugar daddy' phenomenon. Other references include 'slay queen', 'sugar baby', 'good time girl', 'blessed girl' and so on. All these iterations suggest a narrative of choice and freedom that young women desire in a consumerist society. However, the chapter considers the context of violence in which such transgressive women exist. A number of violent encounters are evidence of the violence young women who transgress societal expectations of good feminine behaviour evoke. Recent examples in Kenya include the murders of students such as Mercy Keino, Ivy Wangeci and Sharon Otieno.

In the chapter, I argue that the media structures stories about these transgressive figures as cautionary tales, thereby leading them to be read as warnings, rather than focusing on the harm being done to female bodies. The mobility and independence of young women seems to provoke violence and death. I argue that the persistence of young women to be visible suggests their embrace of their vulnerability. They use their vulnerability as a location of strength.

Notes

1   For an extensive reading of the 'blesser' phenomenon, see Masenya, M. (Ngwan'a Mphahlele). 2017. "Reading Proverbs 7 in the Context of Female 'Blessers' and Sugar Mamas in South Africa." *Scriptura*, 116: 120–132. https://dx.doi.org/10.7833/116-2-1316; Masango, L. 2019. "Johannesburg, Sex, Love and Money: An Ethnography of Phones and Feelings." Unpublished MA thesis, University of the Witwatersrand.

2   A South African slang word that refers to younger men who get into relationships with older, rich women for money. The reference to these young men as 'ben 10' deliberately links to the idea of a 'toyboy'. It refers to men who are young enough to have enjoyed the American franchise and TV series *Ben 10*, which shows on *Cartoon Network*. This reference marks a generational divide between the older women and the young men, often seen to be young enough to be their sons.

3   Read more at: https://www.standardmedia.co.ke/article/2000015282/sugar-daddy-syndrome

4   Shelley Marsden. 25 November 2015. "Teen medical student who is disillusioned with boys her own age has ELEVEN sugar daddies." Accessed 28 October 2019. https://www.mirror.co.uk/news/uk-news/teen-medical-student-who-is-disillusioned-6896443

5   London. 1 December 2015. "Meet female medical student whose 11 sugar daddies are company CEOs." Accessed 28 October 2019. https://www.standardmedia.co.ke/article/2000184170/meet-female-medical-student-whose-11-sugar-daddies-are-company-ceos

6   Rene Otinga. n.d. "16 Crazy Jokes about Kenya slay queens." Accessed 28 October 2019. https://www.tuko.co.ke/255194-16-crazy-jokes-kenya-slay-queens.html#255194

7   KTN Kenya. Accessed 28 October 2019. https://www.facebook.com/KTNKenya/posts/i-am-a-student-and-i-am-hiv-positive-i-swore-i-would-spread-the-thing-because-i-/267589060019487/

8   Originally found on the blog *Jambo News Spot*, this piece has since disappeared. This is to be expected, given the ephemeral nature of the internet.

9   Julian Sonny. 15 March 2014. "Woman In Kenya Infects 324 Men With HIV As Part Of Revenge Act, Plans On Infecting 2,000 More." Accessed 28 October 2019. https://www.elitedaily.com/news/world/woman-kenya-infects-300-men-hiv-part-revenge-act-plans-infecting-2000

10 Kenyan popular music indicates that the suspicion of the modern (educated) woman has long been a part of public culture. Freshley Mwamburi's famous 1995 hit song "Stellah" demonstrates this. The song's protagonist anticipates the return of his lover, Stellah, who left to go and study in Japan. In the song's narrative, Stellah has been gone for three years. The protagonist explains that he had had to sell his property, including a car, to help raise Stellah's fare and upkeep money. He was invested in the relationship. On the day that Stellah was supposed to return, the protagonist goes to the airport with his friends and relatives. When Stellah finally disembarks from the plane, she is holding a baby, with her new lover, a Japanese man in tow. The song is about betrayal and heartbreak at the hands of an educated woman.

11 KTN News Kenya. 31 Aug 2012. "Facebook: a prostitution ring?" Accessed 28 October 2019. https://www.youtube.com/watch?v=mUek7pb1rHA

12 Evelyn Musambi, 2014. "Kenyans criticize 'Campus Diva' girl who prefers dating older men." *Daily Nation*, June 5. Accessed 3 May 2016. http://mobile.nation.co.ke/news/Kenyans-criticise-Campus-Diva-girl/-/1950946/2338106/-/format/xhtml/-/v1ucjw/-/index.html

13 Mzalendo254. "Revealed: NTV Campus Diva Story was fake." Accessed 10 May 2016. https://www.youtube.com/watch?v=MqFO9l1rzvAvideo

14 David Lazer et al. 2018 speak on the crisis of news production in an era where the idea of truth is no longer stable.

15 Mary Wambui and Vincent Achuka. 2019. "Ivy Wangechi's killer: A quiet worker and teetotaller." *Daily Nation*, April 11. Accessed 20 October 2019. https://mobile.nation.co.ke/news/Colleagues-speak-about-Ivy-Wangechi-killer/1950946-5066112-magtc8/index.html

16 The culture of mob justice in Kenya is well documented. See for instance, Yvonne Adhiambo Owuor's *Dust* (2014).

17 Mary Wambui and Vincent Achuka. 2019. "Ivy Wangechi's killer: A quiet worker and teetotaller." *Daily Nation*, April 11. Accessed 20 October 2019. https://mobile.nation. co.ke/news/Colleagues-speak-about-Ivy-Wangechi-killer/1950946-5066112-magtc8/ index.html

18 YouTube video featuring Sheddy Empire's "Pigwa Shoka." Accessed 21 October 2019. https://www.youtube.com/watch?v=kLe2DpqolyY

19 See discussions of Vera Sidika's body in Chapter 6 of this book, in which references are made to her wide hips and slender waist as sites of curiosity and desire. See particularly the discussion of Sidika being featured in specifically sexualised ways in a music video titled 'Dat Dendai'.

20 In this video, the group apologises and condemns femicide, claiming they just wanted to showcase their creativity. They blame the media and bloggers for turning an 'innocent song' into something whose intentions were violent and hurtful. See the full apology online. Accessed 21 October 2019. https://www.youtube.com/watch?v=Li_7A-azRdQ

21 See the discussion of this event in Chapter 3 of this book.

22 Caren Nyota. 10 April 2019. "Photos of Ivy Wangeci, the sexy Moi University student who was hacked to death."Accessed 25 October 2019. https://mpasho.co.ke/photos-ivy-wangeci-moi-university-hacked/

23 Journalist Oyunga Pala runs a blog called "The Modern African Guy" (http://oyungapala. com/) and has long been known for his cynical attitudes towards women. J. Musangi (2008) says of him, 'Oyunga Pala is a Kenyan columnist in the Saturday edition of the newspaper *Daily Nation* known for his humorous, but ironic, masculinist ideas about women' (Musangi 2008, 41).

24 Monica Kimani was a young woman who was found murdered in her house 20 days after Sharon's body was discovered. What connected the deaths was that they were both high-profile deaths because of the relationships those who were murdered had with well-known public figures. In the case of Kimani, her death was linked to TV journalist Jackie Maribe, the fiancée of the key suspect in the murder, Joseph Irungu Kuria. Oyunga Pala. 2018. "Slay queens, socialites and sponsors: the normalisation of transactional sex and sexual violence in Kenya." *The Elephant*, November 1. https://www.theelephant. info/features/2018/11/01/slay-queens-socialites-and-sponsors-the-normalisation-of-transactional-sex-and-sexual-violence-in-kenyan-society/

25 Tamerra Griffin. 8 September 2018. "The Murder Of A Pregnant Woman In Kenya Has Put Sugar Daddy Culture Under The Spotlight." Accessed 27 October 2019. https:// www.buzzfeednews.com/article/tamerragriffin/sharon-otieno-murder-sponsor-culture

26 Nyasha Kadandara. 2018. 'Sex and the sugar daddy.' *BBC*. Accessed 27 October 2019. https://www.bbc.co.uk/news/resources/idt-sh/sex_and_the_sugar_daddy

27 Pala. 2018. "Slay queens, socialites and sponsors."

28 While the gruesome details of Ms Keino's death are important, I do not focus on the actual murder case, but on how her death presented an opportunity for the press to create cautionary tales about the dangers of becoming a good time girl. As such, the narratives

that were created in the media show how the cautionary tale weaves into narratives of good time girls. It is also important to note that the investigation into her death is still ongoing at the time of writing.

29 Koinange Street in Nairobi is known for its high population of sex workers.

30 Keguro Macharia. 2013. On Mercy Keino. Blog post. Gukira. Accessed 20 April 2014. https://gukira.wordpress.com/2011/08/08/on-mercy-keino/

31 These were accessed from the Facebook 'Campus Divas' page, in 2014. The page has since undergone so many changes, and the posts are no longer available. This is partly due to social media's high turnover of information.

32 Onjerika, Makena. 2013. "An Open Letter to Kenyan Men: Feminism Is Good For You." WhatifKenya (blog). Accessed 12 May 2014. http://www.whatifkenya.com/feminism-good-for-kenyan-men/

33 Her blog draws attention to the culture of sexual harassment and sex pests located at universities. A recent BBC exposé titled "Sex for grades: Undercover in West African universities" reveals the difficulties that female students face at universities at the hands of predatory lecturers. Accessed 27 October 2019. https://www.bbc.com/news/av/world-africa-49907376/sex-for-grades-undercover-in-west-african-universities

6

Women celebrities, hypervisibility and digital subjectivity in Kenya

Introduction

In this chapter, I analyse women who, through their bodies, perform defiance and refusal in public. By this, I am referring to women whose bodies are visibly present in ways that go against accepted heteropatriarchal norms of morality. I read hypervisible women as 'difficult women' and to explore the extent to which their visibility can be read as a critical intervention into discourses of freedom and agency in conservative gender contexts I read them through a range of feminist scholarship. In addition, I look at feminine subjectivities that appear in popular texts online. Specifically, I look at Instagram, a social media platform, and focus on three young Kenyan female celebrities, Vera Sidika, Huddah Monroe and Esther Akoth (Akothee). All three women are popular for their exhibitionist performances and self-representations online. They have variously also been referred to as socialites, a term explored further in the chapter. I use a feminist intersectional approach to read these women's bodies as legible in a context that marks them as immoral and therefore dispensable.

Hypervisibility and being difficult

I premise this chapter on the idea of hypervisibility as an agentic strategy for reading the representations of African women in Kenyan popular culture. In black feminist studies, hypervisibility is a way of acknowledging invisibility as well as the culture of stereotyping black women's bodies as abnormal, hypersexual and deviant (Mowatt, French, and Malebranche 2013). The black woman is often either absent completely from discourse or — when she comes into view — as a source of spectacle (Noble 2013; Mowatt, French, and Malebranche 2013). The invisibility can also be achieved through misrepresentation and deliberate objectification of their sexuality over other kinds of identities (Noble 2013). These misrepresentations and eventual marginalisation are the result of both academic research on women and a lack of interest in taking women subjects seriously. Christine Obbo's (1980) research on African women in a different decade laments the lack of women as researchers and participants in African historiographies, leading to a lopsided view of the social realities that affect them directly. Mowatt, French, and Malebranche (2013) urge that any research of black women's bodies adopts an approach that recognises the intersectional politics of race, class and gender and how these affect the inclusion of black women in research. In this chapter, I take into account the context in which I read black women's bodies as a crucial factor in interpreting the practices and choices that the women I analyse engage in. I recognise the location of the research in an African country where gender, class and sexual politics collide to influence how women are represented or how they self-represent. The location of culture is important in situating and exploring the social realities of gender, race, sexuality and class that define black women's bodies in productive ways (Mowatt, French, and Malebranche 2013; Noble 2013).

To read the women I study as hypervisible is to acknowledge that they are difficult subjects. Pumla Dineo Gqola's *Reflecting Rogue* (2017) explores the idea of 'being difficult' as a form of refusal to work in normative confines and expectations of what it means to be 'a good woman' in a heteropatriarchal context. Lynn Phillips (2000, 39) describes 'good womanhood' as the adoption of proper gender roles that celebrate the desire for a woman to be pleasant, genteel, moral, subordinate to men and willing to be of service to others. To be a good woman also means to be a good citizen or a good national subject, as Danai Mupotsa (2014) reminds us. The family and the nation are here seen as institutions whose values mould and offer inspiration to good women subjects. Difficult women defy these pre-determined roles by choosing to present themselves in ways that physically and symbolically cause discursive rupture. Difficult women are not momentary beings who can be cast aside when the novelty wears off. They are consistent in their refusal to disappear. In thinking through this point, I engage with Sara Ahmed's (2014) idea of wilful subjectivity. To be wilful, she argues, is to refuse to conform to authority, or bow to moral correction (Ahmed 2014). If wilfulness is a refusal, then Gqola's invitation to explore the lives of three key women in African political space, for instance Winnie Mandela, Wangari Maathai and Wambui Otieno, is instructive (2017). Importantly, Gqola reads these women against a background of violence on the bodies of women that happens in everyday life, and she explores the public meanings that Winnie, Wangari and Wambui embody in contexts of violence. While their bodies remain vulnerable in the spaces they occupy, their defiance creates space for imagining possibilities for freedom. Gqola argues that 'difficult women, like Winnie, Wangari and Wambui stand as hopeful imagination' for a number of women in different political, social and cultural spaces (2017, 148). Gqola (2004), reading Brenda Fassie, shows how a woman's public performances of non-conformity can be both admired and frowned upon, often because of the symbolic meanings of such public presence.

In reference to the bodies of work cited above, I argue for a theoretical possibility to imagine oneself outside of confining institutionalised boundaries of moral behaviour. I identify the nation space as important for the formation of African subjectivities where individuals learn to become proper humans. To paraphrase Mupotsa, one is a proper human if one has the kind of aspirational politics that performs the self in the confines and demands of the family and the nation (2014, 7). In her work on white weddings, Mupotsa (2014, 7) urges us to think about 'the Oedipalized process of myth-making' that entices us, as subjects of the nation, to become particular kinds of humans whose pursuits sometimes work to our own detriment. I link Mupotsa's ideas of aspirational subjects with Ahmed's idea of the promise of happiness, in order to engage more fruitfully with the problematics of becoming a good citizen. Reading the family in particular as an object of happiness, Ahmed turns our gaze to the constructedness of happiness, where happy objects are read as 'those objects that affect us in the best way' (2010, 22). Demonstratively, Ahmed argues that when things affect us positively, we call it good, and when things affect us negatively, we call it bad, pointing to the subjective ways in which happiness is constructed and interpreted. Yet happiness is but a promise that is very moralising in its makeup — if you do good, you will be happy, and so on. What if one fails to be good? What if one falls outside of that order that is promised through an encouragement to do good? This chapter draws on this supposition, and the possibilities that are created for women when they cease to confine themselves to what is promised in hegemonic femininity.

Digital subjectivities and imagining freedom

Being difficult enables the imaginative possibility of theorising the digital subject in Kenyan public space in ways that signal a shift in gender and sexual debates. According to Mark Poster (2007), the digital subject is a position created in a planetary public sphere that defies the configuration of 'territorial identities' (2007, 390). Present through 'textual, aural and visual uploads', it seeks rather to be located 'automatically in the global space of the network' (2007, 389). For him, if postcolonial subjects are located in the proximity of nation, then digital subjects are outside of it, 'solicited not to stabilize, to centralize, to unify the territorial position, but to invent and construct themselves in relation to others' (2007, 390). The digital self is free to construct a subjectivity that is untethered by the temporal and spatial demands of family and nation. The digital subject offers an opportunity to reconstruct the self in ways that may not always be possible offline. In critical internet studies, there are scholars who have countered this optimistic reading of digital subjectivity by insisting that the digital subject has no agency in the context of the capitalist regime that is digital media. Such scholars remain cynical about the potential that digital media has to contribute to social transformation and argue that the digital subject is a captured subject (Dean 2009; 2010). There is, however, a different body of scholarship that recognises the potential digital media holds for social and political transformation. Eva Giraud (2015, 7), for instance, argues that despite the research into digital media as conduits of capital, they can still be understood as alternative sites of discourse outside of a neoliberal framework. In this chapter, I acknowledge the neoliberal context in which digital subjectivity can be understood. What I am interested in, however, is the symbolic significance of such subjectivities in Kenya's dominant heteropatriarchal world, and how they create a rupture in discourse that is important and worthy of critical attention.

I look at women who use the internet as a platform in which to create their digital selves. Focusing specifically on the social media platform Instagram, I argue that such women circumvent the demands of nationhood by constructing their subjectivities online, thus freeing themselves from the demands of social structures that could be placed on them offline. My reading here is influenced by feminist internet studies that identify the internet as a space through which women can rethink their positions as multifaceted audiences, users and consumers of digital media (Van Zoonen 2001). I read the women I select as fragments of themselves, made available through careful curation in existing neoliberal frameworks of femininity and celebrity culture.

Celebrities as critical commentary

In data collected between 2014 and 2018, Sidika, Monroe and Akothee each maintained an online presence by documenting their lives across a range of social media platforms such as Instagram, Twitter and Facebook, and YouTube. Their stories have appeared in several tabloids online, sourced through interviews, rumour and gossip.[1] The women have been referred to as 'socialites', a term that has gained currency in contemporary media culture to refer to young women who are celebrities because of their social networks.[2] The *Cambridge Dictionary* defines a socialite as someone of high social status who is famous for going to a lot of parties and social events.[3] Historically, socialites had to have wealth to sustain the expensive lifestyles that they led. In the 21st century, the idea of a socialite has become associated with narratives of fame and wealth as circulated through popular culture and the media.

Famous socialites who have entered into the media sphere in recent years include Kim Kardashian, an American reality television star, and Paris Hilton, heir to the Hilton Hotel empire. Popular understandings of socialites are that there are no visible forms of labour or talent that account for their fame. In many cases, socialites' inherited wealth is the basis for their lavish lifestyles.

In the African context, where class remains a contested category, the meaning of socialite links more directly to labour. Women referred to as socialites use digital media to magnify their visibility through the promotion and branding of the self. However, in Kenyan public discourses, the link to capital intersects with the idea of sexual deviance, with reference to women's sexuality in particular. When a reporter at a local television broadcaster interviewed Monroe in 2013, she openly rejected the tag 'socialite' as she claimed it referred to women who made money by offering their bodies in exchange for sex.[4] The easy association of these women's public personas with sexual morality is of course problematic, as it closes off any possibility of interacting with a more varied reading of their public performances. Sidika, Monroe and Akothee, for instance, offer biographical vignettes on Instagram, which consistently emphasise the value of hard work and self-confidence. Nevertheless, these three women exist in a context that locates them as excessive subjects, to be found in tabloid pages and other similarly structured gossip columns, and so not to be taken seriously. Their narratives revolve in an existing repertoire of knowledge about socialite lifestyles. In East Africa, well known socialites include the late Agnes Masogange of Tanzania (Nyamsenda 2014),[5] Uganda's Zari Hassan, and Kenya's Vanessa Cheruto and Corazon Kwamboka.[6] Visual markers of their lifestyles as posted on social media include glossy images in which the women showcase their access to luxury goods. Common images include photos of the women next to, or inside, luxury vehicles, in beautiful homes, inside the first-class sections of airplanes, in faraway resorts next to beaches, and so on. That the socialite lifestyle is sought after can be seen in reproductions through television shows such as *Nairobi Diaries*, a reality show in Kenya in which stars reveal how much they aspire to become socialite celebrities. The first season featured eight women, including Vera Sidika, most of whom described themselves as socialites.[7]

To be a socialite in Kenya, then, is to be a celebrity. A celebrity, according to David Marshall, refers to an individual who is elevated into the public eye in a capitalist context (1997). Following Richard Dyer's conceptualisation of star theory (1979), Marshall recognises the link between celebrities, modernity and capitalism. For him, the celebrity is a metaphor for individuals who exist as a 'celebration of democratic capitalism' (1997, 4). The celebrity is thus a value in modern society, elevated as such through mass audiences who provide individuals with such worth and value (Marshall 1997). The celebrity is constructed in consumer culture to represent aspiration and success. Indeed, arguments against celebrity culture, mostly from Marxist critics, identify the celebrity as a personality cult that uses individuals to proffer the 'promise of capitalism' through 'the myth of universal success' (1997, 9). While acknowledging their location in capital, Marshall urges us to consider celebrity power and the pleasure that mass audiences derive from consuming the individual celebrity, as well as the symbolic role such a celebrity plays in the everyday lives of audiences.

Capitalist entanglements have resulted in attempts by scholars to distinguish between what Joshua Gamson (2011) refers to as the new celebrity and the traditional celebrity. Kevin Marinelli (2015) argues that the new brand of celebrity churned out through reality shows and the internet are a problematic category that ruptures earlier understandings of celebrity culture. The pseudo celebrity, as he refers to it, occupies an ambiguous location in capitalist society. In other words, he argues that pseudo celebrity destabilises the distinction between celebrity status and personal merit so that, in essence, the pseudo celebrity becomes 'famous for being famous' (Marinelli 2015, 1). The vague talents of the socialite figure remain at the centre of this distinction. Marinelli explores the Kardashian celebrity status as one example of a pseudo celebrity in which the Kardarshians attract negative attention as the public tries to understand the reasons behind their fame. Their status as celebrities comes about as a result of being hypervisible, an element of mass media celebration of individuals in the 20th and 21st centuries (Van Zoonen 2006). Van Zoonen emphasises its gendered history, where traditional celebrities are associated with famous men who were brilliant and innovative producers of culture and knowledge, while the new celebrity is associated with a more feminine, consuming culture (2006). I argue that the classed and gendered nature of celebrity discourse obscures the power that celebrities have to impact and engage in everyday life.

Following Marshall, I locate this celebrity power as agentic, where interaction between digital subjects and their publics occurs (Marshall 1997). I also argue that Sidika, Monroe and Akothee's hypervisibility is made possible because of digital media, through which they manipulate their power to influence in order to circulate a message of success as defiance. Sidika's appearance in a music video catapulted her to fame,[8] and she has maintained this celebrity status through an active social media presence, which has led to her getting work as a plus-size model, a social event host, and as a reality television star. Monroe's fame rose after she featured in the eighth season of *Big Brother Africa*.[9] Since then she has hosted social events, worked as a model and made appearances at parties. She has also secured acting jobs in industries such as Nollywood. Akothee's entry into social media is far less direct. She gained notoriety as Kenya's richest musician. She presents a rags-to-riches narrative that explains her rise to fame, narrated variously through her social media accounts. All three women document their lives by selectively showcasing aspects that are the epitome of capitalist success. Akothee's identity online combines her success with accounts of single motherhood. Sidika presents herself as the ultimate neoliberal subject, offering advice on how to gain success as a young woman. Sexual freedom and access to luxury dominate Monroe's timeline, displaying various aspects of her life as 'fabulous'. These female celebrities immerse themselves in the everyday, providing projections of possibility in a capitalist context. Gamson (2011) identifies celebrity culture as a push of 'ordinariness into the cultural forefront' (Gamson 2011, 1062). For him, the new celebrity is embedded in the ordinary. The 'commodity at stake is embodied attention; the value the celebrity inheres is his or her capacity to attract and mobilize attention' (2011, 1062). Nevertheless, Gamson warns that even in its ordinariness, celebrity culture remains part of the larger capitalist machinery.

Can one then make the claim that these women's assertiveness, controversies and presence online necessitate a discussion about agency? Jessalynn Marie Keller (2012) argues that a distinct characteristic of the new media celebrity is the ability to manipulate media for their own purposes. In her work on supermodel Tyra Banks's recent successful uptake of new media in creating a persona that young girls can relate to, she identifies Banks as a celebrity entrepreneur because of her ability to 'invent herself through multiple media platforms and explain her success as indicative of ambition, talent, and hard work' (2012, 147). However, Keller raises concern over Banks's celebration of subjectivity through her portrayals of 'individual choice and self-acceptance while maintaining a disciplined yet naturalized hegemonic femininity acceptable to contemporary American ideals…' (2012, 148). Following Keller, what kinds of questions arise when engaging with Sidika, Monroe and Akothee as complex and potentially problematic agentic subjects?

One way of entering into this discussion is to consider what their location in the public space in a context of patriarchy does to disturb hegemonic patriarchal norms. This in many ways reflects the existing literature on new media and troubling bodies in the era of the internet. I.D. Roberts (2010), writing on Chinese internet sensation Furong Jiejie, argues that Jiejie became famous precisely because she was able to use sexualised language in a conservative Chinese context. Furong Jiejie is a Chinese woman who received worldwide attention in 2005 for her blog posts in which she spoke openly about sex and intimacy in a society that is still extremely conservative. In 2005, as her fame grew, the Chinese government censored her by asking that all information related to Jiejie be pushed to low-profile parts of the internet. A television programme about her was also banned. Even then, Jiejie continued to draw attention to herself in a variety of ways made possible by the internet.

In reading Sidika, Monroe and Akothee, I am aware that arguments have been made regarding their negative influences on society. However, I am interested in engaging with their symbolic significance in the discussion about agency and gender.

While I have relied on a variety of narratives circulating online, either on YouTube or in various tabloid newspapers, I now focus on the women's Instagram accounts because through them it becomes possible to knit together the narrative that the women want to tell the world about themselves. I build a corpus of data from all three women's Instagram accounts in order to establish a narrative of their digital lives.

Spectacular femininities

In this section, I show how Vera Sidika, Huddah Monroe and Akothee have convincingly been able to demonstrate their success through excessive displays of their femininities, in what Simidele Dosekun (2015) has referred to elsewhere as spectacular femininities. These are femininities that embrace

> …hyper-feminine styles characterized by the spectacular use of elements such as cascading hair extensions, long and manicured acrylic nails, heavy and immaculate make-up, false eyelashes and towering high heels. (2015, 970)

Like Dosekun, I argue that these displays of hyperfemininities are an embrace of class privilege that mark these women as different from ordinary working-class women. This is particularly important in the context of the global South, where class differences are stark (Dosekun 2015). Studying women in Lagos, Dosekun argues that such women are quick to point out their financial independence and stress their pleasure at being able to afford luxury items, and that they associate their wealth and success with empowerment (2015). Like their Western counterparts, these women are part of a postfeminist sensibility (Gill 2007). Rosalind Gill (2007) suggests that postfeminism contains distinctive characteristics that enable one to identify it easily, and thus engage with it critically. In the introduction to their book on new femininities, Gill and Scharff (2011, 4) summarize these elements as

> …the notion that femininity is increasingly figured as bodily property; a shift from objectification to subjectification in ways that (some) women are represented; an emphasis upon self-surveillance, monitoring and discipline; a focus upon individualism, choice and empowerment; the dominance of a 'makeover paradigm'; a resurgence of ideas of natural sexual difference; the marked 'resexualization' of women's bodies; and an emphasis upon consumerism and the commodification of difference.

In a postfeminist culture, the sexy body is the ultimate mark of spectacular femininity. This body, while presented as a woman's source of power, is also constantly in need of 'surveillance, discipline and re-modelling' (Gill 2007, 149). Modern cultures have epitomised regimes of self-care that impose notions of beauty on women and men that need maintenance through consumer spending.

Its obvious problematic ties to capital notwithstanding, I focus on the spectacular ways in which Sidika, Monroe and Akothee display their femininities; ways that can be theorised as excessive. Excessive femininity exaggerates, is unapologetic, is consumerist, and completely refuses to align with the normalised versions of femininity (Åsberg 2007). It calls attention to itself, refusing to conform to the norm and therefore offering an opportunity to engage with female agency (Åsberg 2007). I argue for a reviewing of the feminine subject as located at the centre of discourse, and therefore as possessing control over how she curates herself.

I first came across the name Vera Sidika in relation to the Facebook group 'Campus Divas for rich men' while working on an article on good time girls in contemporary Kenyan media in 2014.[10] Interestingly, Sidika, who was not part of the Facebook group, was consistently cited in ensuing discussions by commentators who largely found the behaviour of the women belonging to the Facebook group appalling. The women who participated in the group existed only through posts advertising their availability for transactional relationships with older rich men, and through images depicting raunchy, desiring subjects.

It is in this context that I first encountered Sidika, a 26-year-old video vixen and fashion model for plus-size women who also identifies as a student, having at the time registered for a degree in Art and Design at Kenyatta University, one of Kenya's public universities. Sidika is famous for her big bottom and for publicly acknowledging that she had undergone a skin lightening as well as a breast augmentation procedure.[11] Indeed, she presents herself in the media as the ultimate postfeminist figure. Sidika, like most of the other celebrity socialites, carries the marks of a neoliberal postfeminist subject highly invested in technologising the self (Foucault 1982). Her first encounter with the public is through the music video for the hit song "You guy" (*Dat Dendai*) in 2012, performed by the hip-hop group P-Unit and circulated widely on YouTube. The song lyrics allude to an unnamed woman, referred to throughout the video as *dat dendai* (sheng[12] for 'that girl'), who is apparently so raunchy that the male persona in the song feels compelled to share news of his encounter with her with his friends. This is captured in the chorus of the song:

> *You guy, dat dendai, dendai*
>
> *She can really get a good one*
>
> *You guy, dat dendai, dendai*
>
> *She can give you a good one*

The song uses heavy dancehall beats made popular by the songs of Jamaican artists Chaka Demus & Pliers, such as "Murder, she wrote" produced in 1993 and "bam bam" produced in 1990. "You guy" contains sexually explicit references to a female subject who is beautiful, yet 'nasty', 'dirty', 'sexually perverse' and 'up for anything'. She is the epitome of a modern good time girl, a fantasy, explained in the lyrics as so enticing that the male persona can only desire her. Vera Sidika features in the video dressed in a body hugging mini-dress that accentuates her bottom which is clearly much bigger than those of the other girls appearing in the video. Her body is sexualised through the camera angle which does not focus on any other part of her body. This video was banned by CitizenTV (one of the more prominent television stations in Kenya) shortly after its release because it was deemed sexually explicit. Undaunted, Sidika has gone on to feature in several other music videos, including local hip-hop star Prezzo's "My gal" in 2014,[13] and Nigerian KC, Skiibii and Harrysong's video for the song "Ebaeno".

Some scholars and commentators argue that Sidika is problematic because she works in the service of patriarchy (Warah 2015) and capital (Nyamsenda 2014). They argue that she embraces the individualist approach to feminine success while lacking reflection on how her visibility promotes the continuation of violent cultures against women. Rasna Warah (2015), for instance, considers Sidika an agent of her own oppression, citing the elaborate work that Sidika has put into looking a certain way in order to meet standardised ideas of beauty. She accuses Sidika of participating in a world that uses a neoliberal argument to erase histories of violence on the woman's body. Warah's lamentations point to the element of sexualisation as well as the increasing ways in which the current discourse of femininity reasserts notions of sexual difference, thereby undoing the work of feminism from the 1970s and 80s. These arguments are part of a larger body of work on postfeminism and neoliberalism that identifies elements in today's contemporary culture and its representations of femininities as problematic (Gill 2007; Gill and Scharff 2011). For instance, in the hundreds of pictures of Sidika posted on Instagram, she always appears in expensive clothes, the pictures being carefully curated to depict glamour, gloss and luxury. Her self-representation feeds into what Mehita Iqani (2016), reading Sidika and other female celebrities, has referred to as commoditised beauty in the global South. Sidika's lightened skin and augmented breasts emphasise the 'sleek, toned, controlled figure' considered 'essential for portraying success' (Gill 2007, 150).

While Warah may have a point, I argue instead that Sidika pushes against the very violent public canvas against which women's bodies are read through her bold embrace of herself. I pay attention to her active selection of particular images for public circulation through Instagram. Her use of selfies is instructive. Following the work of Lauren Smith and Jimmy Sanderson (2015), I argue that the selfie 'enables the [subjects] to counteract how they are being portrayed in mass media...and to disclose information that prompts identification and potentially parasocial interaction with fans' (2015, 343). Sidika's selection of particular images of herself counteracts those that appear in tabloids that allude to her as being a deviant. A popular image of Sidika that circulates shows her as a dark-skinned, timid-looking young woman with a poor sense of fashion, juxtaposed with a different image of her as she looks today — light-skinned, bigger breasts and hips and in more expensive clothes.[14] As Theresa Senft and Nancy Baym (2015) show, selfies, those 'self-generated digital photographic portraiture spread primarily through social media', are deliberate forms of representing the self. Beyond reading them as narcissistic and pathological, the authors urge a consideration of selfies as important indices of popular culture. Sidika constructs her own public persona because she thinks of her body as a moneymaker. Through a series of interviews carried out between 2012 and 2016, she maintained that she had no problems with how her body navigates the public space. In an interview with a local television anchor, for instance, she says, 'Looking good is my business, my body is my business, nobody else's business but mine.'[15] She was also featured on *BBC Trending* where she defended her choice to lighten her skin, claiming that it was her choice to do so.[16] In 2016, when I first accessed her account, there were nearly 700 photographs — mostly consisting of selfies — focusing on her physical beauty, always in close proximity to a luxury article, whether a phone, beautiful surroundings or a luxurious form of transportation. In her pictures, she is the embodiment of a modern, wealthy woman. Sidika is aware of the way that she projects her wealth and is quick to issue a warning in one of her posts:

> Don't let Instagram fool you. There are people with only 5–10 likes who have plenty of friends. People with 1,000+ likes who are lonely as fuck! Couples, who look so happy together, yet are miserable as hell. People who don't post pictures of themselves and their significant other, but are in a beautiful loving relationship. People who know each other very well but appear as strangers. People who are up to their necks in debt yet live lavish Instagram life. Always remember that this is not real life.[17]

Most of Sidika's Instagram visuals are therefore curated to project success. This is quite contrary to images and narratives of her that circulate in other popular media such as tabloids. Although she is a successful businessperson, most of what is captured in the news about her concerns either a sexual scandal or has something to do with her relationship status.[18] Her selfies are a rewriting of these narratives.

Huddah Monroe, like Sidika, uses her Instagram page to self-curate. Her fame rose in 2013 after she featured in the eighth season of *Big Brother Africa*. Despite being evicted in the first week, videos of her naked body during shower hour circulated widely online. Tabloids have focused on her use of vulgar language and bold commentary on issues related to sexuality. Controversial headlines such as "Women let's marry each other"[19] and "Socialite Huddah Monroe finds love and is screaming about the good sex"[20] provide a snippet of how her persona appears in tabloid stories. Born Sonie Alhuda Njoroge, she publicly adopted the name Monroe to show her admiration of Hollywood celebrity Marilyn Monroe because of her status as a sex symbol.[21] Controversy is a key element in Huddah Monroe's project of self-promotion. As Lynette Mukhongo (2014) observes, Monroe has capitalised on the initial attention she received from appearing on *Big Brother Africa* by posting controversial images of her body, and sustaining interest by means of her body and by showing how to use it to make money. According to information gleaned from interviews she has given, Monroe makes her money through modelling. She is also a businessperson.[22] Like Sidika, Monroe is seemingly rich, with Instagram pictures showing off expensive cars, clothes and general lifestyle.[23]

Huddah, like Sidika and Akothee, has several Instagram pages, some containing pictures of her promoting her business, others about her everyday life. There are also a number of secondary pages on Instagram that use a hashtag to earmark Huddah's life, particularly moments of scandal. One consistent narrative from Huddah's pages is that she is not shy about exposing her body. She has posted pictures of herself without underwear and pictures showing aspects of her body that may be sexualised, including one with a nipple showing. Huddah, one would argue, advocates sexual freedom through her interaction with her publics.

Instagram as autobiography

While Huddah and Vera rely on their body aesthetics to draw attention to themselves, the third celebrity studied here, Akothee, presents herself differently. Unlike her counterparts, she draws attention to herself as a self-made woman. She sells a rags-to-riches narrative that she sustains by juxtaposing before and after images of her life's journey. Akothee is a single mother to five children. Her Instagram tagline is 'President of single mothers'. Indeed, this narrative frames her public self-presentation. Her biographical details reveal that she got married at the age of 14, and had four children in quick succession after dropping out of school and eloping with the father of her children.[24] During those years she says she had to stay with the boy's mother, working 'as a domestic worker', while her spouse continued with his education, eventually receiving his first degree. After the death of her second child, and betrayal by her partner, Akothee eventually left to begin her life afresh. The success of Akothee's life rests on this history of struggle. It is apparent that life was hard for her as a young mother, particularly as she had not finished high school. She often confesses that meeting a wealthy French diplomat changed her life.[25]

Akothee's main Instagram account, @akotheekenya, shows that she navigates social media through visuals and texts detailing her story as a young mother: a story of survival and of self-reliance. These stories are juxtaposed with others that show her as conspicuous consumer of luxury goods and lifestyle. An Instagram post on 22 April 2018,[26] for instance, shows a picture of a young but tired version of herself, sitting on the edge of a seat. To her left are her three children — two older girls and a new-born baby. Below the photograph is a short caption explaining the picture. The Kiswahili text denounces men who, according to her, made her pregnant then left her to fend for herself. She then announces her new position of agency, stating that should anyone want to make babies with her, they would need to sign contracts, and open 'pregnancy bank accounts'. She is specific in her demands. These accounts will vary, from 'pregnant account', 'post-natal account,' 'school fee account', 'holiday account', 'upkeep account'. She continues that anyone not willing to follow her rules is free to go look for children elsewhere, away from her. In a recent interview, she reinforces this message saying that if she is with someone who does not love her, she will leave the person, 'with her uterus'. This insistence on her reproductive power, and the way in which she is able to insist on speaking about it in public, is empowering and agentic. Akothee breaks a common myth held against women, especially mothers, about an inability to leave a bad relationship when one has children. She is an exception to the rule, and she uses social media to explore this.

That she has had children with more than one man is often illuminated as a sign of her immoral existence. Even worse, she is highlighted as a perfect example of a blessee, having received her wealth through relations with a rich European man. Clouded in a discourse of shame, narratives of 'transactional sex', as explored in the previous chapter, are meant to discipline women in some way. She refuses to see herself in ways that are limiting. Rather, she speaks about these same men abandoning her, and failing to meet her expectations. Her husband, for instance, cheated on her, after she had had four children with him and made huge sacrifices. Rather than stay in the marriage, she chose to leave. She had three children to feed, and little money. She then met a Swiss man who promised to marry her and take her with him to Switzerland. While pregnant with his child, Akothee realised that the man had no intention of legally marrying her, and according to an interview, she packed her bags and went back to Kenya. She refuses to submit to what she sees as substandard conditions. She refuses to settle. She holds her stories as examples of her refusal to conform, a way of showing how to navigate impossible terrains.

Akothee chooses to share her intimate stories in public. So, for instance, in one post, also posted on 22 April 2019, there is a picture of her with her fiancé. It is a picture taken outdoors. Both of them are wearing dressing gowns over their pyjamas. Their bodies are close together, with Akothee standing in front of the man. The background shows palm trees and sand on one side, and a beach front on another. From the picture, one can conclude that the two of them are on holiday. In the accompanying text, Akothee celebrates her fiancé, stating that because of him, 'wazungu' (white men) are 'feeling sick with jealousy' (possibly referring to her two previous relationships with European men). At this point, one commentator 'polices' Akothee by stating that 'these are bedroom matters' and that she (Akothee) should not announce her life thus. The commentator adds, 'Oyoo and Ojwang will see this one day' (these are the names of her two youngest sons). Akothee's response is quick: 'Life is too real to pretend. Unless you are living a fantasy!' These kinds of responses are typical from Akothee, who refuses to feel cowardly about how she imagines her life. She refuses to adhere to common parameters through which women, and especially mothers, are judged. She uses the very instruments used to judge and silence women to her advantage.

This trait comes through in most of her posts. In one Instagram post she says in Luo (her mother tongue), '*Akoth chumbi chuo, kama otuone ema otuchee*', which roughly translates as 'Akothee, salt of men, wherever there is scarcity, she will appear'.[27] The accompanying photo shows her in white attire, shoes and bag, standing next to an expensive car. This kind of staging reinforces the wealthy lifestyle narrative hinted at before. However, her words also hint at her desire to provoke people's moral sensibilities by shocking, rather than hiding away. She also uses the opportunity to announce an upcoming business event.

On being outrageous: Conclusion

Women's bodies situate themselves variously in public. As I have argued in previous chapters, the media is complicit in shaping how these bodies should be based on a dominant hetero-patriarchal perspective. Transgressive bodies are often punished, using scandal or other forms of silencing. The three women I discuss in this chapter, Sidika, Monroe and Akothee, go against the societal norm that defines decency within narrow frames. They are vocal and hypervisible in challenging societal norms of femininity. While their lives are publicly accessible because of their celebrity status, these three women have chosen to use various social media platforms to curate selves in ways that are often non-conforming and seemingly outrageous. Vera Sidika, well-known for posting videos of herself dancing provocatively with her bottom facing the camera, is a good example. The dance she performs is twerking, which has become globally popular and is associated with sex. I acknowledge the difficulty of claiming agency in the cases of these women, in this instance, particularly because of their immersion in a strong consumerist culture. I am also aware that their exercising of sexual freedom is seen by some as a sign of their own sexual immorality. I, however, insist that these women are breaking moral boundaries and making it possible for women to re-categorise themselves as public subjects who can speak for themselves and control how their narratives circulate. These women are hardly normative role models, yet they embody the kind of freedom that can only come from their refusal to remain confined in the demands of society.

An Instagram image of Huddah Monroe posing naked and circulated in mainstream platforms will cause outrage because it demands that the public confronts the meaning of her body as deviant. Equally, a video of Vera Sidika twerking in her bathtub is meant to provoke. Akothee posts several pictures of herself in skimpy clothing, either dancing by herself or rubbing herself against her boyfriend. The comments such posts receive show the extent to which these women maintain their public notoriety through controversies.

It is my contention that these provocations contribute to a broader dialogue about women's freedom in public. This freedom is as much physical as it is discursive. Tabloid reports on these three women indicate a closed narrative of sexual immorality. A closer look at their self-narratives shows a different story, with a focus on a much more complex interiority.

Notes

1 See for instance *Pulse Live*. Accessed 21 January 2019. https://www.pulselive.co.ke/news/politics/kenyan-female-celebrities-who-rocked-in-2018/gdv1jcx

2 This is one example on socialites in Kenya. Accessed 21 January 2019. https://www.sde.co.ke/thenairobian/article/2000207935/revealed-how-kenyan-socialites-make-millions

3 *Cambridge Dictionary* online. Accessed 3 May 2016. http://dictionary.cambridge.org/dictionary/english/socialite

4 Television interview on K24, a local commercial television station. 6 May 2016. https://www.youtube.com/watch?v=gNQ010hXsBA

5 I here refer to an article by Sabatho Nyamsenda, published in 2014 as a blog post with the title: "Ubidhaishaji wa maumbile ya binadamu: toka Sarah Baartman mpaka Agnes 'Masogange'." Wajenga Dunia Blog Post. http://wajengadunia.blogspot.com/2014/07/ubidhaishaji-wa-maumbile-ya-binadamu.html.

6 https://www.sde.co.ke/thenairobian/article/2000207935/revealed-how-kenyan-socialites-make-millions

7 *Nairobi Diaries* seems to be modelled on the American *Real Housewives* franchise, particularly, *The Real Housewives of Atlanta*, and has highlighted other women's desires to be publicly known as socialites.

8 KenyanPoetsLounge. P-Unit. 'You Guy' YouTube video. Accessed 2 May 2016. https://www.youtube.com/watch?v=DE-MtRUsp9E

9 Grace Kerongo. 23 May 2013. "Is Huddah Kenya's rep to big brother?" Accessed 25 January 2019. https://allafrica.com/stories/201305240349.html

10 Ligaga, Dina. 2014. "Mapping Emerging Constructions of Good Time Girls in Kenyan Popular Media.' *Journal of African Cultural Studies* 26 (3): 249–261.

11 See for instance, Cate Mukei's article "Vera Sidika opens up on her new boobies." Accessed 2 May 2016. ttps://www.sde.co.ke/thenairobian/article/2000129374/vera-sidika-opens-up-on-her-new-boobies

12 Sheng is a hybrid language that draws from dominant Kenyan languages including English and Swahili, as well as from local vernacular languages.

13 HB Online. 2014. "Prezzo – My gal." Accessed 2 May 2016. https://www.youtube.com/watch?v=qQHujEdlvJY

14 See one such comparison on Instagram pictures. Accessed 2 May 2016. https://www.instagram.com/p/Bfe_Lq0gcV2/?hl=en&tagged=verasidika *Pulselive*

15 As is the nature of online material, the original interview has been removed due to third party copyright infringement. It now appears in snippets online. However, one can still find a few videos that reference the original, such as this: https://www.youtube.com/watch?v=1YEdTBh0Y3c

16 BBC trending. 16 June 2016. Access 3 August 2016. "Kenya's #BleachedBeauty speaks out." https://www.youtube.com/watch?v=6RoIjOBzVAU

17 Vera Sidika. Instagram. Accessed 18 May 2016. https://www.instagram.com/p/BAe2u1DA2-P/?taken-by=queenveebosset&hl=en

18 See for instance https://www.sde.co.ke/article/2001310493/no-love-lost-otile-goes-for-vera-sidika-s-waist-in-new-song

19 Nyota, Caren. 2018. *Mpasho*, May 10. Accessed 25 January 2019. https://mpasho.co.ke/women-lets-marry-huddah-monroe-says-bashing-black-men/

20 Kasujja, Mwende. 2018. *Nairobi News*, August 29. Accessed 25 January 2019. https://nairobinews.nation.co.ke/chillax/socialite-huddah-monroe-finds-love-screaming-good-sex/

21 Norma Jeane Mortenson, famously known as Marilyn Monroe, also reinvented herself in order to build her modelling and acting career in Hollywood.

22 https://informationcradle.com/kenya/huddah-monroe/

23 Both women charge a lot of money for their participation in events. Monroe reveals that she gets paid approximately $1 860 to attend a single event. Vera Sidika's fees are exponentially higher. In an interview for the Kenyan daily newspaper, *Daily Nation*, she reveals that she charges $2 500 an hour.

24 Details of Akothee's life can be found on websites such as *SOFTKENYA*. Accessed 25 January 2019. https://informationcradle.com/kenya/akothee/

25 https://informationcradle.com/kenya/akothee/

26 Monicah, Shanniq. 2018. "The first baby daddy gives her a hard time by going to court." *eveDIGITAL*, January 25. Accessed 25 January 2019. https://www.standardmedia.co.ke/evewoman/article/2001267213/akothee-and-her-baby-daddy-fight-over-custodial-rights-for-their-son

27 The reference she makes to her sexual appeal to men here is obvious. To refer to herself as the salt that men need in order to function (implied in the original vernacular statement), she is drawing attention to her attractiveness and desirability. She is not shy about advertising herself as a commodity that men need, one that is guaranteed to satisfy their needs (scarcity).

7

Conclusion

This book is about public cultures in Kenya that focus on gender, sexuality and morality. Specifically, I critique public constructions of femininity at the moment of circulation. I argue that in circulating particular ideas about women, there is a process of constructing femininity that is often violent and harmful. The centrality of my argument is that the public interfaces of these circulations ought to be interrogated if one is to understand fully the significance of how violence against women in the public sphere occurs. I ask the question: what does a woman's visibility in public mean? I consider what women's presence in public spaces means in contexts of violence; and whether one can read their presence as a refusal to be typecast and violated. I advocate alternative ways of envisioning women's agentic power in conditions that make living and existing in public difficult. As such, this suggests firstly: that women's bodies are significant in generating discourses of morality in Kenya, and that such discourses are based predominantly on these women's sexualities. Secondly, it shows that for such discourses to circulate effectively, they must operate in melodramatic, spectacular and scandalous ways. I argue that a pattern of representation that emerges is a violent one that emphasises the idea of disciplining the female body in public, whether symbolically or physically. This is how these texts remain generative of morality discourses.

A core concern I have is the idea of popular culture as mediator of problematic discourses. I argue though, that in order to understand fully the role that popular culture plays, one has to read popular culture in relation to conventional cultural thought, state ideology and patriarchy. Popular media take the form of drama, advice columns, gossip and entertainment, tragic news blown out of proportion, news that intends to shock, and so on. I am interested in how these various forms come to transmit conventional and institutional knowledges in such a way that women become circulated and eventually translated as moral subjects. I argue that public constructions and circulations of femininity work through pre-convened public scripts, which I describe as publicly endorsed moral narratives supported by existing colonial and traditional patriarchal structures. The idea of the public script is based on the idea of sexual scripts as conceptualised by John Gagnon and William Simon

(2017) who argue that these scripts shape how sexuality is interpreted as ideological constructs.

I am also concerned with questions of sexuality and morality, as two ideas that converge and diverge in interesting ways throughout the book. Sexuality is often married to morality in contexts where social conventions on behaviour reign. Behaviour is sanctioned privately and publicly. Indeed, I focus on the intersections between public sentiment, disciplinary regimes and subjective positions on sexuality as constructed within texts. If we engage with a nuanced reading of these two dynamics, and understand how the very process of becoming and unbecoming is gendered, how might we read women who have to exist in spaces that mete out violence as modes of correcting 'bad' behaviour? How can a productive reading of texts that circulate familiar stereotypes of femininity provoke a counter-reading, or disruptive publics? How might one read visibility as a location of agency, even where visibility makes subjects vulnerable?

I chose three platforms that I felt would offer adequate spaces for interrogation across a range of media. Drawing on ideas of transmediation that define contemporary media, I argued that the public script works across texts in ways that go beyond specificities of genres. I looked at a radio programme that was produced for the state broadcaster, but that also linked to colonial Kenya in ways that allowed me to make arguments about the role radio played in the construction of African womanhood. Radio drama in Kenya is part of state ideology, as it has historically been produced for the state. Radio drama is also steeped in the domestic sphere, in a way de-politicising it by bringing it back to the politics of the home. In the book, however, I look at the ways in which radio drama systematically aligns itself with the domestic space as a way of navigating the national space. In doing so, women become categorised as either proper or deviant. Little space is provided to engage with the myriad other possibilities of womanhood that allow for a more complex engagement with such meanings. Radio drama, as I have shown, becomes one of the key sites for regulating femininity, and though circulated as edutainment, remains embedded in strict expectations of heteronormative belonging. I look at women who transgress these spaces, where they appear in the media, how they become sources of spectacle and humour, and how the work of the media remains consistently that of containing these women. Lastly, I look at the women who refuse to be contained. This last category of women draws our attention to the fragile state of the heterosexual nation. The nation is dependent upon a politics of heteronormativity, with the family as its core centre. Women who refuse punishment, as has been argued by a myriad of feminists and other cultural thinkers, become important sites for imagining change.

To understand how these discourses unfold, it is useful to engage with the idea of the heterosexual nation, or what Lauren Berlant and Michael Warner term 'national heterosexuality', which they define as 'the mechanism by which a core national culture can be imagined as a sanitised space of sentimental feeling and immaculate behaviour, a space of pure citizenship' (1998, 549). In this model, the family is central, as a site for the 'aspirations of national belonging', so that those aspiring to this idea of the nation become separated from their critical roles in the public sphere as citizens. In other words, the family becomes a way of diverting any crucial discussions about sexual discrimination, exclusion and sexual rights. In his chapter on sexual minorities, law and policy in Kenya, Keguro Macharia (2013) expands on the idea of national heterosexuality. He assesses three pivotal legal and policy documents in Kenya: the Sexual Offences Act (2006), the National Policy on Culture and Heritage (2009) and the new constitution (2010). In his analysis, Macharia argues that the family unit has been used to structure bills and policy documents meant to protect all citizens of Kenya. Macharia challenges a claim made by advocates of the Sexual Offences bill (before it was passed into law in 2006) that the family is the foundation of the Kenyan society. For him, such a claim 'rewrites and erases Kenya's urban histories of prostitution, class-based histories embodied in Kenya's very important trade unions, multi-ethnic coalitions that function outside of kin-based frameworks, and the violent histories of colonialism that forged unities out of disparate groups' (2013, 279). The claim refuses to attend to the differences and diversities that form the Kenyan nation.

I also engage with the complexities presented by femininity discourses in Kenya. I assess a number of media sources in order to determine the ways in which the media remain embedded in the project of regulation. I use different examples to engage critically with ways in which unbelonging for the woman is defined inside of the heteronormative nation. My work is deliberately about femininity. I chose femininity as a way of signalling a problematic culture that targets women. However, it is impossible not to engage with queer scholarship in thinking through the idea of heteronormativity. In Kenya, for instance, laws about LGBTQIA individuals are often quite telling in terms of who is a part of the heteronormative family. It is therefore important to underline the significance of the body of scholarship in the field of queer studies. It is my hope that this book contributes to a much more nuanced debate about women and the construction of femininity in the public sphere. The morality angle that continues to dictate the very tenet of being for woman in Kenya needs to be properly interrogated.

To engage radio, tabloids and entertainment newspapers, and social media platforms is to engage media at specific historical and political standpoints. While other forms of media exist, I found these three platforms offered range both in terms of the mode – aural, written and visual texts – and in terms of the various media's 'place' in history. Each mode produces particular historical narratives that enable one to build a narrative of Kenyan public cultures, however general. While radio drama is attached to state policy and ideology, tabloids and entertainment newspapers trace a different kind of public culture that is embedded in shame, scandal, gossip and sensation. Signalling the melodramatic moral narrative in radio drama, I have shown how tabloid stories that carry gossip or scandal about a woman creates a public that is receptive to its simplified mode. Similarly, the element of the spectacle is contained in the way women's bodies are exhibited online.

I deconstruct the dominant ideologies that present themselves as natural by engaging in the power of popular culture to disrupt, to re-write and to re-articulate. For instance, I argue that tabloids tap into informal networks of knowledge that make it possible to form alternative knowledges and to address a counterpublic. I consider the digital public script and ways in which women create disruptive publics. These disruptive publics are generated through women's presentations of their bodies in the context of expected notions of respectability. As such, hypervisibility becomes an embrace of difficulty, even in the face of vulnerability. Agency is located in the violence, not outside of it. This agency can be read as ambiguous, given its location in the vulnerable exposed body. I have argued elsewhere in an article on vulnerability and trafficked bodies (Ligaga 2019) that vulnerability need not be interpreted as helplessness. Rather, following Judith Butler (2010), I argue that vulnerability can be troubled in order to relocate the woman's body to a place of presence and visibility. By becoming present and visible, vulnerability offers a woman the opportunity to survive the precarious conditions of life (Butler 2010). It exposes one to violence, but in doing so, 'allows one to gather the will to live, survive, and endure' (Ligaga 2019, 76). The modes of transgression as contained in texts become the points at which visibility becomes possible.

Politics of respectability in Africa are tied to religion, colonialism and traditional patriarchy. In the book, I unpack the meanings of Victorian sexuality and its influences on respectability politics. I read Victorian notions of sexuality in contexts of formation in Africa, and engage with how these ideas of sexuality travel and are re-appropriated in the building of empire (Stoler 1989). I engage scholarship that explores what this re-appropriation meant in Africa. In the construction of African womanhood, respectability politics meant that one had to be civilised. Scholars such as Tabitha Kanogo (2005) show though, that African women have negotiated terrains presented to them, using their existing agencies to navigate stringent laws about their bodies. I point out that mobility became the most threatening aspect of womanhood in Africa, given that it allowed women to break several laws. As Stoler (1989) argues, white women in the context of colonialism were presented to African women as the ideal feminine figures. The African woman was meant to emulate this femininity in order to be recognised as civilised. In the context of colonial modernity, however,

African women challenged suggestions to become 'proper' women who were civilised by moving away from traditional patriarchal set-ups and religious dogma found in newly constituted Christian churches. Mobility became a way of exercising freedom (Kanogo 2005). Narratives of sexual promiscuity, generated from different temporal locales, eventually defined how African womanhood would be read.

The control of women's bodies was embedded in the surveillance of women's movement in order to create governable citizens and manage sexual behaviour. I have explored what it would mean to read disruptive subjectivities within such contexts. Reading texts as capable of generating disruptive publics, I consider visibility a crucial methodological tool for assessing such disruptions. I read disruption in oppressive and unequal contexts. I use feminism to rupture the dominant discourses and to emphasise the displacement of these discourses. In my methodology, I deliberately select taken-for-granted myths, precisely because, I argue, the genre in which they circulate — tabloids and other popular culture sites — prevents them from being interrogated for the harm they cause. They seem obvious. This book contributes towards a critical dismantling of dominant frameworks that frame femininities.

While I have tried to engage a series of examples from Kenya, I am aware that this book is far from exhaustive in its engagement with the issues affecting women. I would, for instance, have liked to spend more time assessing the violence occurring in several other spaces defined by public sentiment. Violence in the workplace, Kenya's #MeToo moment and other examples are yet unexplored. I also know that platforms such as Twitter offer rich sources of data that demonstrates ways in which women are 'fighting back' systems of violence. Strong voices of Kenyans on Twitter (KOT) are emerging to challenge existing structures of violence within public institutions as well as in private spaces. The work of scholars, such as Nanjala Nyabola (2018), is shifting the terrain for engaging change and pushing for transformation in various facets of Kenyan life. In closing, I am aware that I take a heteronormative approach in the assessment of women in Kenyan popular media. This bias is partly the result of the examples I selected, which epitomize public conversation in the platforms that I have engaged with. There is, however, room for expansion and for a much more extensive reading of women's bodies inside and outside of heteronormative spaces.

Bibliography

Abu-Lughod, L. 2002. "Egyptian Melodrama: Technology of the Modern Subject." In *Media Worlds: Anthropology on New Terrain,* edited by Faye D. Ginsburg, Lila Abu-Lughod and Brian Larkin, 112–133. Berkeley: University of California Press.

Achebe, C. 1966. *A Man of the People*. London: Heinemann.

Ahmed, S. 2010. *The Promise of Happiness*. Durham: Duke University Press. doi:10.1215/9780822392781.

Ahmed, S. 2014. *Wilful subjects*. Durham: Duke University Press. doi:10.1215/9780822376101.

Ahmed, S. 2017. *Living a Feminist Life*. Durham, NC: Duke University Press. doi:10.1215/9780822373377.

Akech, A. 2010. "(Re)turn of Women: Post-Moi's Kenya and Electoral Politics in Kalenjin Rift Valley." In *Tensions and Reversals in Democratic Transitions: The Kenya 2007 General Elections,* edited by K. Kanyinga and D. Okello. Nairobi: Society for International Development (SID) and Institute for Development Studies (IDS), University of Nairobi.

Akujobi, R. 2011. "Motherhood in African literature and culture." *CLCWeb: Comparative Literature and Culture* 13 (1): 2–7.

Amadiume, I. 1987. *African Matriarchal Foundations: The Case of Igbo Societies*. London: Karnak House.

Amutabi, M. 2007. "Neither Bold nor Beautiful: Interrogating the Impact of Western Soap Operas on Africa." Paper presented at the Conference on Popular Cultures in Africa, University of Texas at Austin, March 30–April 1.

Andersson, F. B. 2002. "Isidingo: Between Memory Box and Healing Couch." MA thesis, University of the Witwatersrand, Johannesburg.

Andrade, S. Z. 2011. *The Nation Writ Small: African Fictions and Feminisms, 1958–1988*. Durham: Duke University Press. doi:10.1215/9780822393740.

Bibliography

Ang, I. 1985. *Watching Dallas: Soap Opera and the Melodramatic Imagination*. London: Routledge.

Ang, I. 2007. "Television Fictions Around the World: Melodrama and Irony in Global Perspective." *Critical Studies in Television* 2 (2): 18–30. doi:10.7227/CST.2.2.4.

Appadurai, A. 1995. "Playing with modernity." In *Consuming Modernity: Public Culture in a South Asian World*, edited by C. A. Breckenridge, 23–48. Minneapolis: University of Minnesota Press.

Arnfred, S., ed. 2004. *Re-thinking sexualities in Africa*. Uppsala: Nordic Africa Institute.

Åsberg, C., 2007. "Spectacular Queens and the Morals of Excessive Femininity: A Feminist Approach to Public History." *Linköping Electronic Conference Proceedings*. Linköpings Universitet: Linköping University Electronic Press.

Atieno-Odhiambo, E. S. 2000. *Luo Perspectives on Knowledge and Development: Samuel G. Ayany and Paul Mbuya. African Philosophy as Cultural Inquiry*. Bloomington: Indiana University Press.

Aubrey, L. M. 1997. *The Politics of Development Cooperation: NGOs, Gender and Partnership in Kenya*. New York: Routledge. doi:10.4324/9780203442302.

Bakhtin, M. M. 1981. *The Dialogic Imagination: Four Essays*. Translated by Caryl Emerson and Michael Holquist and edited by Michael Holquist. Austin: University of Texas Press.

Banet-Weiser, S. 2015. "Keynote Address: Media, Markets, Gender: Economies of Visibility in a Neoliberal Moment." *Communication Review* 18 (1):53–70. doi:10.1080/10714421.2015.996398.

Barber, K. 1987. "Popular Arts in Africa." *African Studies Review* 30 (3): 1–78. doi:10.2307/524538.

Barber, K. 1997. "Preliminary Notes on Audiences in Africa." *Africa* 67 (3): 347–62. doi:10.2307/1161179.

Barber, K. 2000. *The Generation of Plays: Yoruba Popular Life in Theater*. Bloomington: Indiana University Press.

Barber, K. 2018. *A History of African Popular Culture*. UK: Cambridge University Press. doi:10.1017/9781139061766.

Barker, C. 2004. *The SAGE Dictionary of Cultural Studies*. London: SAGE publications. doi:10.4135/9781446221280.

Barlow, T., M. Yue Dong, U. Poiger, P. Ramamurthy, L. M. Thomas, and A. E. Weinbaum. 2005. "The Modern Girl Around the World: A Research Agenda and Preliminary Findings." *Gender & History* 17 (2): 245–94. doi:10.1111/j.0953-5233.2006.00382.x.

Barnes, T. A. 1992. "The Fight for Control of African Women's Mobility in Colonial Zimbabwe, 1900–1939." *Signs: Journal of Women in Culture and Society*, 17 (3): 586–608.

Bastian, M. L. 1993. "'Bloodhounds who have no friends': Witchcraft and Locality in the Nigerian Popular Press." In *Modernity and its Malcontents: Ritual and Power in Postcolonial Africa*, edited by J. Comaroff and J. Comaroff, 129–166. Chicago: University of Chicago Press.

Baum, M. A. 2002. "Sex, Lies, and War: How Soft News Brings Foreign Policy to the Inattentive Public." *American Political Science Review* 96 (1): 91–109. doi:10.1017/S0003055402004252.

Berger, I. 2016. *Women in Twentieth-century Africa*. Cambridge, United Kingdom: Cambridge University Press. doi:10.1017/CBO9780511979972.

Berlant, L. G. 2011. *Cruel Optimism*. Duke University Press. doi:10.1215/9780822394716.

Berlant, L., and M. Warner. 1998. "Sex in Public." *Critical Inquiry* 24 (2): 547–66. doi:10.1086/448884.

Bey, M. 2017. "Beyoncé's Black (Ab)Normal: Baaad Insurgency and the Queerness of Slaying." *Black Camera* 9 (1): 164–78. doi:10.2979/blackcamera.9.1.10.

Bhabha, H. 1994. *The Location of Culture*. London: Routledge.

Bingham, A., and M. Conboy. 2015. *Tabloid Century: The Popular Press in Britain, 1896 to the Present*. Oxford: Peter Lang. doi:10.3726/978-3-0353-0700-9.

Bjorkman, I. 1989. *Mother, Sing for Me: People's Theatre in Kenya*. London: Zed Books.

Brooks, P. 1976. *The Melodramatic Imagination: Blazac*. New Haven: Yale University Press.

Brown, M. E. 1994. *Soap Opera and Women's Talk: The Pleasure of Resistance.* Thousand Oaks: Sage.

Bryce, J. 1997. "Women and Modern African Popular Fiction." In *Readings in African Popular Culture*, edited by K. Barber, 118–124. Bloomington, Indiana: Indiana University Press.

Buiten, D., and E. Salo. 2007. "Silences Stifling Transformation: Misogyny and Gender-based Violence in the Media." *Agenda (Durban, South Africa)* 21 (71): 115–21.

Burke, T. 1996. *Lifebuoy Men, Lux Women: Commodification, Consumption, and Cleanliness in Modern Zimbabwe.* Durham: Duke University Press.

Butler, J. 1990. *Gender Trouble: Feminism and the Subversion of Identity.* New York: Routledge.

Butler, J. 2010. *Frames of War: When is Life Grievable?* London: Verso.

Cabral, A. 1970. *National Liberation and Culture.* Eduardo Mondlane Memorial Lecture. Issue 57 of Occasional Paper, Syracuse University Program of Eastern African Studies.

Cai, B. 2008. "A trickster-like Woman: Subversive Imagining and Narrating of Social Change." *Communication Studies* 59 (4): 275–90. doi:10.1080/10510970802257580.

Chandler, D. 2002. *Semiotics: The Basics.* Routledge. doi:10.4324/9780203166277.

Cloete, E. 2006. "A Time of Living Dangerously: Flanking Histories to Wambui Waiyaki Otieno's Account of Mau Mau." *English in Africa* 33 (1): 113–35.

Cohen, D. W., and E. A. Odhiambo. 1992. *Burying SM: The Politics of Knowledge and the Sociology of Power in Africa.* Portsmouth, NH: Heinemann.

Cohen, S. 1972. *Folk Devils and Moral Panics: The creation of the Mods and Rockers.* London: MacGibbon & Kee.

Cohen, W. A. 1996. *Sex Scandal: The Private Parts of Victorian Fiction.* Durham: Duke University Press. doi:10.1215/9780822398028.

Cole, J. 2010. *Sex and Salvation: Imagining the Future in Madagascar.* Chicago, IL: University of Chicago Press. doi:10.7208/chicago/9780226113326.001.0001.

Cole, J., and L. M. Thomas, eds. 2009. *Love in Africa.* Chicago: University of

Chicago Press. doi:10.7208/chicago/9780226113555.001.0001.

Collins, P. H. 2000. "Gender, Black Feminism, and Black Political Economy." *Annals of the American Academy of Political and Social Science* 568 (1): 41–53. doi:10.1177/000271620056800105.

Cooper, M Lynne. Mar 2002. "Alcohol Use and Risky Sexual Behavior among College Students and Youth: Evaluating the Evidence." *Journal of Studies on Alcohol* 63 (14): 101–17. doi:10.15288/jsas.2002.s14.101. PMID:12022716.

Cornell, D. 1995. "What is Ethical Feminism?" In *Feminist Contentions: A philosophical exchange*, edited by S. Benhabib, J. Butler, D. Cornell and N. Fraser, 75–106. New York: Routledge.

Cornwall, A., ed. 2005. *Introduction. Readings in Gender in Africa*. Oxford: James Currey.

Crook, T. 1999. *Radio Drama: Theory and Practice*. London: Routledge.

Cutrufelli, M. 1983. *Women of Africa: Roots of Oppression*. London: Zed Press.

De Certeau, M. 1984. *The Practice of Everyday Life*. Translated by Steven Rendall. Berkeley: University of California Press.

Dean, J. 2009. *Democracy and Other Neoliberal Fantasies: Communicative Capitalism and Left Politics*. Durham: Duke University Press. doi:10.1215/9780822390923.

Deem, M. 1999. "Scandal, Heteronormative Culture, and the Disciplining of Feminism." *Critical Studies in Media Communication* 16 (1): 86–93. doi:10.1080/15295039909367074.

Diop, C. A. 1978. *The Cultural Unity of Black Africa: The Domains of Patriarchy and Matriarchy in Classical Antiquity*. Chicago: Third World Press.

Dosekun, S. 2015. "For Western Girls Only?" *Feminist Media Studies* 15 (6): 960–75. doi:10.1080/14680777.2015.1062991.

Dyer, R. 1979. *The Stars*. London: British Film Institute.

Fabian, J. 1978. "Popular culture in Africa: Findings and conjectures." *Africa* 48 (4): 315–34. doi:10.2307/1158799.

Fairhurst, G., and R. Sarr. 1996. *The Art of Framing*. San Francisco: Jossey-Bass.

Fardon, R. and G. Furniss, eds. 2000. *African Broadcast Cultures: Radio in Transition*. Oxford, UK: J. Currey.

Farganis, S. 1996. *Social Reconstruction of the Feminine Character*. Lanham, Maryland: Rowman & Littlefield.

Farvid, P., and V. Braun. 2013. "Casual Sex as 'Not a Natural Act' and other Regimes of Truth about Heterosexuality." *Feminism & Psychology* 23 (3): 359–78. doi:10.1177/0959353513480018.

Finlay, S. J., and V. Clarke. 2003. "'A Marriage of Inconvenience?' Feminist Perspectives on Marriage." *Feminism & Psychology* 13 (4): 415–20. doi:10.1177/09593535030134002.

Finn, M. 2012. "Monogamous Order and the Avoidance of Chaotic Excess." *Psychology and Sexuality* 3 (2): 123–36. doi:10.1080/19419899.2011.551834.

Finnegan, R. 2012. *Oral Literature in Africa*. Cambridge, UK: Open Book. Publishers. doi:10.11647/OBP.0025.

Fluck, W. 1987. "Popular Culture as a Mode of Socialization: A Theory about the Social Functions of Popular Cultural Forms." *Journal of Popular Culture* 21 (3): 31–46. doi:10.1111/j.0022-3840.1987.2103_31.x.

Forsyth, F. 1982. *No Comebacks*. New York: Corgi.

Foucault, M. 1972. *The Archaeology of Knowledge*. Translated by A. M. Sheridan Smith. New York: Pantheon.

Foucault, M. 1982. "The Subject and Power." *Critical Inquiry* 8 (4): 777–95. doi:10.1086/448181.

Foucault, M. 1988. "Technologies of the Self." In *Technologies of the Self: A Seminar with Michel Foucault*, edited by L. H. Martin, H. Gutman, and P. H. Hutton, 16–49. Amherst : University of Massachusetts Press.

Franklin, B. 1997. *Newszak and News Media*. London: Arnold.

Frederiksen, B. F. 2000. "Popular Culture, Gender Relations and the Democratization of Everyday Life in Kenya." *Journal of Southern African Studies* 26 (2): 209–22. doi:10.1080/03057070050010075.

Freeman, E. 2005. "Time Binds, or, Erotohistoriography." *Social Text* 23 (3-4 (84-85)): 57–68. doi:10.1215/01642472-23-3-4_84-85-57.

Fuchs, C. 2015. "Surveillance and Critical Theory." *Media and Communication* 3 (2) doi:10.17645/mac.v3i2.207.

Gagnon, J., and W. Simon. 2017. *Sexual Conduct: The Social Sources of Human Sexuality*. 2nd ed. New Brunswick, London: Aldine Transaction. doi:10.4324/9781315129242.

Gamson, J. 2001a. "Normal Sins: Sex Scandal Narratives as Institutional Morality Tales." *Social Problems* 48 (2): 185–205. doi:10.1525/sp.2001.48.2.185.

Gamson, J. 2001b. "Jessica Hahn, Media Whore: Sex Scandals and Female Publicity." *Critical Studies in Media Communication* 18 (2): 157–73. doi:10.1080/07393180128082.

Gamson, J. 2011. "The Unwatched Life is Not Worth Living: The Elevation of the Ordinary in Celebrity Culture." *PMLA* 126 (4): 1061–1069. doi:10.1632/pmla.2011.126.4.1061.

Gauvin, L. R. 2013. "In and Out of Culture: Okot p'Bitek's Work and Social Repair in Post-Conflict Acoliland." *Oral Tradition* 28 (1). doi:10.1353/ort.2013.0008.

Genz, S. 2009. *Postfemininities in popular culture*. Basingstoke: Palgrave Macmillan. doi:10.1057/9780230234413.

Geraghty, C. 1991. *Women and Soap Opera: A Study of Prime Time Soaps*. Cambridge: Polity Press in association with Blackwell.

Gergen, M. M. 1990. "Finished at 40: Women's Development within the Patriarchy." *Psychology of Women Quarterly* 14 (4): 471–93. doi:10.1111/j.1471-6402.1990.tb00225.x.

Gikuru, S. 2014. "The battle of the tabloids." Blog entry. Accessed 28 October 2019. https://samwagik.wordpress.com/2014/07/09/battle-of-the-tabloids/

Gill, R. 2007. "Postfeminist Media Culture: Elements of a Sensibility." *European Journal of Cultural Studies* 10 (2): 147–166. doi:10.1177/1367549407075898.

Gill, R., and C. Scharff, eds. 2011. *Introduction. New Femininities: Postfeminism, Neoliberalism and Subjectivity*. Basingstoke, UK: Palgrave Macmillan. doi:10.1057/9780230294523.

Giraud, Eva. 2015. "Subjectivity 2.0: Digital Technologies, Participatory Media and Communicative Capitalism." *Subjectivity* 8 (2): 124–46. doi:10.1057/sub.2015.5.

Githiora, W. 2007. *Wanjira*. Indianapolis: Dog Ear Publishers.

Goro, V. and S. Muluka-Lutta. 1991. "An Analysis of the Roles portrayed by Women in Television Advertising: Nature and Extent of Sexism Present." Unpublished research paper, School of Journalism, University of Nairobi.

Gqibitole, K. 2002. "Contestations of Traditions in Xhosa Radio Drama under Apartheid." *English Studies in Africa* 45 (2): 33–46. doi:10.1080/00138390208691313.

Gqola, P. D. 2004. "When a Good Black Woman is your Weekend Special: Brenda Fassie, Sexuality and Performance." In *Under Construction: 'Race' and Identity in South Africa Today*, edited by Natasha Distiller and Melissa E. Steyn. Oxford: Heinemann.

Gqola, P. D. 2015. *Rape: A South African Nightmare*. Johannesburg: MF Books.

Gqola, P. D. 2017. *Reflecting Rogue: Inside the Mind of a Feminist*. Johannesburg: MF Books.

Gunner, L. 2000. "Wrestling with the Present, Beckoning the Past: Contemporary Zulu Radio Drama." *Journal of Southern African Studies* 26 (2): 223–37. doi:10.1080/03057070050010084.

Gunner, L. 2019. *Radio Soundings: South Africa and the Black Modern*. Johannesburg: Wits University Press. doi:10.1017/9781108556903.

Gunner, L., D. Ligaga, and D. Moyo. 2011. *Radio in Africa: Publics, Cultures, Communities*. Johannesburg: Wits University Press.

Hall, S. 1993. "What is this 'Black' in Black Popular Culture?" *Social Justice* 20 (1/2) (51-52), Rethinking Race (Spring-Summer 1993): 104–114.

Hall, S. 1997. "The Work of Representation." In *Representation: Cultural Representations and Signifying Practices*, edited by S. Hall, 13–72. London: Sage in association with the Open University.

Heath, C. 1986. "Broadcasting in Kenya: Policy and Politics, 1928–1984." Doctoral dissertation, University of Illinois, Urbana, IL.

Hilmes, M., and J. Loviglio, eds. 2002. *Radio Reader*. Great Britain: Routledge.

Hodgson, D., and S. McCurdy. 2001. *Wicked Women and the Reconfiguration of Gender in Africa*. Portsmouth, NH: Heinemann.

hooks, b. 1996. *Reel to Real: Race, Sex and Class at the Movies*. London: Routledge.

hooks, b. 1997. *Wounds of Passion: A Writing Life*. New York City: H. Holt.

Hunter, M. 2002. "The Materiality of Everyday Sex: Thinking Beyond Prostitution." *African Studies* 61 (1): 99–120. doi:10.1080/00020180220140091.

Insaidoo, K. A. 2011. *Moral Lessons in African Folktales*. Bloomington, Indiana: AuthorHouse.

Iqani, M. 2016. *Consumption, Media and the Global South: Aspiration Contested*. Pietermaritzburg: University of KwaZulu-Natal Press. doi:10.1057/9781137390134.

Jackson, S., and S. Scott. 2004. "Sexual Antinomies in Late Modernity." *Sexualities* 7 (2): 233–48. doi:10.1177/1363460704042166.

Jamieson, L. 2004. "Intimacy, Negotiated Non-monogamy and the Limits of the Couple." In *The State of Affairs: Explorations in Infidelity and Commitment*, edited by Jean Duncombe, Kaeren Harrison, Graham Allan, and Dennis Marsden, 35–57. Mahwah, New Jersey: Lawrence Erlbaum Associates.

Jenkins, H. 2006. *Fans, Bloggers, and Gamers: Exploring Participatory Culture*. New York: NYU Press.

Jones, J. L., and B. R. Weber. 2015. "Reality Moms, Real Monsters: Transmediated Continuity, Reality Celebrity, and the Female Grotesque." *Camera Obscura: Feminism, Culture, and Media Studies* 30 (1 (88)): 11–39. doi:10.1215/02705346-2885431.

Kahiu, W., dir. 2018. *Rafiki*. Film.

Kalulu, N. 19 December 2006. Interview. Nairobi.

Kanogo, T. 2005. *African Womanhood in Colonial Kenya, 1900–1950*. Oxford: James Currey; Nairobi: EAEP; Athens: Ohio University Press.

Kassilly, B. J. N., and K. Onkware. 2010. "Struggles and Success in Engendering the African Public Sphere: Kenyan Women in Politics." *Kenya Studies Review* 3 (3): 71–83.

Kehrer, L. 2019. "Who Slays? Queer Resonances in Beyoncé's Lemonade." *Popular Music and Society* 42 (1): 82–98. doi:10.1080/03007766.2019.1555896.

Keller, J. M. 2012. "Fiercely Real? Tyra Banks and the Making of New Media

Celebrity." *Feminist Media Studies* 14 (1): 147–64. doi:10.1080/14680777.201
2.740490.

Kellner, D. 2003. *Media Spectacle*. London: Routledge. doi:10.4324/9780203166383.

Kenyatta, J. 1964. *Harambee! The Prime Minister of Kenya's Speeches 1963–1964*.
Nairobi: Oxford University Press.

Kinder, M. 1991. *Playing with power in movies, television, and video games: from
Muppet Babies to Teenage Mutant Ninja Turtles*. California: Univ of California
Press.

Kiriamiti, J. 1984. *My Life in Crime*. Nairobi: EAEP.

Klein, V. 1971. *The feminine character: History of an ideology*. vol. 298. Illinois:
University of Illinois Press.

Kristeva, J. 2002. "'Nous Deux' or a (Hi)story of Intertextuality." *Romanic Review* 93
(1/2): 7–13.

Langland, E. 2002. *Telling Tales: Gender and Narrative Form in Victorian Literature
and Culture*. Ohio State University Press.

Leclerc-Madlala, S. 2003. "Transactional sex and the pursuit of modernity." *Social
Dynamics* 29 (2): 213–33. doi:10.1080/02533950308628681.

Lewis, J. 2000. *Empire State-building: War and Welfare in Kenya 1925–1952*. Oxford:
James Currey.

Ligaga, D. 2005. "Enacting the Quotidian in Kenyan Radio Drama: Not Now
and the Narrative of Forced Marriage." *Radio Journal: International Studies in
Broadcast & Audio Media* 3 (2): 107–19. doi:10.1386/rajo.3.2.107/1.

Ligaga, D. 2012. "'Virtual expressions': Alternative Online Spaces and the
Staging of Kenyan Popular Cultures." *Research in African Literatures* 43 (4)
in *Measuring Time: Karin Barber and the Study of Everyday Africa*, edited by
Onookome Okome and Stephanie Newell (Guest Editors), 1–16.

Ligaga, D. 2019. "Ambiguous Agency in the Vulnerable Trafficked Body: Reading
Sanusi's 'Eyo' and Unigwe's 'On Black Sisters Street'." *Tydskrif vir Letterkunde*
56 (1): 74–88. doi:10.17159/2309-9070/tvl.v.56i1.6274.

Lonsdale, John, Otieno, Wambui, and Presley, Cora. 2001. "Mau Mau's Daughter:
A Life History." *Canadian Journal of African Studies* 71 (2): 325–327.

doi:10.2307/1161531.

Lorde, A. 1982. *Zami: A New Spelling of My Name*. New York: Trumansburg.

Lorde, A. 1984. *Sister Outsider*. Berkeley, California: Crossing Press.

Loughran, G. 2010. *Birth of a Nation: The Story of a Newspaper in Kenya*. London, New York: IB Tauris.

Lutta, Sophie-Muluka and Victoria Goro. 1991. "An Analysis of the Roles Portrayed by Women in Television Advertising: Nature and Extent of Sexism Present." Research Thesis. School of Journalism, University of Nairobi.

Maathai, W. 2007. *Unbowed: A Memoir*. London: William Heinemann.

MacDonald, M. 1995. *Representing Women: Myths of Femininity in the Popular Culture*. London: Edward Arnold.

Macharia, K. 2013. "Queer Kenya in Law and Policy." In *Queer African Reader*, edited by S. Ekine and H. Abbas, 273–289. Dakar: Pambazuka Press.

Macharia, K. 2015. "Archive and Method in Queer African Studies." *Agenda (Durban, South Africa)* 29 (1): 140–46. doi:10.1080/10130950.2015.1010294.

Macharia, K., 2011. On Mercy Keino. *Gukira*. Accessed September 30, 2013. http://gukira.wordpress.com/2011/08/08/on-mercy-keino/

Maitland, S. 2014. *How to be Alone*. Basingstoke: Macmillan.

Makholwa, A. 2017. *The Blessed Girl*. Johannesburg: Pan Macmillan.

Mangua, C. 1971. *Son of Woman*. Nairobi: East African Publishing House.

Marinelli, K. 2015. "The Material Labour of Pseudo Celebrity: Rethinking Use and Exchange Value in Late Capitalism." Paper presented at the fourth annual Celebrity Project, Mansfield College, University of Oxford, 26 July.

Marshall, D. P. 1997. *Celebrity and Power: Fame in Contemporary Culture*. Minneapolis: University of Minnesota Press.

Masango, L. 2019. "Johannesburg, Sex, Love and Money: An Ethnography of Phones and Feelings." Unpublished MA research report, University of the Witwatersrand, South Africa.

Masenya, M (Ngwan'a Mphahlele). 2017. "Reading Proverbs 7 in the Context of Female 'Blessers' and Sugar Mamas in South Africa." *Scriptura* 116 (2):

120–132. doi:10.7833/116-2-1316.

Masvawure, Tsitsi. 2010. "'I Just Need to be Flashy on Campus': Female Students and Transactional Sex at a University in Zimbabwe." *Culture, Health & Sexuality* 12 (8): 857–70. doi:10.1080/13691050903471441. PMID:20069476.

Mbure, W. G. 2018. "Heroic Transverser: A Rhetorical Analysis of Representations of Wangari Maathai in Kenyan Press." In *The Rhetorical legacy of Wangari Maathai: Planting the Future*, edited by Eddah M. Mutai, Alberto Gonzalez and Anke Wolbert, 63–82. Lanham: Lexington Books.

McClintock, A. 1995. *Imperial Leather: Race, Gender and Sexuality in the Colonial Contest*. New York: Routledge.

McCombs, M. 2002. "The Agenda-setting Role of the Mass Media in the Shaping of Public Opinion." University of Texas at Austin. Accessed at https://www.infoamerica.org/documentos_pdf/mccombs01.pdf.

McFadden, P. 2003. "Sexual Pleasure as Feminist Choice." *Feminist Africa* 2: 50–60. Accessed at http://www.agi.ac.za/sites/default/files/image_tool/images/429/feminist_africa_journals/archive/02/fa_2_standpoint_1.pdf.

McGee, M. C. 1990. "Text, Context, and the Fragmentation of Contemporary Culture." *Western Journal of Communication* 54 (3): 274–89.

McKee, A. 2005. *The Public Sphere: An Introduction*. Cambridge: Cambridge University Press.

McKinnon, S. 2014. "Text-Based Approaches to Qualitative Research." In *The International Encyclopedia of Media Studies*, 1st ed., general editor Angharad N. Valdivia, vol. VII: *Research Methods in Media Studies*, edited by Fabienne Darling-Wolf. Hoboken, New Jersey: John Wiley & Sons, Ltd.

McRobbie, A. 2007. "Postfeminism and Popular Culture: Bridget Jones and the New Gender Regime." In *Interrogating Postfeminism: Gender and the Politics of Popular Culture*, edited by Yvonne Tasker and Diane Negra, 27–39. Durham: Duke University Press. doi:10.1215/9780822390411-002.

McRobbie, A. 2011. *Preface in R. Gill and C. Scharff, New Femininities: Postfeminism, Neoliberalism and Subjectivity*. Basingstoke: Palgrave Macmillan.

Mohammed, S. A. 2000. *Kitumbua Kimeingia Mchanga*. Nairobi: Oxford University Press.

Mohammed, S. M. 1972. *Kiu*. Nairobi: East African Publishers.

Mojola, S. 2014. *Love, Money, and HIV: Becoming a Modern African Woman in the Age of AIDS*. Oakland, California: University of California Press. doi:10.1525/california/9780520280939.001.0001.

Motsemme, N. 2004. "The Mute Always Speak: On Women's Silences at the Truth and Reconciliation Commission." *Current Sociology* 52 (5): 909–932. doi:10.1177/0011392104045377.

Mowatt, R., B. French, and D. Malebranche. 2013. "Black/female/body Hypervisibility and Invisibility: A Black Feminist Augmentation of Feminist Leisure Research." *Journal of Leisure Research* 45 (5): 644–60. doi:10.18666/jlr-2013-v45-i5-4367.

Mowatt, Rasul A., Bryana H. French, and Dominique A. Malebranche. 2013. "Black/Female/Body Hypervisibility and Invisibility." *Journal of Leisure Research* 45 (5): 644–660. doi:10.18666/jlr-2013-v45-i5-4367.

Muema, N. 2018. "Ways and Mannerisms of Slayqueens Revealed." *Eve Digital*, January 27. https://www.standardmedia.co.ke/evewoman/article/2001267442/era-of-slayqueens-how-to-spot-a-slayqueen-from-miles-away

Mukhongo, L. L. 2014. "Reconstructing Gendered Narratives Online: Nudity for Popularity on Digital Platforms." *Ada: A Journal of Gender, New Media, and Technology* 5. doi:10.7264/N3K64GB3.

Mupotsa, D. 2014. "White Weddings." PhD thesis, University of the Witwatersrand, Johannesburg.

Mupotsa, D. S. 2011. "'From Nation To Family': Researching Gender And Sexuality." In *Researching Violence in Africa*, edited by Christopher Cramer, Laura Hammond and Johan Pottier, 95–109. Leiden: BRILL. doi:10.1163/ej.9789004203129.i-184.44.

Muriungi, A. 2004. "Romance, Love and Gender in Times of Crisis: HIV/AIDS in Kenyan Popular Fiction." PhD thesis, University of the Witwatersrand, Johannesburg.

Murray, J. 2018. "Disciplining Women: South African Literary Representations of Gendered Surveillance and Violence." *English Academy Review* 35 (2): 71–82. doi:10.1080/10131752.2018.1519922.

Musangi, J.B. 2008. "A Walk Through the Criminal's City: John Kiriamiti's 'My Life in Crime' and 'My Life in Prison'." MA dissertation, University of the Witwatersrand, Johannesburg.

Musila, G. A. 2005. "Age, Power and Sex in Modern Kenya: A Tale of Two Marriages." *Social Identities* 11 (2): 113–29. doi:10.1080/13504630500161490.

Musila, G. A. 2009. "Phallocracies and Gynocratic Transgressions: Gender, State Power and Kenyan Public Life." *Africa Insight* 39 (1): 39–57. doi:10.4314/ai.v39i1.51238AJOL.

Musila, G. A. 2015. *A Death Retold in Truth and Rumour: Kenya, Britain and the Julie Ward Murder.* Suffolk: Boydell & Brewer.

Mutahi, W. 1991. *Three Days on the Cross.* Heinemann Kenya. Ltd, Nairobi.

Mutongi, K. 2007. *Worries of the Heart: Widows, Family, and Community in Kenya.* Chicago: University of Chicago Press. doi:10.7208/chicago/9780226554228.001.0001.

Mwangi, M. W. 1996. "Gender Roles Portrayed in Kenyan Television Commercials." *Sex Roles* 34 (3-4): 205–14. doi:10.1007/BF01544296.

Mwangi, W. 2013. Silence is a Woman. *The New Inquiry,* June 4. Accessed at https://thenewinquiry.com/silence-is-a-woman/

Nasong'o, S. W., and T. Ayot. 2007. "Women in Kenya's Politics of Transition and Democratization." In *Kenya: The Struggle for Democracy*, edited by G. Murunga and S. Nasong'o, 164–196. New York: Zed Books.

Nead, L. 1988. *Myths of Sexuality: Representations of Women in Victorian Britain.* Oxford: B. Blackwell.

Nelson, N. 2002. "Representations of Men and Women, City and Town in Kenyan Novels of the 1970s and 1980s." In *Readings in African Popular Fiction,* edited by Stephanie Newell, 108–116. Oxford: James Currey:.

Newell, S. 2000. *Ghanaian Popular Fiction: 'Thrilling Discoveries in Conjugal Life' and Other Tales.* Oxford: James Currey.

Newell, S., ed. 2002. *Readings in African Popular Fiction.* Oxford: James Currey.

Ngula, Kyalo wa, Hellen K Mberia, and Ann Neville Miller. 2016. "Parental Mediation of Adolescent Media Use and Demographic Factors as Predictors of Kenyan High School Students' Exposure to Sexual Content in Television." *African Journal of AIDS Research* 15 (1): 1–8. doi:10.2989/16085906.2015.113 1727. PMID:27002353.

Ngunjiri, F. W. 2009. "Servant Leadership and Motherhood: Kenyan Women Finding fulfillment in Serving Humanity." Gender, Development and Globalization Working Paper No. 294. Available at www.wid.msu.edu/ resources/papers/pdf/WP294.pdf

Nnaemeka, O., ed. 2005. *Female Circumcision and the Politics of Knowledge: African Women in Imperialist Discourses*. Westport, Connecticut: Praeger, Greenwood Publishing Group.

Noble, S. U. 2013. "Hyper-visibility as a Means of Rendering Black Women and Girls Invisible. *InVisible Culture: An Electronic Journal for Visual Culture* 19 . http://hdl.handle.net/1802/28018.

Nwoga, D. 2002. "Onitsha Market Literature." In *Readings in African Popular Fiction*, edited by Stephanie Newell, 37–44. Oxford: James Currey.

Nyabola, N. 2018. *Digital Democracy, Analogue Politics: How the Internet Era is Transforming Politics in Kenya*. London: Zed Books.

Nyairo, J. 2004. "'Reading the referents': The Ghost of America in Contemporary Kenyan Popular Music. *Scrutiny2*, 9 (1): 39–55.

Nyamsenda, S. 2014. "Ubidhaishaji wa maumbile ya binadamu: toka Sarah Baartman mpaka Agnes Masogange'." Unpublished paper.

Nyanzi, S. 2011. "Unpacking the [Govern]mentality of African Sexuality." In *African Sexualities: A Reader*, edited by Sylvia Tamale, 477–501. Cape Town: Pambazuka Press.

Nzegwu, N. 2011. "'Osunality' (or African eroticism)." In *African Sexualities: A Reader*, edited by Sylvia Tamale, 253–270. Cape Town: Pambazuka Press.

Nzomo, M. 1997. "Kenyan Women in Politics and Public Decision Making." In *African Feminism: The Politics of Survival in sub-Saharan Africa*, edited by Gwendolyn Mikell, 232–254. Philadelphia: University of Pennsylvania Press.

Obbo, Christine. 1980. *African women: their struggles for economic independence*. London: Zed Books.

Obiechina, E. 1972. *Onitsha market literature*. London: Heinemann.

Ochwada, H. 2002. "Church Missionary Society and the Reconstruction of Gender Roles in Western Kenya, 1919–1939." In *Historical Studies and Social Change in Western Kenya: Essays in Memory of Professor Gideon S. Were*, edited by William R. Ochieng', 158–180. Kampala: East African Educational Publishers.

Ochwada, H. 2007. "Negotiating Difference: The Church Missionary Society, Colonial Education, and Gender among Aβaluyia and Joluo Communities of Kenya, 1900–1960." Doctoral dissertation, Indiana University.

Ogola, G. 2017. *Popular Media in Kenyan History: Fiction and Newspapers as Political Actors*. United Kingdom: Palgrave Macmillan. doi:10.1007/978-3-319-49097-7.

Ogundipe-Leslie, M. 1994. *Re-creating Ourselves: African Women & Critical Transformations*. Trenton: Africa World Press.

Okemwa, J.O. 2016. "The Role of Women in the Making of Kenyan Political History: A Case of Chelagat Mutai among the Nandi, 1949–2013." MA thesis, Kisii University, Kisii.

Okome, O. 2012. "Nollywood, Lagos, and the Good-time Woman." *Research in African Literatures* 43 (4): 166–86. doi:10.2979/reseafrilite.43.4.166.

Okpewho, I. 1992. *African Oral Literature: Backgrounds, Character, and Continuity*. Indiana University Press.

Onsagrio, D., 2013. "Case Files: Black Sunday." *KTN News Kenya*. Accessed 20 October 2019. https://www.youtube.com/watch?v=1YMr75331Sc.

p'Bitek 1963 . "Oral Literature and its Social Background among the Acoli and Lango." Unpublished. B.Litt. thesis, Oxford, St. Peter's College.

p'Bitek, O. 1972. *Song of Lawino*. Oxford: Heinemann.

Parkins, I., and E. Karpinski. 2014. "In/Visibility in/of Feminist Theory. *Atlantis: Critical Studies in Gender, Culture & Social Justice*, 36 (2): 3–7.

Phillips, L. M. 2000. *Flirting with danger: young women's reflections on sexuality and domination*. New York, London: New York University Press.

Plummer, K. 2017. *Foreword in J. Gagnon and W. Simon Sexual Conduct: The Social Sources of Human Sexuality*. 2nd ed. New Brunswick, London: Aldine Transaction.

Poster, M. 2007. "Postcolonial Theory in the Age of Planetary

Communications." *Quarterly Review of Film and Video* 24 (4): 379–93. doi:10.1080/10509200500526810.

Presley, C. A. 1988. "The Mau Mau Rebellion, Kikuyu Women, and Social Change." *Canadian Journal of African Studies/La Revue canadienne des études africaines*, 22 (3): 502–527.

Quayson, A. 2000. *Postcolonialism: Theory, Practice or Process*. Cambridge: Polity.

Radway, J. A. 2009. *Reading the Romance: Women, Patriarchy, and Popular Literature*. Chapel Hill: University of North Carolina Press.

Rich, A. 1980. "Compulsory Heterosexuality and Lesbian Existence." *Signs* 5 (4): 631–60. doi:10.1086/493756.

Ringrose, J., and E. Renold. 2012. "Slut-shaming, Girl Power and 'Sexualisation': Thinking through the Politics of the International SlutWalks with Teen Girls." *Gender and Education* 24 (3): 333–43. doi:10.1080/09540253.2011.645023.

Ritchie, A., and M. Barker. 2006. "'There aren't words for what we do or how we feel so we have to make them up': Constructing Polyamorous Languages in a Culture of Compulsory Monogamy." *Sexualities* 9 (5): 584–601. doi:10.1177/1363460706069987.

Roberts, I. D. 2010. "China's Internet Celebrity: Furong Jiejie." In *Celebrity in China*, edited by L. Edwards and E. Jeffreys, 217–236. Hong Kong: Hong Kong University Press. doi:10.5790/hongkong/9789622090873.003.0011.

Rotman, D. 2009. *Historical Archaeology of Gendered Lives*. Heidelberg: Springer Science & Business Media. doi:10.1007/978-0-387-89668-7.

Rubin, G. 1984. "Thinking Sex: Notes for a Radical Theory of the Politics of Sexuality." In *Social perspectives in Lesbian and Gay Studies: A Reader*, edited by Peter M. Nardi and Beth E. Schneider, 100–133. New York: Routledge.

Samuelson, M. 2007. *Remembering the Nation, Dismembering Women? Stories of the South African Transition*. Scotsville: University of KwaZulu-Natal Press.

Scheufele, D. A. 1999. "Framing as a Theory of Media Effects." *Journal of Communication* 49 (1): 103–22. doi:10.1111/j.1460-2466.1999.tb02784.x.

Senft, T. M. and Baym, N. K. 2015. "What does the Selfie Say? Investigating a Global Phenomenon." *International Journal of Communication*, 9 (Feature): 1588–1606.

Singhal, A., and E. M. Rogers. 2003. *Combating AIDS: Communication Strategies in Action*. New Delhi: Sage Publications.

Singhal, A., M. J. Cody, E. M. Rogers, and M. Sabido, eds. 2004. *Entertainment-education and Social Change: History, Research, and Practice*. New York: Routledge.

Sipalla, F. 2004. "Dangerous Affair: Narrating Popular Experiences in Kenya." MA thesis, University of the Witwatersrand, Johannesburg.

Skeggs, B. 2005. "The Making of Class and Gender through Visualizing Moral Subject Formation." *Sociology* 39 (5): 965–82. doi:10.1177/0038038505058381.

Smith, L. R., and J. Sanderson. 2015. "I'm going to Instagram it! An Analysis of Athlete Self-presentation on Instagram." *Journal of Broadcasting & Electronic Media* 59 (2): 342–58. doi:10.1080/08838151.2015.1029125.

Snyder-Hall, R. C. 2010. "Third-wave Feminism and the Defense of choice." *Perspectives on Politics* 8 (1): 255–61. doi:10.1017/S1537592709992842.

Spencer, L. G. 2014. "Writing Women in Uganda and South Africa: Emerging Writers from Post-repressive Regimes." Doctoral dissertation, Stellenbosch University, Stellenbosch.

Spencer, L. G., D. Ligaga, and G. A. Musila. 2018. "Gender and Popular Imaginaries in Africa." *Agenda (Durban, South Africa)* 32 (3): 3–9. doi:10.1080/10130950.2018.1526467.

Spronk, Rachel. 2012. *Ambiguous pleasures: sexuality and middle class self-perception in Nairobi*. New York: Berghahn Books.

Steenveld, L., and L. Strelitz. 2010. "Trash or Popular Journalism? The Case of South Africa's *Daily Sun*." *Journalism* 11 (5): 531–47. doi:10.1177/1464884910373534.

Steeves, L. 1997. *Gender Violence and the Press: The St. Kizito Story*. Athens, Ohio: Ohio University Press.

Stoler, A. L. 1989. "Making Empire Respectable: The Politics of Race and Sexual Morality in 20th-century Colonial Cultures." *American Ethnologist* 16 (4): 634–60. doi:10.1525/ae.1989.16.4.02a00030.

Stratton, F. 1994. *Contemporary African Literature and the Politics of Gender*. London: Routledge. doi:10.4324/9780203202975.

Strelitz, L., and L. Steenveld. 2005. "Thinking about South African Tabloid Newspapers." *Ecquid Novi* 26 (2): 265–68. doi:10.1080/02560054.2005.9653337.

Summers, C. 2002. *Colonial Lessons: Africans' Education in Southern Rhodesia, 1918–1940.* Portsmouth: Heinemann.

Tamale, S. 1999. *When Hens Begin to Crow: Gender and Parliamentary Politics in Uganda.* Boulder, Colorado: Westview Press.

Tamale, S., ed. 2011. *African Sexualities: A Reader.* Cape Town: Pambazuka Press.

Tanenbaum, L. 2015. *I am not a Slut: Slut-shaming in the Age of the Internet.* New York, NY: Harper Collins.

Tappan, M., and L. M. Brown. 1989. "Stories Told and Lessons Learned: Toward a Narrative Approach to Moral Development and Moral Education." *Harvard Educational Review* 59 (2): 182–206. doi:10.17763/haer.59.2.d364up55vx875411.

Tasker, Y., and D. Negra, eds. 2007. *Interrogating Postfeminism: Gender and the Politics of Popular Culture.* USA: Duke University Press. doi:10.1215/9780822390411.

Tcheuyap, A. 2005. "African Cinema and the Representation of (Homo)sexuality." In *Body, Sexuality and Gender: Versions and Subversions in African Literatures* 1, edited by F. Veit-Wild and D. Naguschewski, 143–154. Amsterdam: Editions Rodopi B.V.

Thomas, L. M. 2003. *Politics of the Womb: Women, Reproduction, and the State in Kenya.* Berkeley: University of California Press.

Thomas, L., and J. Cole. 2009. "Introduction: Thinking through Love in Africa." In *Love in Africa*, edited by J. Cole and L. M. Thomas, 1–30. Chicago: University of Chicago Press. doi:10.7208/chicago/9780226113555.003.0001.

Tibbetts, A. 1994. "Mamas Fighting for Freedom in Kenya." *Africa Today* 41 (4): 27–48.

Ticknell, E., D. Chambers, J. Van Loon, and N. Hudson. 2003. "Begging for It: 'New Femininities,' Social Agency, and Moral Discourse in Contemporary Teenage and Men's Magazines." *Feminist Media Studies* 3 (1): 47–63. doi:10.1080/1468077032000080121.

Turner, J. S. 1991. "To Tell a Good Tale: Kierkegaardian Reflections on Moral Narrative and Moral Truth." *Man and World* 24 (2): 181–98. doi:10.1007/BF01249551.

Ugangu, W. 2012. "Normative Media Theory and the Rethinking of the Role of the Kenyan Media in a Changing Social Economic Context." Doctoral dissertation, University of South Africa, Pretoria.

van Zoonen, L. 2001. "Desire and Resistance: Big Brother and the Recognition of Everyday Life." *Media Culture & Society* 23 (5): 669–77. doi:10.1177/016344301023005007.

van Zoonen, L. 2005. *Entertaining the Citizen: When Politics and Popular Culture Converge.* Lanham: Rowman and Littlefield Publishers.

van Zoonen, L. 2006. "The personal, the Political and the Popular: A Woman's Guide to Celebrity Politics." *European Journal of Cultural Studies* 9 (3): 287–301. doi:10.1177/1367549406066074.

Vaz, P., and F. Bruno. 2003. "Types of Self-surveillance: From Abnormality to Individuals 'At risk'." *Surveillance & Society* 1 (3): 272–91. doi:10.24908/ss.v1i3.3341.

Wa Thiongo, N. 1986. *Decolonising the Mind: The Politics of Language in African Literature.* London: James Currey.

Wa-Mungai, M. 2003. "Identity Politics in Nairobi Matatu Folklore." Doctoral dissertation." The Hebrew University of Jerusalem, Jerusalem.

Warah, R. 2015. "OpEd: Kim Kardashian and Vera Sidika — in the Service of Patriarchy." *Sahan Journal.* Access ed 13 January 2017. http://sahanjournal.com/vera-sidika/#.V0ImxeTD9wh.

Warner, M. 2002. "Publics and counterpublics." *Public Culture* 14 (1): 49–90. doi:10.1215/08992363-14-1-49.

Wasserman, H. 2010. *True Story! Tabloid Journalism in South Africa.* Bloomington, Indiana: Indiana University Press.

Weeks, J. 1981. *Sex, Politics and Society.* London: Longman.

Weeks, J. 2014. *Sex, Politics and Society: The Regulation of Sexuality since 1800.* 3rd ed. London: Routledge. doi:10.4324/9781315833330.

Were, M. N. 2017. "Kenyan Women in Androcentric Political Culture: From Julia Auma Ojiambo to Affirmative Action." *Social Dynamics* 43 (3): 487–504. doi:10.1080/02533952.2017.1416975.

White, L. 1990. *The Comforts of Home: Prostitution in Colonial Nairobi*. Chicago: University of Chicago Press. doi:10.7208/chicago/9780226895000.001.0001.

White, L. 2008. "Between Gluckman and Foucault: Historicizing Rumour and Gossip. *Social Dynamics*: *A Journal of African Studies* 20 (1): 75–92. doi:10.1080/02533959408458562.

Index

C

cabinet of Kenya 80n7
Cai, Bei 94
Cambridge Dictionary 129
"Campus Divas for rich men" Facebook page 109–110, 120–121, 134
capitalism 130–132, 135
casual sex 91
Catholic Church 65–66
cautionary tales 106, 111, 114, 122
celebrities
    as critical commentary 129–133
    'difficult women' 126–128
    digital subjectivities 128–129
    freedom 126, 128–129, 139–140
    hypervisibility 126–128, 139
    Instagram as autobiography 137–139
    new vs traditional 131
    outrageousness 139–140
    politicians as 42
    pseudo 131
    scandals 97
    spectacular femininities 133–137
censorship 62, 66, 132, 135
chamas (women's group meetings) 75, 96–97
charmed circle model 10
Cheruto, Vanessa 130
Christianity 9, 63–64, 73, 80, 110
chrononormativity 66, 70, 72
citizenship 49
CitizenTV 135
'civilised' 57, 145–146
class 37, 127, 133
clitoridectomy (genital excision) 36, 39, 58
Cloete, Elsie 43
clothing 39
Cocktail Ladies 28–29
Cohen, Stan 8
Cohen, William 91–92
Cole, J. 35, 101
Collins, Patricia Hill 13
colonialism
    Christianity and 64
    femininity and 24, 36–41, 50, 69, 145–146

    gender oppression and 84–85
    otherness 26
    radio and 4, 56–60, 79
    resistance to 23, 30
    sexuality and 9
Colonial Lessons 58
colonial modernity 38, 103, 145–146
community builders, women as 74–75
Community Development programmes 57–58
'compensated relationships' 100–101
    see also 'blessers'/'blessees'
Conboy, Martin 87
constitution of Kenya 61–62, 144
consumerism 101, 104–106, 122, 133–139
contemptuousness 113
control 24, 27–28, 60–62, 146
controversy 49, 137, 140
Cornell, Drucilla 67
Cornwall, Andrea 68
counterpublics 2, 11, 17, 145
coup d'état attempt (1982) 62
Crazy Mondays 86
Crazy World column 93–95
credibility 90
'cross-generational partnerships' 100
    see also 'blessers'/'blessees'
'cruel optimism' 70
Cruel Optimism 103
cult of domesticity 24, 32, 37

D

Daily Mirror 106
Daily Nation 1, 84–85, 115–118
Dangerous Affair (film) 64
death 110–119
De Certeau, Michel 14
'deviant' women *see* 'proper' and 'deviant' women
"Diary of a Kenyan campus girl" (blog) 121
'difficult women' 126–129, 145
digital media 6, 16, 88, 110–111, 128–131
    see also social media
discipline 2, 27–28, 40, 45–46, 118, 138, 142–143
disruptive publics 7, 10–14, 145

division of labour 57

domesticity 24, 31–34, 37, 60, 63, 67, 143

Doob, Leonard 56

Dosekun, Simidele 133

'double entanglement' 36

"Double lives of university students, The"
  115–117

Dyer, Richard 25, 130

E

'East African song school' 30

economic success 93, 131, 136, 137

education 30–31, 37, 56–58, 65–66, 79, 80n8,
  107–119

Egypt, soap operas in 31

Ekine, Sokari 35

emotional realism 31, 78

empowerment 105

equality *see* inequality

erotohistoriography 66, 70, 72

everyday life 3–4, 14

excessive femininity 133–137

F

Fabian, Johannes 17

Facebook 47–48, 109–110, 112, 118, 120–121,
  134

faithfulness 69, 76

fake news 110

family 62–63, 128–129, 143–144

Farganis, Sonia 31

Farvid, Pantea 91

Fassie, Brenda 128

'female fear factory' 46

female friendships 68

Feminine Character, The 31

femininity
    meaning of 31–33, 50
    myths of 18
    new femininities 34–36, 133

feminism 4, 12–13, 90–91, 135, 146

fertility 49, 58, 71, 138

fixity 26

Fluck, Winfried 17

'Formation' (song) 106–107

Forsyth, Frederick 74–75

Foucault, Michel 10, 32–33

Frederiksen, Bodil 18

freedom 93, 105–109, 126, 128–129, 139–140,
  146

Freeman, Elizabeth 66–67, 70–72

French, B. 12, 127

friendships 68

Furong Jiejie 132

G

Gagnon, John 2–3, 142–143

Gamson, Joshua 41, 92, 131, 132

Gauvin, Lara 30

gender
    colonialism and 38
    domesticity and 32
    media coverage and 83–85, 92–93
    performativity 33–34
    politics and 41–49
    roles and celebrities 127
    sexuality and 4
    state and 41–49

Gender Violence and the Press 84

genital excision (clitoridectomy) 36, 39, 58

Genz, Stephanie 33–34, 48

Ghafla! 1, 49, 86

Ghana 17

Gikuru, Samuel 88

Gill, Rosalind 36, 105, 133

Giraud, Eva 129

Giriama people 43

'Girl Power' 34

Gisesa, Nyambega 115–117

Githiora, Wambui 108

'global postmodern' 13–14

'good' and 'bad' women 1, 66–68, 70, 72,
  75–76, 80, 95, 127

'good time girls' 1, 28–29, 39, 102–110,
  114–118, 120, 122, 135

gossip 88–90, 97, 145

governmentality 10

www.ingramcontent.com/pod-product-compliance
Lightning Source LLC
Chambersburg PA
CBHW081739270326
41932CB00020B/3333